Power and Politics in Education

Deakin Studies in Education Series

General Editors: Professor Rob Walker and Professor Stephen Kemmis, Deakin University, Victoria, Australia

1 CURRICULUM: PRODUCT OR PRAXIS?
Shirley Grundy

2 CRITICAL REFLECTIONS ON DISTANCE EDUCATION
Edited by Terry Evans and Daryl Nation

3 CRITICAL PERSPECTIVES ON EDUCATIONAL LEADERSHIP
Edited by John Smyth

4 TOWARDS A THEORY OF SCHOOLING
David Hamilton

5 PHYSICAL EDUCATION, CURRICULUM AND CULTURE: CRITICAL ISSUES IN THE CONTEMPORARY CRISIS
Edited by David Kirk and Richard Tinning

6 THE SOCIAL PRODUCTION OF MERIT: EDUCATION, PSYCHOLOGY AND POLITICS IN AUSTRALIA, 1900–1950
David McCallum

7 HEARTS AND MINDS: SELF-ESTEEM AND THE SCHOOLING OF GIRLS
Edited by Jane Kenway and Sue Willis

8 POWER AND POLITICS IN EDUCATION
Edited by David Dawkins

Deakin Studies in Education Series: 8

Power and Politics in Education

Edited by
David Dawkins

The Falmer Press
(A member of the Taylor & Francis Group)
London · New York · Philadelphia

UK The Falmer Press, 4 John St, London WC1N 2ET
USA The Falmer Press, Taylor & Francis Inc., 1900 Frost Road, Suite 101, Bristol, PA 19007

First published 1991

British Library Cataloguing in Publication Data
Dawkins, David
Power and politics in education.
1. Education. Political aspects
I. Title
379

ISBN 1-85000-889-2

Library of Congress Cataloging-in-Publication Data
Power and politics in education/edited by David Dawkins.
p. cm.
Includes index.
ISBN 1-85000-889-2: — ISBN 1-85000-890-6 (pbk.):
1. Education and state—Australia. 2. Politics and educational—Australia. 3. Education—Social aspects—Australia. I. Dawkins, David, 1939– .
LC96.P69 1991
379.94—dc20

90-42319
CIP

Jacket design by Caroline Archer

Typeset in 10.5/13 pt Bembo by
Graphicraft Typesetters Ltd, Hong Kong

Printed in Great Britain by Burgess Science Press, Basingstoke on paper which has a specified pH value on final paper manufacture of not less than 7.5 and is therefore 'acid free'.

Contents

General Editors' Introduction

The Deakin Studies in Education Series aims to present a broad critical perspective across a range of interrelated fields in education. The intention is to develop what might be called a 'critical educational science': critical work in the philosophy of education, curriculum, educational and public administration, language education, and educational action research and clinical supervision. The series strives to present the writings of a rising generation of scholars and researchers in education.

A number of researchers based at Deakin University have been closely associated with the development of the critical perspective across these fields. For such reasons, people in the field have sometimes spoken of a 'Deakin perspective'. We do share some common views from which we hope to contribute to contemporary debates about the future development of educational enquiry; at the same time, our disagreements seem as fruitful for us as our agreements.

The Deakin Studies in Education Series provides an opportunity for extending this debate about the nature and future development of education and educational enquiry. It will include the writings of a variety of educational researchers around the world who, like ourselves, are interested in exploring the power and limitations of the critical perspective in the analysis of educational theory, policy and practice.

The central themes of the series will not be dictated by the alleged boundaries between 'foundational' disciplines in education, nor by an unexamined division of the tasks of education and educational research between 'practitioners' and 'theorists', or between 'practitioners' and 'policy-makers'. On the contrary, one of the tasks of the series is to demonstrate, through careful research and scholarship across a range of fields of practical, political and theoretical endeavour, just how outmoded, unproductive, and ultimately destructive these divisions are both for education and for educational research. Put positively, the central themes and questions to be addressed in the series include:

> the unity of educational theory and practice — expressed, for example, in the work of educational practitioners who research their practice as a basis for improving it, and in the notion of collaborative, participatory educational research, for example, in educational action research;
>
> the historical formation, social construction and continual reconstruction of education and educational institutions and reforms through processes of contestation and institutionalization — expressed, for example, in the work of critical researchers into the curriculum and educational reform; and
>
> the possibilities of education for emancipation and active and productive participation in a democratic society — expressed, for example, in the development of critical pedagogy and the development of communitarian perspectives in the organization of education.

These are enduring themes, touching upon some of the central questions confronting our contemporary culture and, some would say, upon the central pathologies of contemporary society. They are all too easily neglected or obscured in the narrow and fragmented views of education and educational research characteristic of our times. Yet education is one of the key resources in what Raymond Williams once described as our socicties' 'journey of hope' — the journey towards a better, more just, more rational and more rewarding society. Education has always aimed to nurture, represent, vivify and extend the values and modes of life which promise to make the best in our culture better. Finding out how this can be done, interpreting our progress, and appraising and reappraising the quality of our efforts at educational improvement are the tasks of critical educational research. They are the tasks of this series.

Stephen Kemmis and Rob Walker

Introduction

David Dawkins

While the chapters of this book were being put together there was a Federal election in Australia. Education, as one of the biggest departments of government absorbing a large slice of the fiscal cake, has always been one of the focal points of electioneering, usually over how much public money will be given to private schools and the perennial 'standards' debate. This time, however, in the current mode, it was the state of the economy which dominated events as the central election issue, and education was pushed into the wings as a minor side issue. On the hustings it featured mainly in two ways which may strike a chord of familiarity in other countries; on one hand it was touted as being centrally important for the nurturing of those 'skills' perceived to be necessary for the nation's economic well-being, while on the other, underlining the current fiscal condition, it was debated in terms of budgetary cuts and cost effectiveness.

Within the more carefully considered policy statements on education there seemed to be little to choose between the two major parties. The conservatives published a policy statement which contained a preamble laced with familiarly vague generalizations about Australia's long-term future being 'guaranteed only if we become a knowledge-intensive nation', and that education 'should inculcate the desire for learning (and) encourage the pursuit of excellence and ingenuity', and that students should 'develop their full capacity . . . if Australia is to achieve an internationally competitive standard of schooling.' Who would dare disagree with that?

They also promised to establish a National Standards Monitoring Program. This would ensure that the best of education would be provided (had they become the government) because 'objective measures' would be gathered throughout the country to monitor 'teacher training, school curricula, methods of testing and assessment, standards of educational performance, and standards of physical fitness, so that States and non-government school authorities can target action for improvement on the basis of objective information.' A manifesto for tackling the problems of the future with the discarded solutions of the past, it reads in a remarkably similar vein to the Labor Party document, *Strengthening Australia's Schools*, which proposed a common approach to measures of student achievement and performance throughout the country.

The other major conservative policy promised to 'restore parental choice' in education; this was a way of saying that they were willing to provide more money for private schools than the Labor Party. This merely shows that even in this the choice was between the parties' relative funding commitment rather than real policy differences. Both parties have policies which support the privatization of education but perhaps for different reasons; for one it appears to be based on ideological views supporting meritocratic assumptions, for the other it seems to be more of a pragmatic response to difficult times.

Besides playing on common fears about educational 'standards', which themselves are largely generated through the media by politicians seeking to create 'issues', and unsubtle offers of funding for private schools, what do the parties have to offer education in Australia? Fundamentally, both parties are commited to the development of 'skills' through education; skills believed necessary to ensure Australia's future economic success. Thus education policy in Australia is increasingly geared towards instrumental goals thought to be in the best interests of the economy, with the assumption that this is what is best for all of us. Again, readers may find similarities between this and what is happening in other countries.

The emphasis on economic goals is not new. For decades past, the streaming of students into academic, commercial and trade oriented curricula, with particular skills being taught within each, was geared towards future employment in occupations believed relevant to economic needs. The critique of this practice had little to do with its occupational focus but was more concerned with its biases. Besides questions raised about which groups actually sent their children to what type of school, the critics questioned the use of simplistic measures such as IQ tests to determine which stream students would follow, for both processes with few exceptions directed occupational choices. However, it was generally taken for granted that along with 'occupational skills' students should also be given a 'good education', vaguely stated perhaps but with fairly agreed notions about allowing students to develop their intellectual and critical potential.

What should be of concern in the present context is the inequitable closing of options through oligarchic decisions about which 'skills' are thought appropriate. Where once students were denied access to particular types of knowledge because of assumptions based upon aptitude testing that they were destined to follow menial or servitor occupations, consequently not having the need (nor, it was assumed, the ability) to appreciate 'higher' cultural forms, now there appears to be a move to constrain access to kinds of knowledge thought to be less important on the grounds that they are dysfunctional to techno-economic needs. In our contemporary situation the imposition of a corporate management model of educational administration goes hand-in-hand with the imposition of assumptions about the appropriateness of particular skills. These assumptions, by which forms of knowledge ('skills') are chosen, translate into funding decisions which promote the availability of subject areas in schools through staffing and resource provisions, which are then popularized through advertizing, both in school and through the mass media. The new assumptions upon which school curricula are based give pre-eminence to skills perceived as serving economic needs, and make a mockery of those oratorical statements about encouraging 'the desire for learning' and for students to 'develop to their full capacity', paraded before us at election time.

What is especially problematic about this new situation is the way in which decisions about what skills are appropriate are arrived at. Who decides what is appropriate? From what ideological bases? On what evidence? Essentially it is a question of whom the government chooses to take its advice from, and in our current situation it seems that this comes from a small coterie of economic rationalists. The current fascination with 'skills' and long discredited testing instruments runs counter to the claims of the recent OECD report, *New Technologies in the 1990s: A Socioeconomic Strategy*, that new technological changes require an education and training system which will 'foster initiative, creativity, and responsibility among young people.'

Of course it is not just a matter of governments, commonwealth or state, taking advice and making policy, which then translates into action. There is a vast education industry to be taken into account: teachers, and their professional organizations, the teacher unions. Although teachers are engaged in a struggle about their own pay and conditions surrounding award restructuring within the education industry, they are professionals as well as unionists, and engaged in a larger struggle which will determine the shape of education in the 1990s. Much of the interface between teachers and government has to do with how the latter's policy intentions will be translated into classroom reality.

Australia is currently undergoing a period of great change. Most obvious is the process of economic restructuring as the government seeks to place less reliance on agriculture and mining for the nation's economic base and more on technologically advanced manufacturing. These changes require concomitant changes in the workforce, most notably in the development of multi-skilling, accompanied by award restructuring. Crucial to this is the role of education as the feeder system to ensure the supply of adequately prepared labour, which is why education has become even more than ever a site of struggle. If the discourse of reform is to lead to a liberatory education system, it must not be subverted to serve instrumental objectives created in the name of economic rationalism and managerial efficiency.

It is to join with teachers in shaping the discourse of reform that this book has been written. The issues raised here reflect our thoughts and concerns as we consider the present state of education in Australia. We do not claim to have raised all the issues, nor to have provided all the answers, but as co-workers in education we hope to contribute jointly to the discourse, mindful of what Michael Apple, reflecting on the separation of academic work from that of teachers, has said:

> I would like to claim that, in not just a metaphorical way, unless it takes its democratic politics seriously such work can tend to reproduce on an ideological level the separation of conception from execution that lies at the heart of the division of labour in our economy. 'We' will generate the 'correct' criticisms; 'you' will be 'taught' how to operate in educational institutions. This is why it is so very important that those who engage in critical scholarship in education should have constant and close ties to the real world of teachers, students, and parents, and why they need to be closely connected to feminist groups, people of colour, unions, and to those teachers and curriculum workers who are now struggling so hard in very difficult circumstances to defend from rightist attacks the gains that have been made in democratising education and to make certain that our schools and the curricular and teaching practices within them are responsive in race, gender, and class terms. After all, teaching is a two-way street and academics can use some political education as well.

The first two chapters focus on education within the macro-social context. Paige Porter begins with a discussion of social reproduction and change intersected by human agency, ideology and the role of the state, as the foreground to a brief history of the official ideology about the family held by the Western Australian Education Department. She argues that the central contradiction in the education systems of advanced capitalist societies arises because although education has a central role in reproducing the political structure of the capitalist production process and property rights, and a key role in the patriarchal family and male rights, it also has a role in defending human rights. This understanding explains how education, a key arm of the state, can be both progressive and conservative with regard to class and gender divisions.

Porter also argues for a 'joint dynamic' or 'doubled vision' of gender and class. Theory oriented solely around the labour-capital relationship obscures power based on other sources, and we need to see how gender and class structures have developed in interaction with each other. Allied to this is the relationship of the family, the economy and education; gender differentiation and our ideas about the economy shape our idea of the family, thus governing female-male relationships, and education is implicated in reproducing traditonal views. In these we find there to have been a view of the 'proper' form of the family, and of the function education plays in training children to fit into their appropriate roles in the family and the workplace.

In Chapter 2 Jill Blackmore is concerned with how the structure and ideology of the corporate state relate to educational governance, and how the hegemony of consent is constructed and maintained. She argues that the incorporation of teacher unions into policy-making committees and advisory boards at both central and regional levels has affected the 'quieting' of oppositional discourse. The incorporation of 'key' leaders and 'peak' unions raises two questions: first, to what extent does this selective incorporation exclude competing interpretations; second, who represents the views of those not included within the scope of selective incorporation?

Within schools, incorporation has a capacity to capture the discourse of educational reform in the name of consensus. The emphasis on joint decision-making with consensus as the desired outcome has favoured governmental arbitration when agreement is not reached, giving legitimacy to state intervention which might produce unfavourable and undemocratic decisions. Thus control is maintained by more subtle and indirect means. Blackmore concludes by considering possibilities for recapturing the discourse of reform.

The next two chapters link macro and micro aspects of education. In Chapter 3 the question of why little has changed in education despite national reform programs is raised. Besides briefly looking at the political contexts within which two national education reform programs were developed, the chapter questions the usefulness of studying education systems and school practices in isolation from their sociocultural contexts. Thus, although evaluation studies of the two programs have suggested that they have introduced considerable educational reform into schools in Victoria, when examined within a sociocultural framework, they may be seen to have made very little difference.

To suggest why national reform programs make so little difference, several aspects of one program are re-examined to determine the extent to which they may be regarded as having reproduced or contested cultural hegemony in education. Two specific situations are looked at: the contestation of patriarchic hegemony, and the contestation of hegemony in the mental/manual dichotomy of the school curriculum. Examples drawn largely from school-based case studies reveal significant differences within the cultural contexts of various educational sites, and suggest that for reform programs to effect changes which contest hegemony in education there needs to be greater awareness that education is a site of social struggle.

In Chapter 4 Jane Kenway examines the use of consumption, particularly the consumption of private schooling, as a mechanism for social structuring. She questions the 'categorical approach' of investigating and describing the social class of private school clients, which derives from theories of social stratification 'characterized by an absence of overt theorizing, accompanied by an eagerness to identify male parents according to certain criteria.' An alternative 'relational approach', which finds its origins in Marxist class theory and Gramsci's notion of hegemony, is put forward as a more adequate way of thinking about education, especially private schooling, as a mechanism for the reproduction of gendered class formation and relations.

Kenway highlights some connections between class culture, gender, consumption and private schooling. With media support, the loose amalgam of the educational Right and New Right has propagated the notion that educational excellence is best guaranteed by subjecting education to market forces. This gives opportunity for the loud extolling of the 'success' of private schooling compared with state schools, which are presented as being 'in crisis'. Besides questioning this view, Kenway warns that this 'consumer sovereignty ethic' has also 'led to the subtle privatization of state schools.' She argues that the more state governments transfer educational authority to 'consumers' at the local level, the more they relinquish their capacity to direct education in socially just ways. She attributes to this shift the trend to see education less as a means of individual development and more as an investment for individuals to obtain a job and the nation to obtain economic growth.

Chapters 5 and 6 examine two of the most prominent current issues in education. In Chapter 5 Fazal Rizvi argues that the idea of ethnicity, on which the official policies of multiculturalism rest and which informs the various practices of multicultural education, is flawed because it is derived from an inadequate account of social relations. It thus constitutes an inadequate basis for developing egalitarian politics.

Rizvi argues that multicultural policies, including multicultural education, are the product of assumptions drawn from a number of prominent theories of ethnicity. However, the 'revival' of ethnicity is regressive, and multicultural education is ideological, because the emphasis on ethnic heterogeneity obscures and legitimates the essential class inequalities which produce the disadvantages that migrants in Australia face. He argues that multicultural education should not focus on ahistorical and apolitical studies of ethnic customs, religions, music and languages. Rather than simply cataloguing ethnic differences, students should be encouraged to examine the structure of their society; the emphasis should be on the constituted similarities of social experience that migrants and other disadvantaged groups share, in order to produce a challenge to the structural and symbolic forces of inequality in our society.

In Chapter 6 Peter Watkins argues that the fascination with high technology as the source of new jobs may be highly mistaken. His central argument is that future job opportunities for most young people will be with low tech rather than high tech forms of work, even within high tech industries.

He compares the deterministic linear approach to technological change in the work of Ellul and Winner, which sees virtually no interconnection between human beings and technology and has no consideration of values not subordinate to technical rationality, with the dialectic approach of Marx and Weber. The dialectic approach takes the view that technological change is neither autonomous nor value-free but is the result of a socially influenced chain of options. Technology is neither ideologically neutral nor introduced in a neutral or random fashion, and generates hostility. Yet even the Luddites were not opposed to technology. They were opposed to technological innovation which failed to meet two criteria: the enhancement of the quality of manufactured products, and an improvement in the quality of work.

Although many argue that children must be educated to create and work the new technology, Watkins argues that the appropriate educational response should not be to respond in a functional way to the needs of industry. Instead, schools should facilitate the examination of the practices and repercussions emanating from human choice in the creation and implementation of technology.

In the final chapter, Lawrence Angus takes us back to question the role of education in society. He points to some themes in early Australian education, democracy, social harmony, equality and the possibility for social mobility, but adds that the very notion of education is a historical and political construct and thus inescapably ideological in nature. These early themes became entrenched as part of a traditional liberal democratic view of education and society. It required only a small step to move from this to embrace the ideology of meritocracy and notions of human capital. He argues that Australian education has consistently offered a liberatory and egalitarian promise which has never been realized. There has been a shift to the Right in Australian education characterized by moves to manage schools more tightly, test teacher competence, impose centrally determined curricula and test children's learning of the curriculum.

Angus argues for the restoration of democracy and equality in schools. In such an education 'the basics' would not be understood in simplistic terms of technical competency in literacy and numeracy, but in standards of respect for fellow human beings, justice and autonomy. The problematic nature of the notion of quality schooling, a loosely defined term employed as part of the slogan system which symbolizes a conservative educational ideology, needs to be emphasized by teachers, and the shift in the educational debate which has occurred to accommodate conservative New Right themes must be contested.

This book is about power and politics in education. It touches on the *realpolitik* of political parties which shapes education policy as a means to power, both the intrinsic power of political office and the arrogated power in which education serves the interests of particular social groups. It is also about the politics of social life in which education is a site of the struggle to build a more just society, and the power of individuals to help shape the discourse of reform.

Chapter 1

The State-Family-Workplace Intersection: Hegemony, Contradictions and Counter-Hegemony in Education

Paige Porter

In 1971 Michael Young, a well-known British sociologist and educationalist, edited his influential book on the sociology of knowledge, *Knowledge and Control*. In this book authors delineated the ways in which much of what we accept as everyday 'knowledge', including school 'knowledge', is socially constructed, meaning that it is a creation of particular dominant groups in a particular society at a particular time and serves to help maintain those groups in power.The air of truth and of traditon that is conveyed with regard to such socially constructed knowledge ensures that for the most part we do not ordinarily question whether these assumptions really are the best or indeed the only way to understand the world, whether they mask hidden power relationships and structures, or even whether they limit our own perspectives in ways which might be detrimental to ourselves.

In the preamble to that book Young (1971) included a short poem by Robert Desnos, a French poet, which illustrates in simple form some of the related social theories and concepts which will be referred to in this chapter on the relationship between gender and education.

One day young Captain Jonathan,
he was eighteen at the time,
Captured a Pelican
On an island in the Far East.
In the morning,
This Pelican
of Jonathan's,

Laid a white egg
and out of it came
A Pelican
Astonishingly like the first.
And this second Pelican
laid in its turn
A white egg,
From which came inevitably
Another
Who did the same again.
This sort of thing can go on
a very long time,
if you don't make an omelette.

(Desnos, in Young, 1971, p. i)

The parable of the pelican draws our attention to the taken-for-granted fact that pelicans keep producing white eggs which keep producing pelicans which keep producing white eggs and so on — unless someone makes an omelette. Within both the education system and the gender order it often seems as though as much as everything changes, everything also stays the same. Despite a century of significant social change in both areas much appears to remain the same. This chapter offers some explanations for the coexistence of both change and stability in these areas; further, it offers some insights on why it is important to understand that the nature of the late twentieth century education system cannot be adequately understood without recognizing its interaction with the late twentieth century gender order.

Social Reproduction Theories and Education

Social reproduction theories developed as an attempt to understand how societies seemed to be able to hold themselves together and to continue in many important aspects relatively unchanged, or how they were able to 'reproduce' themselves. In some ways this is the old Hobbesian question of why the world is not constantly in a state of war of all against all. As such, it reflects a basic preoccupation of sociology, the analysis of social order and social disorder. However, the role of education in either process has assumed a new ascendancy in this analysis in recent years.

For example, Louis Althusser (1918–), a French philosopher, in an influential essay argued that all societies are based on a particular mode of economic production; to continue to exist, they must reproduce both the labour power necessary to maintain that system *and* the relations of production, or the world view, necessary for people to continue to believe in that particular economic system (Althusser, 1971). Althusser viewed education as 'relatively autonomous' 'ideological apparatus' of the state which had become, in mature capitalism, the key means by which this reproduction occurs. He stressed the way in which the school, through an ideology of neutrality with regard to its function, actually reproduces both the labour power and the relations of production. It does this through its teaching of basic knowledge and skills, and through the inculcation of the behaviour and attitudes required to facilitate submission to the rules of the established order. Althusser also identified the 'family-education couple' as an example of an ideological apparatus (replacing the family-church couple of the past) whose function it has become to help maintain and reproduce the social and sexual division of labour *in tandem*.

Bourdieu and Passeron (1977), contemporary French sociologists studying the French education system, stressed another element of reproduction theory: how in a class-based social system the relevant social practices are perpetuated. They argued that not only does the education system maintain and stabilize the class structure, but it does this, together with the family, by inculcating within the growing child a system of dispositions or 'habitus', which will facilitate the ability to behave in class-appropriate ways in later life. Furthermore, the kinds of acceptable knowledge, attitudes and behaviour that belong to the upper classes are the same as those which are increasingly required the higher one goes in the educational system. Conversely, knowledge, attitudes and behaviour that are prevalent in the lower classes are increasingly *less* acceptable within the education system the higher one goes. The modes of knowledge and thought that characterize different classes are referred to as 'cultural capital'. The cultural capital of the bourgeois class is that which is valued by the education system. Hence schools mask their arbitrary nature and appear 'natural' — they just reward merit — thus legitimating not only themselves but the whole social structure as well.

Basil Bernstein, the British sociologist, has also produced influential work describing the role of schools in cultural reproduction (1971). Bernstein uses the concepts of 'classification' and 'framing' to discuss the process of knowledge transmission in schools. Through the transmission of knowledge in 'codes' certain knowledge is legitimated and other knowledge is not, in particular, school knowledge and language reflect the 'elaborated code' of the middle class, while working-class children operate at a disadvantage in schools with their 'restricted code'. Thus schools reproduce the existing class system through the 'neutral' employment of certain knowledge and language which is in reality class- and interest-based.

The most comprehensive analysis of an education system within a reproductive framework is in the work of American economists Samuel Bowles and Herbert Gintis. *Schooling in Capitalist America* (1976) is a historical study which traces the relationship between changes in the American system of economic production and educational reforms. Bowles and Gintis (1976) see this relationship in terms of a 'correspondence principle', in which a close connection between education and the capitalist production system is ensured, not through the content of education but through the correspondence between the social relations of the workplace and those of the school. Specifically, the authority and control system in schools replicates the hierarchical division of labour in the vertical power structure of the workplace. Students' lack of control over their curriculum is similar to workers' lack of control over the content of their jobs. The motivational system in schools, based as it is on grades and the threat of failure, is similar to the worker's situation with regard to wages and the spectre of unemployment. The compartmentalization of academic knowledge in schools is similar to the fragmented nature of jobs in most industries. The emphasis on competition between individual students in schools is similar to the stress on individual competition in the workplace.

These reproduction theories have provided considerable incentive to rethink the role of education in contemporary society. They have been a welcome relief from either the traditional, self-congratulatory approaches about the grand historical march of social progress led by schools, or the blame-the-victim approaches which accept without question the basic economic and political structures of a society and go on to consider solutions to the educational 'problems' of those seen to be 'deficient' in terms of the dominant social system.

However, reproduction theories have some weaknesses. With Captain Jonathan and his pelican in mind again, they do not explain how omelettes are ever made. Furthermore, while it should be obvious that both a male and female pelican must in some way be involved in the production of the fertile egg, there is no consideration whatsoever of the sex of the pelican or of the relevant interaction that must have occurred. Social reproduction theories have two major problems: their determinism and their sexism. (These are not the *only* social theories that suffer from these weaknesses.)

The deterministic nature of these theories means that the stronger one argues for the power of the social structures, that harder it is to explain how an individual or group ever escapes their impact or, indeed, how any social change ever occurs. Human behaviour is seen to be determined by powerful social forces. The implications within such perspectives are that people do not understand what is happening to them, that they cannot change their own lives, that they are not active human agents, but objects, to be acted upon.

The theories are sexist in that they do not consider different male and female life experiences; their entire interpretation of social life is dictated by the typical *male* life pattern, in particular, participation in the world of paid work. Insofar as they begin their theorizing from a mode of production which is taken entirely to be that of the market workplace, they ignore a huge hidden infrastructure of the economy in unpaid work and hence the work and lives of many women. They also ignore gender as a set of power relationships as significant as social class. They relegate the most crucial aspect of social reproduction — the organization of sex and procreation — to theoretical non-existence. Women, insofar as they are considered at all, are dealt with by attaching them to males; but mostly they are invisible. Following sections consider ways in which both the determinism and sexism of social reproduction theories can be moderated.

Conceptualizing Social Change and Human Agency

The search for an understanding of how the *determinism* of the social reproductive perspective, both theoretically and in 'real life', can be moderated has preoccupied a number of writers. Henry Giroux (1981), an Amercian sociologist, has explored the concept of 'resistance' and how both individuals and class groups are sometimes able to oppose the hegemony of the dominant groups in education. Willis (1977) has provided an insightful interpretation of how working-class English boys are able to 'resist' the middle-class culture of the school, although this is also interpreted as part of the hidden process eventually *confirming* their own class position. Australian sociologist Bob Connell has breathed life into the relationships between schools, kids and their families by describing the dynamic interplay of class relations and gender relations in education. Both the content and accessible style of his and his co-workers' research and writing works against determinism (Connell *et al.*, 1982). In an essay on social reproduction theories Connell talks tantalizingly about 'liberating practices' and how they must be seen to emerge from the mundane and not the exceptional: 'Illumination is in no sense an exotic event, to be achieved only by the arcane. It arises in the midst of the everyday, and that is part of what is astonishing. So with culture, no realm separate from one of power; and so with the breaks and reconfigurations, large and small, that we are gesturing towards with a clumsy word like "liberation"' (Connell, 1983, p. 161).

Another approach develops the concept of 'ideology' as an area in which the potential for social change may be observed. Briefly, the concept of ideology, as it has been primarily used in sociology, derives from Marx's notion that the ruling class succeeds in having its ideas accepted as the 'legitimate' way to understand the world, thus disguising the basic ways in which it is already exploiting those who do not own or manage the means of production and must sell their labour for wages. Ideology in this sense provides a false, or at least partially false, understanding of the world; it disguises the actual social relations of material production.

For German sociologist Max Weber (1864–1920) 'ideology' was a 'world view' which legitimated underlying power structures which included, but were not limited to, those having an *economic* base. He saw power as also emanating from *political* and *social* bases. Furthermore, he argued for the possibility of tensions in society between some prevalent ideas and the interests of dominant groups. When, and if, such ideas eventually corresponded, Weber called this 'elective affinity'. Some ideas have an affinity with the interests of powerful groups, and, if so, they are likely eventually to become part of their world view, and hence the world view that is promoted as the 'natural' one. This Weberian understanding of ideology allows for the possibility of ideas which do not correspond with dominant interests existing, and indeed even coming to be seen to reflect dominant interests and hence being incorporated into the hegemonic ideology. Thus we can conceptualize the operation of a hegemonic ideology and at the same time other ideas — and people — who are challenging the status quo (Weber, [1904] 1958).

This perspective can be taken further through reference to German/British sociologist Karl Mannheim's (1893–1947) concept of 'utopia'. Mannheim distinguished between ideology, which he saw as ideas reflecting dominant groups, and 'utopia', which he saw as ideas reflecting the interests of a subordinate but ascendant group. Wearing (1984), commenting on Mannheim's perspective (in the context of understanding the ideology of motherhood), points out that

> For Mannheim . . . the bearers of ideology represent the prevailing social and intellectual order and they experience that structure of relationships of which they are the bearers. But he sees that within any given society there are groups 'driven into opposition

> to the present order' who are oriented towards the first stirrings of the social order for which they are striving and which is being realised through them. These groups are bearers of utopian ideas which, unlike ideology, 'transcend the existing order' and attempt to 'break the bonds' of such an order 'while at the same time containing in condensed form the unrealised and unfulfilled tendencies which represent the needs of the age' and which 'become the explosive material for bursting the limits of the existing order'. (Wearing, 1984, pp. 25–6)

Mannheim's concept of utopian ideas allows us to explain not only *individual* resistance to dominant groups and the hegemonic ideology but also organized *group* resistance. It also provides a way of conceptualizing both the possibility of individuals directing their own lives *and* social change.

Perhaps the most useful work of all in contemplating the possibilities of human agency amidst powerful social forces is that of Italian theorist and activist, Antonio Gramsci. Writing in the context of revolutionary struggle in post-World War I Italy, Gramsci was concerned to explain the rise of a reactionary fascism supported by much of the working class. Gramsci developed the concept of hegemony — and counter-hegemony — and provided an analysis of 'consciousness' which explains both the ability of dominant groups to control without force and the potential source of social change.

The concept of hegemony refers to the successful efforts of the dominant classes to unify potentially different interests within their own ranks, thereby creating powerful allies, who are able to establish *their* view of the world as universal, thus imposing their own conception of reality on all subordinate classes. Yet individual human beings' thought, or consciousness, is capable of critique and transformation and is consequently also an area of political struggle. Individuals are shaped by hegemonic ideas, but they also have the power to contest those ideas and the covert control they reflect. The dominant classes may also be continually struggling to *maintain* their hegemonic position. The concept of hegemony also defines counter-hegemony. It is not only individuals through their active consciousness but subordinate social *groups* as well which may struggle with dominant groups for hegemonic control. Thus both individuals and groups are influenced by hegemonic world views, but because they have consciousness, they can and do sometimes resist and develop counter-hegemonic ideas. The Gramscian analysis is a dynamic one which highlights the enormous possibilities inherent in schooling and in the concepts of active learners and critical education.

Yet another way in which we can understand the social reproduction process without getting lost in determinism and sexism is through our conception of the role of the state. In traditional Marxian sociological thought the state is a superstructure built upon the exploitative economic base which reflects the interests of capitalists. Its basic role is to help reproduce the means and relations of capitalist production. Some theorists, in trying to account for the existence of a much more complex state in mature capitalism, have presented an interpretation which accords the state some autonomy from its economic base. For example, Bowles and Gintis developed their views beyond the simple correspondence theory discussed earlier. In more recent work they elaborated on the contradictions which existed within the state and between the state and the production system (Bowles and Gintis, 1981). They now see society as an 'ensemble of structurally articulated sites of social practice' in which a site is a 'cohesive area of social life characterized by a specified set of characteristic social relations or structures' (Bowles and Gintis, 1981, p. 229). The sites which are most apparent in advanced capitalistic democratic social formations are those of capitalistic production, the patriarchal family and the liberal democratic state.

The site of capitalist production is characterized by private property in the means of production, market exchange, wage labour and capitalistic control of production and investment. The patriarchal family is characterized by a structure based on gender, kinship and age relations. 'The liberal democratic state is characterized by near universal suffrage and general civil liberties' (Bowles and Gintis, 1981, p. 230). These three social sites are seen as fundamental in defining the major relations individuals have *vis-à-vis* their society. 'None of these can be understood as reducible to or derivative from the others' (Bowles and Gintis, 1981, p. 230). Each site is capable of relations of domination and subordination. Capitalist production is a site of domination of capital over labour, the patriarchal family is a site of domination of men over women. But the liberal democratic state, while central to the reproduction of the conditions of domination and subordination in the economy and the family, is not *necessarily* a site of domination itself.

A 'contradictory totality' flows from the articulation of these three sites, and the dynamics of education emerge from this. Specifically, the central contradiction in the education systems of advanced capitalist societies is that education has a central role in reproducing the political structure of the capitalist production process and thus property rights, it has a key role in helping to reproduce the patriarchal family and thus male rights, but as a subsystem of the state it also has a role in defending what are perceived to be general human rights. Thus contradictions are inherent in the action of educational systems and policy can be, at one and the same time, progressive and reproductive. In this formulation the state is given both reflectivity *and* autonomy from the economic base. Furthermore, it is credited with some real progressive impact via its liberal democratic discourse of natural rights. Given that education is a key arm of the state, this conception allows us to explain how educational authorities can be both progressive and conservative with regard to class and gender divisions. It also illuminates the way the state is both a site of social struggle *and* the prize itself.

Finally, American economists Martin Carnoy and Henry Levin, in their work on the relationship between *Schooling and Work in the Democratic State* (1985), have drawn attention to the historical and dialectic character of this process. In a somewhat similar vein to Bowles and Gintis (although emphasizing the primacy of the economic base more strongly than Bowles and Gintis) they suggest that schools as public institutions must guarantee citizens' rights to some extent, while private institutions are more proscribed by the imperatives of property rights. The expansion of the state in this century into a variety of areas, including education, is seen as increasing the protection of citizens' rights, not decreasing them as suggested by conservatives, precisely because the 'growth of the public sector seems to have developed largely in response to demands for services and guarantees not available from the free market' (Carnoy and Levin, 1985, p. 13). They develop a model of educational change which includes this dialectical element.

> The dynamic of the American educational system, we suggest, can best be understood as part of a much wider social conflict arising in the nature of the capitalist production, with its inequalities of income and power. These inequalities lead to struggles by subordinate, relatively powerless groups for greater equality, economic security, and social control. In a politically democratic society, the State provides space for such struggles. In public education, as our historical sketch has shown, the social conflict is expressed in the conflict between reforms aimed at reproducing the inequalities required for social efficiency under monopoly capitalism and reforms aimed at equalizing opportunities in pursuit of democratic and constitutional ideas. (Carnoy and Levin, 1985, p. 24)

Thus it is through these concepts that frameworks that both facilitate the analysis of social reproduction *and* provide a way of seeing people as subjects, not objects, and the possibilities of social change are made evident. The anti-deterministic concepts include 'resistance' by individuals to hegemonic ideas, the 'consciousness' of human thought that is capable of critique, 'counter-hegemonic' activities by subordinate groups, 'utopian ideas' pushed by subordinate but ascendant groups, the reality of 'contradictions' and potentially 'liberating practices' embedded in the hegemonic order of the dominant groups, and a view of society which sees the state as not only helping to reproduce social divisions, but also capable of progressive attitudes and actions in a dynamic struggle in which it is not only the arena but also a prize. These concepts are relevant in understanding both class and gender in education. Yet considerable clarification is still needed if we are to understand the interaction of *gender* with education as well as with class.

Conceptualizing Gender: Making Women Visible

The basic tenet in most feminist theory is that gender is as important a source of power as class, and that any theory which orients itself totally around the means of production (defined as the labour-capital relationship) must inevitably obscure or submerge power based on other sources. As Heidi Hartmann, in her comprehensive paper on the unhappy marriage between socialism and feminism, succinctly put it: 'Marxism and feminism are one and that one is Marxism' (Hartmann, 1981, p. 2). The debate is extensive, but essentially the point is that it is very difficult to deal with women in socialist theory by doing anything other than — again — attaching them to the men who are presumed to support them via the paid workplace. If the labour-capital relationship is the central and determining feature of society, then anyone not in the paid workforce is taken account of only by virtue of their attachment to someone who is — a father, husband or the state.

However, social theorists who see gender as an equally competing if not *more* pervasive source of power in society than class, chronicle the long history of gender-based exploitation, argue that such exploitation is based on the organization of sexual relations and procreation (instead of the organization of the means of production), and that the most salient part of the hegemonic ideology perpetuated by the dominant group (adult males) is that of biology as destiny for women, with society's prevalent notions about 'the family' and 'motherhood' seen as 'natural' and inevitable.

Without going into the extensive debate between so-called socialist feminists and radical feminists (who differ generally on the primacy given to the power structures which emanate from the organization of production versus the organization of sexuality), many theorists would suggest that a binocular approach is needed, i.e. a way of seeing how gender and class structures have developed in *interaction* with each other. Bob Connell has argued for the need for an account of a 'joint dynamic' between the class structure and the sexual power structure which focuses on historical change. 'It is a question of the interplay between the generative processes that produce capitalism and patriarchy, their processes of transformation, and their tendencies toward crisis' (Connell, 1983, p. 38). Joan Kelly, in advocating a 'doubled vision' in this regard, stressed the public importance of personal relations and the personal importance of public relations. She points out that

> *woman's place is not a separate sphere or domain of existence but a position within social existence generally.* It is a subordinate position, and it supports our social institutions at the same time that it serves and services men. Woman's place is to do women's work — at home and in the labor force. And it is to experience sex hierarchy — in work relations and personal ones, in our public and our private lives. Hence our analyses, regardless of the traditions they originate in, increasingly treat the family in relation to society; treat sexual and reproductive experience in terms of political economy; and treat productive relations of class in connection with sex hierarchy. (Kelly, 1979, p. 221, original emphasis)

Thus public and private are not separate spheres but intimately related. How private lives are organized is directly related to how public lives are organized, and how public life is organized is directly related to how private life is organized.

In the 'joint dynamic' or 'doubled vision' of gender and class it is, for the most part, the effects of gender which are the least understood, particularly by male social and political theorists. Dale Spender (1982), in her book on the effects of the 'invisibility of women' in the education system, discussed the way in which much of what we think of as human experience is really male experience. Spender argues that many of our understandings of the world as seen in our culture, our institutions and our economy are based on a male experience of the world. Because of the historically based hierarchy between men and women, women experience the world differently from men, but this is not generally recognized. Male experience is taken as universal, but in fact it is only part of human experience. This perspective is important in developing an understanding of the processes of social reproduction in respect of gender.

It is useful to elaborate the argument. Spender argues that the male definition of the world occurs in three ways. First, the way in which *male* experience is seen as *all* experience is related to the way in which *female* experience is not seen at all but is *invisible*. Women's experience of life has largely disappeared from our knowledge of the past. Most people are ignorant of past women's achievements and of their everyday lives. This omission grows and becomes the ostensible reason for the continuation of the ignorance. The result is a distorted history but one which is not seen to be distorted.

The second mechanism that facilitates a male definition of the world is the way in which *male* experience is seen as *central* to life and *female* experience is seen *in relation* to male experience and hence peripheral. Men make meanings of life as it appears to them and they name it accordingly. Thus their experience is central and women are defined in relation to men's experience. This can be seen in our distorted sociology and economics, for example, in the way in which 'work' is defined as what men do but not what women do, no matter how many hours are actually spent in chores. This means that women find themselves saying nonsensical things like, 'Oh I don't work, I'm just a housewife.' It also means that women's work is not dealt with in economic theories and statistics; consequently, economists can describe how our economy supposedly operates while completely ignoring a huge hidden and essential economic infrastructure in terms of the unpaid work done by women in servicing men and homes, raising children, consuming, caring for the ill and aged and providing social welfare services to a wide cross-section of the community. Furthermore, international agencies like the United Nations which gather large amounts of data on different facets of work in different countries have been responsible for categorizing data in essentially illogical ways, such as their practice of counting agricultural work done by men as contributing to the gross national product but not agricultural work done by women.

The third mechanism that facilitates a male definition of the world according to Spender is the way in which *male* life-cycle development is seen as the *norm* for human development and *female* development is seen consequently as *deviant*. The male is seen as the normal, representative, paradigmatic human being, and women are judged against this standard and found wanting. For example, psychologist Carol Gilligan (1982) has described the impact of this way of thinking on our psychological theories. She argues that most of the major developmental theorists, such as Piaget, Erikson, Bettleheim and Freud, have all equated male development with human development, particularly insofar as their theories stress the concept of 'separation' as a milestone of childhood/adolescent development. Attaining psychological separation is seen as the key to maturity. But the reality is that due to our historically based family structure in which women are the primary child-carers, little boys *do* have to distinguish themselves from their mothers and other female care-givers in order to assume an adult and male identity, but little girls do not to the same degree. Yet girls are then seen as having greater 'problems' with separation than boys. However, the problem lies in the definition. Normal male development is taken as universal, and girls' inability to separate is then seen as a failure to develop normally. In conjunction with this, girls' developed ability to 'attach' rather than separate is seen as a weakness. When the focus on separation and individual achievement extends into adulthood, and maturity is equated with personal autonomy, then concern with relationships appears as a weakness of women rather than a human strength. Yet surely while individuation is one important aspect of mature human development, so too is attachment.

The point of this kind of work is that it draws our attention to the effects of the past which are embedded in the present. Historically, our social institutions developed in a way which was directly related to the existing hierarchy between men and women. Thus all of our present social structures are likely to reflect that historical relationship. But because they seem to have 'always been', because this has suited particular dominant groups, it is very hard now to 'see' how our modern institutions — and attitudes — are gendered. Analyses like Spender's and Gilligan's are useful for helping to perceive the world differently.

Many writers have also tried to describe the role that the education system plays in the process of social reproduction in relation to gender. For example, Ann Marie Wolpe (1978) argued that the education system functions to satisfy the requirements of both the division of labour within the family and the sexual division of labour in employment. It does this through providing basic training in the necessary skills and transmitting the appropriate ideologies which will fit girls into, at one and the same time, the 'female' labour market and the traditional wife and motherhood roles within the family. Thus the two systems are linked together, and the education is functional for both. Michele Barrett (1980) has also argued that schools contribute to reproducing women's dual relationship to the class structure through ideology, the structure and organization of schools, the mechanisms of channelling girls into the sexual division of labour, and the definition of the curriculum and legitimate knowledge.

Miriam David has examined the relationship of the state, the family and education in the United Kingdom, arguing that: 'the family and the education system are used in concert to sustain and reproduce the social and economic *status quo*. Specifically, they maintain existing relations within the family and social relations within the economy — what has sometimes been called the sexual and social divisions of labour' (David, 1980, p. 1). In a historical analysis David looks at the growth and specification of parental responsibilities and rights in connection with the development of mass compulsory education, and the political aims of education with regard to the division of labour in the family and the workplace. In particular, she looks at the development of curriculum to teach girls about mothering and sexual division of labour in the home, the 'familial ambiance' in the organization of schooling and the treatment of women in teaching. Rosemary Deem has also illuminated the 'familial ambiance' in schooling through her emphasis on the continuity of women's work as mothers in the family and as teachers especially in primary schools. The continuum reflects the existing doubled and gendered division of labour in the home and the workplace. She argues that 'education does not create the sexual division of labour, nor the kinds of work available in the labour market, nor the class relationships of society, but it rarely does anything to undermine them' (Deem, 1978, p. 20).

There has also been considerable work which has described and analyzed the resistance of girls and groups of girls to schooling, to social concepts of appropriate femininity and sexuality, and to class expectations. In particular, the doubled reality of class and gender domination is highlighted for working-class girls (McRobbie and McCabe, 1981; Anyon, 1983). However, schools are understood as contradictory sites for girls and for women teachers. Resistance *may* liberate girls or it may embed them more firmly in subordinate gender or class systems. It is precisely because of the contradictions *between* class and gender, and *between* such 'private' social systems and the 'public' nature of state education that the reality of schools is complex, tense and undetermined. The pressures for reproduction and the potential for change are both always present because social systems are always in process.

Madeleine Arnot has stressed the importance of avoiding the determinism of feminist as well as class reproduction theory. She argues that Gramsci's concept of hegemony should replace the concept of reproduction.

> By putting the concept of hegemony, rather than 'reproduction' at the fore of an analysis of class and gender, it is less easy in research to forget the *active* nature of the learning process, the existence of dialectical relations, power struggles, and points of conflict, the range of alternative practices which may exist inside, or exist outside and be brought into the school. (Madeleine Arnot, 1982, p. 66)

Thus in conceptualizing how gender operates in education it is important to 'double our vision' by always keeping the operation of *class* in mind as well. Class differences and gender differences have developed together in ways that make it impossible to separate them for the purposes of understanding either. It is also important to utilize concepts like resistance and counter-hegemony so that the dynamic aspect of social processes and the active agency of human beings is not overlooked. Placing the present in the context of the past and seeking the historical base also helps to avoid a dissolving away to biology for explanations. We must also keep trying to make women visible in our analyses by continually asking about the public importance of personal relations and the personal importance of public relations. Given the strength of the public-private dualistic view of the world in our present society, and the ideological attachment of women to the private sphere and men to the public sphere, it is likely that by continually questioning the implications and effects of this social division we can 'demystify' it and 'see' more clearly how the lives of men and women interact.

Arenas for Analysis: The Development of Bureaucracy in Education and the Relationship of Family, Economy and Education

In analyzing gender and education one could look at many areas. The preference here is to examine two areas which are seen as crucial to an understanding of what has gone on, and is now going on, in the lives of boys and girls in schools, their teachers and their parents. One is the way in which gender differentiation has been related to the development of bureaucracy in education; the other is the relationship of education, the economy and the family.

The Development of Bureaucracy in Education

In Australia, as in North America and Great Britain, the development of mass compulsory education systems provided by the state occurred at the same time that business and governments were developing bureaucratic forms of organization during the period of early capitalism in the latter half of the nineteenth century and the early half of the twentieth century (see Tyack, 1974, for example.) One of the features of bureaucratic organization is the division of tasks so that a separation occurs between conception and execution. Those who conceive of the task may not be those who are responsible for its execution. Richard Bates (1983) and others have argued that in education this appeared as a separation of administrative concerns from educational concerns. Some people became exclusively concerned with organizing, planning and administering schooling and others became almost exclusively responsible for providing the education itself. Furthermore, Bates has suggested that the separation of administrative and educational concerns was accompanied by the development of a 'cult of efficiency' in education in which a narrow definition of the provision of educational services became the paramount concern of educational administrators. Closely connected with this was the growing concept of expertise in education, or the idea that only certain kinds of people with specific credentials, experiences or skills could be responsible for the social engineering of which the development of compulsory education was a part.

How do the gender issues relate to the development of bureaucracy in education? There are at least three ways of observing this interaction: in gender-linked job types, in gender-linked job descriptions, and in gender-linked job opportunities and power. Gender-linked job types in educational bureaucracies are the easiest to observe. Kathy Ferguson (1984) has argued in a similar vein for the links between bureaucratic structures and processes and masculine values. The development of large-scale bureaucracies in education went hand-in-hand with gender-linked jobs within them. Essentially, men became responsible for the conception, and women the execution, of schooling. Men became the administrators and women the teachers. As one moved up the educational status ladder of primary through secondary and tertiary education, the more likely one was to find more men and fewer women. Even the important clerical support systems for schools and educational bureaucracies repeated the same pattern with female secretaries and male managers. David Tyack (1974), writing about the development of American urban education at the turn of the century, has demonstrated how in that country the developing bureaucratic forms of organization were able to use the existing gender stratification system to the advantage of male administrators (and also to the advantage of white, Anglo-Saxon, Protestant administrators).

The development of bureaucracy in education went hand-in-hand with gender-linked job descriptions. This is a somewhat more subtle manifestation and has to do with the ways in which gender-linked jobs are defined officially in non-gender-linked ways but structured to nurture the gender link. It is a good example of the 'sexism you have when you aren't having sexism'. Rosabeth Moss Kantor (1977), in her study of *Men and Women of the Corporation*, has made some interesting observations on the organizational structure of secretaries' jobs and the relationship between female secretaries and male bosses. Kantor argues that what it takes to be a good secretary perpetuates differentiation between clerical and managerial hierarchies and prevents secretaries from job mobility. In her view the social organization of secretarial work involves three aspects: secretaries derive their status from their bosses and the boss' status determines the power of the secretary; there are very few limits on managerial discretion with regard to secretaries' work as secretaries must respond to a constant flow of orders and are expected to provide personal services; there is an expectation of strong personal loyalty from the secretary to the boss.

Kantor argues that these characteristics of the organization of secretarial work cause secretaries to display behaviour and attitudes which are taken to be female attributes but which are really the orientations of people whose strategies for achieving recognition and control are constrained by the social organization of their job. For example, in one study the female secretaries in a large organization eventually became parochial in the sense that they narrowed their interests to their own small part of the organization as this was what their bosses encouraged; they became timid and self-effacing about their own skills or potential talents; they became addicted to praise as that was a central element in the reward structure of their job (as opposed to money or mobility); and they became prey to emotionality and gossip as a classic way in which the powerless get something from the powerful through emotional manipulation. But what is important is that the attitudes and behaviours that they were rewarded for as good secretaries were exactly the opposite of the attitudes and behaviours they needed to move into management (which were thinking broadly about the whole organization, being confident about their abilities, being able to take criticism as well as praise). The social organization of the secretaries' jobs also encouraged them to resist organizational change.

In education it is possible that the social organization of the job of primary school teachers works against job mobility into administration, in that the attitudes and behaviours that are needed to be seen to be a good primary school teacher are quite different from those that are needed to be seen to be a good manager, e.g. a principal. It is also possible that the attitudes and behaviours that are needed to be seen to be a good primary teacher are quite different from those needed to be seen to be a good secondary teacher. It is even possible that the attitudes and behaviours needed to be seen to be a good school teacher in general are quite different from those needed to be seen to be a good tertiary academic. Furthermore, it is a fact that each of the 'lower' levels is more femalc-dominated than the 'higher' levels. Thus the jobs may be socially organized and structured to maintain the gender link, while seeming to maintain only what is perceived to be essential job descriptions. Finally, since women mostly hold the jobs lower in the hierarchy, the job descriptions and related job characteristics are also seen to be female characteristics and not just job-related expectations. The circle closes.

With regard to the relationship between the social organization of the job and resistance to change, Michael Apple (1982) has argued that one can understand little about educational change without recognizing the significance of the gendered labour force of teaching. He suggests that the history of reform in schools has been largely the history of 'patriarchal politics' in which male academics and male administrators try to intervene in the work of a largely female teaching workforce. It is through this dimension that he interprets much of the (gendered) resistance to curricular reform. His basic argument is 'that it is nearly impossible to understand why curricula and teaching are controlled the way they are unless we understand who is doing the teaching' (Apple, 1988, p. 10). On the other hand, in terms of resistance, Kathleen Weiler (1988) has documented the activities and achievements of feminist teachers who have struggled against this control.

The third way in which gender interacts with the development of bureaucracy in education lies in gender-related job opportunities and power. An important point here is the extent to which having opportunities and power, versus not having them, creates a self-fulfilling prophecy for both the haves and the have-nots. Kantor (1977) argues that power in bureaucracies is all about getting for the group, for subordinates and followers, a favourable share of the resources, opportunities and rewards possible in the organization. Power begets power, and people prefer to associate with the powerful. Bureaucracies are complex organizations which ensure dependency upon many others for decisions to be made. Powerful people can help to short-circuit the dependency by creating some certainty. With regard to women in bureaucracies Kantor argues that the preference for male managers is to a large extent a preference for perceived power.

It is not difficult to envision this argument applying to educational bureaucracies as well. In organizations like schools, where women have not had the same historical opportunities for power and hence efficacy, it is not surprising that males are more powerful and seen to be more powerful. In building a career in education it has been safer to form alliances with males rather than females in that the reality has been that males were more likely to become powerful, and hence facilitate more certainty, in these complex organizations.

The Relationship of Family, Economy and Education

Gender differentiation is based on our ideas — our ideology — about the family; our ideas about the economy significantly define the family; and the education system is implicated in reproducing traditional views in these areas. The importance of the family lies in the reality that this institution is most basic in governing male-female relationships. It is with regard to the family that the status of men and women is most clearly determined. Thus our notions about the 'proper' kind of family are important in understanding the status of men and women in society. In reality there are, of course, many different kinds of families in which men and women play many different roles in many different ways. Yet it is in the ideal rather than real that ideology about the family is most obvious and most powerful. In our society for about the last one hundred years the ideal family has been seen as one in which there exists one male wage-earner who brings outside income into the family and one female who remains at home and whose responsibilities are basically to service the male and offspring. This notion of the family was enshrined and entangled in the concept of the 'family wage' which in Australia was given considerable impetus through the Commonwealth Arbitration Court in 1907.

This type of family is different from the one which existed prior to the industrial revolution, in which the entire family unit was responsible for bringing income into the family, and looking after family members was the responsibility of several members of a larger and often extended family unit. Many observers have pointed out that with the development of the factory system came an increasing division of labour in which economic production was shifted out of the home and away from women and children (see Kuhn and Wolpe, 1978; Eisenstein, 1978). It became the domain of individual men who were paid a wage on which the entire household was expected to survive. Consequently, women were increasingly perceived as non-contributors to the economy, yet the new system was dependent upon the unpaid work of women as well as the paid work of men. The roles of women within the family in caring for men, children and aged relatives, in providing social welfare services to the community and in consuming are key economic roles. They must be fulfilled for society and the economy to function. If there is not an unpaid woman in the family to do them, then someone from outside is hired and paid to perform exactly these tasks. Furthermore, it is clearly in the interests of private capitalists and governments for as much of this to remain *in* the family and out of the state as possible, otherwise they might be called upon for financial support. This is the distinction between the public and private spheres, and this is the way in which women are actually *part* of the economy but not *seen* to be part of the economy.

The importance of our ideas about how the economy operates in relation to the family is brought home most strongly by arguments such as that of Jill Matthews who points out, for example, that popular economic interpretations of the post-war period describe a 'working women's revolution' in which women are portrayed as rushing into the paid workforce — even when married and with young children. Matthews argues that

> To a large degree, the post war 'working women's revolution' was a trick of perspective, not a radical change in women's experiences.
>
> The trick lay in the definition of work, its nature and its place. By and large, masculine economists have classified as work only that which is clearly performed within the masculine capitalist marketplace — the commanding heights, that which is directly organised by the traditional processes of that marketplace — as in large corporate or state enterprises, and that which is defended by the traditional institutions of the male working class — the trade unions. (Matthews, 1984, p. 55)

Matthews points out that women have always worked within the 'local economy' but were invisible to economists because the 'commanding' economy did not move to control the 'local economy' until the 1960s. Now women have become visible as workers, yet all that is happening is that women are now producing jam, bread, shirts, minding children and nursing the infirm for remuneration in the marketplace rather than out of sight for no pay at home (Matthews, 1984, p. 58).

Thus the definitions of what is work, what is part of the economy, the role of the family and gender differentiation are inextricably interwoven. The education system is clearly implicated in this process. As mass compulsory education expanded in the last part of the nineteenth century and in the early twentieth century, schooling contributed to altering the relationships between men and women, adults and children, and the division of labour in the family. For example, the withdrawal of children's contribution to the family economy, the reduction of the parental role in education in favour of specialization in schools, the impossibility of older school children minding younger ones, the increased pressure on mothers to stay at home for small children and to be at home for older ones since school hours did not fit work hours, the increased professional surveillance of parenting, especially mothering, enshrined in child-welfare provisions, the increased cultural attention to the educational extras that 'good mothers' could provide children — these are all illustrations of the links between the education system, the economy and the family.

Schools themselves confirm these links by the hundreds of little acts which encourage girls towards academic areas and future jobs which are likely to ensure their future economic dependency on men or on the state, the continuing lack of women in decision-making roles in schools in which modelling of independence could be observed, the teaching of a history which portrays the 'productive' members of the society to have been primarily men, the various ways in which the higher status of men is confirmed, such as the well-known research showing that teachers spend far more time and attention on boys in classrooms than on girls, and so on (see Spender, 1982). It is important to recognize that this is not just mindless discrimination. The spoken and unspoken justification lies squarely in our ideology of the family. That is *why* it happens; and that is the reason it is not solved simply by the large number of genuine reforms introduced in schools in this area in the last two decades. Sexism in education has to be confronted directly in terms of its relationship with the ideology of the family and its links to the economy.

Many theories and concepts have been considered in this discussion of the interaction of gender and education. Initially, the usefulness of social reproduction theories as providing a basic understanding of how gender and class were mediated through education was discussed. However, the determinism and sexism inherent in these theories were indicated, and ways in which some of these problems could be moderated conceptually were suggested. Social production of both class and gender can be seen to operate through the hegemony of dominant groups — both capitalist and adult males. This hegemony is heavily dependent upon ideology, which legitimates these power relations. Yet ideas do exist in society which are not aligned with these dominant interests, including relatively organized sets of ideas representing alternatives, or 'utopias'. Utopian ideas are usually held by subordinate, but often ascendant, groups. In addition there are many incidences of individual resistance because of individual consciousness. There are also likely to be contradictions and liberating practices which exist within the hegemonic structures and processes. If one focuses on counter-hegemonic tendencies, the reality of points of conflict and power struggles are not lost, and alternatives are clearer.

The state has increasingly become both a site of social struggle between dominant and dominated groups and a prize itself. In the conceptualization of this process it is also important to keep firmly in mind the *joint* dynamic of gender and class and to be aware of the historical origins of present practices. In making women more visible in this process, the relationship and interaction between the public and private spheres, particularly the economy and the family, are crucial for a fuller understanding of the interaction of gender and education.

The State-Family-Workplace Intersection: Illustrations

This section provides some historical examples of ways in which the state, the ideology of the family and the workplace intersect in educational spheres. In particular, the concepts of resistance, contradictions and counter-hegemony are illustrated through examples in twentieth century Australian public schools.

The Domestic Education Curriculum and Resistance. 'Domestic economy' was a subject offered to virtually all girls in the upper years of Australian primary schools from the beginning of state-provided education in the late eighteenth century. Together with manual training for boys, these 'practical' subjects were seen to provide important eye-hand coordination practice, accuracy and tidiness skills, as well as equipping children — particularly girls — for their future lives (Education Department, Western Australia, 1906, p. 10). For example, household management centres, which were set up as much like a home as possible and to which girls came for sessions from contributory schools, were established in Western Australia in 1907. The curriculum was intended to include cooking, the care of the sick, the care of children, household furnishing, cleaning, food purchasing and budgeting. When laundry work was introduced to the course, it became controversial, as many parents objected to their daughters doing such a subject at school. Their concerns included the fear that the girls were being exploited (in terms of doing the laundry of other public institutions), the unacademic nature of work, the lack of desirability of girls eventually finding employment in this area anyway (Education Department, Western Australia, 1908, p. 80). Keeping in mind that government-provided schools were particularly for working-class children at this time (middle-class children attending private schools), one might attribute the parental resistance to a feeling that middle-class Education Department officials were attempting to 'keep them in their place'. It is likely that the parents had ideas of prospective employment for their daughters which had more status. They may have also felt that to be good homemakers girls did not need a school course in laundry work. In any event it is likely that both gender and class were in interaction in this area.

The Western Australian Education Department regularly noted the objections of parents in their annual reports between 1900 and 1930 but continued to pursue the course they felt was most desirable. Their rationale focused on the importance of the training of future wives and mothers of the state, and they eventually made laundry work a compulsory part of the household management curriculum. They had continued to defend their domestic course and laundry work over this thirty-year period. Some of the ideology of the family which underscored their rationale can be seen in the following excerpts from annual departmental reports:

> In the schools an attempt is being made to combat with the evils of drink and smoking. . . . A superficial knowledge of the matter is sufficient to provide that a very common cause which drives a man from his home to the hotel is a badly cooked dinner or a mismanaged washing day. Therefore it seems to be of more importance to provide instruction in practical cookery and laundry work for the girls who will develop into wives and mothers than to teach theoretically the evils of excessive drinking and smoking. (Education Department, Western Australia, 1909, p. 92)
>
> It is to be hoped that girls who receive instruction in these most necessary arts will be the better fitted for their future destiny as wives and mothers than would have been possible for the large majority of them had they not received such instruction in the schools. (Education Department, Western, Australia, 1915, p. 49)

During the early twentieth century needlework was another part of the curriculum considered essential for girls, yet it too was often a problem area (Porter, 1983). In this case there was a lack of enthusiasm by some students and objections by the female teachers responsible for the lessons. Female teachers typically had no choice as to whether they would teach sewing. It was assumed by state Education Departments that it was a normal part of their duties, despite many complaints by female teachers about both having to teach it and not being paid extra for it. For example, a statement by the Western Australian Department of Education to its teachers in the *Education Circular* clearly lays out the perceived importance of needlework both for the home and workplace for working-class girls, and the ambivalence of middle-class female teachers in devoting time to this non-academic subject:

> There is a strong temptation to push needlework into a corner, and to look up on it as unimportant compared with other subjects. To many teachers ... it does not figure in the list of subjects required for Bursary, or University examinations, and does little towards raising the status of the school.... State education exists primarily for the benefit of the working classes, whose children have to make their own way in the world; and therefore for these girls the ability to make and mend is of the utmost importance. If we look to 'the relative value of subjects' in after life, a woman will rarely be called on to work a sum in square root or analyze a sentence; but nearly every day of her life rents will require mending, and stockings have to be darned. The woman who can do these things well will be a thriftier, tidier, and therefore more useful member of society than the one who cannot. (Education Department, Western Australia, 1900, p. 71)

The lack of interest by teachers, as well as the poor quality of student work, was regularly commented upon by the Western Australian Education Department in annual reports. The possibility of salary reduction was brought to the attention of teachers through the *Education Circular*: 'Teachers are reminded that under Regulation 64 section (a), female teachers not qualified to teach sewing are subject to a reduction in their salaries' (Education Department, Western Australia, 1901, p. 96). Furthermore, the issue reflected differences and disputes between male and female teachers, as men were paid extra for teaching manual work but women were not in the case of sewing. The Western Australian Education Department was not impressed with this protest by some of its teachers.

> Many of our teachers, especially the younger ones, seem to think that sewing is not part of their usual work; they look on it as an extra subject, and some have even asserted that those who teach sewing should be paid extra for doing so, as men are for manual work. It is well to remind such that sewing is an integral part of women teachers' work in every civilised country, and such a claim is as irrational as being paid extra for teaching any other class subject. (Education Department, Western Australia, 1910, p. 101)

The departmental Inspectress also lamented: 'In many schools it is to be feared that senior girls are robbed of their sewing lessons in order to coach them for University subjects' (Education Department, Western Australia, 1910, p. 101). Her view was that the 'ability to teach it [sewing] should be required of every woman student' and that female teacher trainees should have their college certificate withheld until they satisfactorily passed an examination in needlework.

There is little doubt that needlework for girls prepared them jointly for the sexual division of labour in the home and the workplace. It is also clear in this illustration that the Education Department in Western Australia had a quite visible ideology about women in this regard and that resistance by female teachers for reasons either of academic status or of equity with male teachers would not change their convictions. It is also apparent that the Education Department did recognize the economic role of women in the family. In 1921 there was an evaluation of technical education in Western Australia and the subsequent report recommended, among other things, that instruction should not be provided free of charge except for courses for industrial purposes only. It recommended that dressmaking and millinery should only be provided for those in the trades. The Western Australian Education Department debated this, pointing out that the university offered many courses free of charge which were not directly related to employment. Furthermore, they argued that industry was also *in* the home: 'it must be remembered that the largest single industry in the world is that of home making. It cannot be said that classes which render the women of the community more efficient in their life work are to be considered as of no value to the State' (Education Department, Western Australia, 1922, p. 15)

The Choice of Course by Students and Resistance. Another example in which we can ascertain the ideology underlying school programs for girls and boys is curricular choice. Until World War II most Australian states provided differentiated courses in categories usually termed professional commercial, industrial and domestic. Industrial courses were typically reserved for boys, and domestic courses were reserved for girls. However, both girls and boys could do the professional courses, and girls were increasingly allowed to do the commercial courses. This was often seen as a problem. For example, from 1915 to 1928 the Education Department in Western Australia stressed its concern that too many girls were doing the commercial course instead of the domestic course (see Table 1.1). The issue was raised in annual reports and the Inspector stressed that the domestic course was a strong one and that girls who

Table 1.1 Enrolment in Central Schools, Western Australia, 1913–29[1]

	Commercial course			Industrial course	Domestic course	Professional course			
Year	Boys	Girls	Total	Boys	Girls	Boys	Girls	Total	Total
1913	297	346	643	277	119	—	—	—	1 039
1917	583	823	1 406	531	197	203	307	510	2 644
1920	490	611	1 101	658	367	275	418	693	2 819
1924	366	544	910	837	389	522	233	755	2 891
1927	378	673	1 051	784	429	612	356	968	3 232
1929	690	873	1 563	823	393	793	309	802	3 581

Note: 1 Central schools were schools which congregated older primary pupils (Years 7 and 8) into one institution.

Source: Compiled from Education Department, Western Australia, *Annual Reports*, 1917–30.

took it 'should prove thoroughly capable housewives in the future'. The problem was that 'this course, however, does not attract the numbers which its value warrants.' The reasons were clear to him and to the Western Australian Education Department.

> One cannot be blind to the fact that at the present day work in the home is not attractive to the great majority of the growing girls.... They prefer almost any other kind of employment. Large numbers of them desire to enter offices as female clerks... Still the shorter hours of labour, the greater freedom, the less strenuous work, and what is still unfortunately falsely considered as the greater social dignity, are attracting too many of our girls from women's natural sphere in the home, and bringing them into competition with men. There is a very large number of girls who are attracted, too, by the professional course.... Still there remains the consideration that for nearly all women the home, and all that the term 'home' signifies, is their natural destiny, and it is somewhat difficult to see how girls who drift into commercial and professional work are even going to acquire the training which will make them efficient as wives and mothers in the future ... the outlook for the future is not thoroughly satisfactory. It seems to me if the present tendency for 80 per cent of our girls to rush into office or kindred work is maintained, that the homes of the future will be composed of an efficient male wage-earner and a more or less efficient wife. (Education Department, Western Australia, 1917, p. 56)

The domestic course for girls was intended to prepare working-class girls for both their work in their own homes and work in the homes of the middle and upper classes. Western Australia, like other states, had always had an insufficient supply of domestic servants. Again the gender and class dimensions of this issue are inseparable. The Education Department recognized the problem of the low social prestige of domestic work in other people's homes but stressed the efficiency of their program.

> The trouble seems to be that work of a domestic nature has generally in the past carried with it a sort of stigma of social inferiority and has generally been the refuge of those who are uneducated.
>
> Such a condition need no longer apply. We have in connection with our Household Management Classes all over the State facilities for training girls to be just as efficient workers in a home as we have in our Commercial Classes to train them to be efficient workers in an office. (Education Department, Western Australia, 1917, pp. 65–6)

The popularity of the commercial course compared with the domestic course for girls remained an issue for the Western Australian Education Department throughout this period, and comments continued in the annual reports until 1930 that not only did the girls appear to avoid the domestic course but that their parents were also unconvinced of its value. 'The course is undoubtedly one of great value for the future housewives and mothers. The attention of parents has been drawn to the importance of this training, but many of them are doubtful about the possibility of it leading to directly remunerative work' (Education Department, Western Australia, 1922, p. 5).

The next thirty years saw little change in Australia in this general approach to domestic education for girls. In Western Australia annual reports continued to talk about the value of both the subject and the course in terms of their importance for future 'mothers of the State' and in terms of their potential 'commercial value'. Domestic economy became domestic science in 1944, home science in 1951 and home economics in 1968, name changes which raise some interesting speculation about the perceptions of such an area as science versus economics, as well as possibly reflecting the subject's lack of 'fit' with the more typical academic curriculum. The subject remained compulsory for all girls through the 1960s, when it became an option at the secondary level (remaining compulsory for one year at the primary level). In the 1970s it became generally possible for both boys and girls to take either home economics or manual arts. However, timetabling, peer pressure, teacher and parental expectation still ensure that for the most part girls and boys follow the traditional pattern. Certain areas of home economics, such as food and nutrition, have become more popular with boys, while areas like clothing and fabric remain almost exclusively in the girls' domain. Home economics has also become an examinable subject for tertiary admittance. This 'professionalization' of the subject became more possible in Western Australia after the Western Australian Institute of Technology (now Curtin University of Technology) opened a course in home economics in 1975.

Vocational Opportunities, Career Guidance and Contradictions. Another area where the state-family-workplace intersection can be observed is in the vocational opportunities perceived by schooling authorities to be open to boys and girls and the career guidance advice consequently provided to children and their families. This area is typically filled with contradictions.

For example, in Western Australia in 1938, during the depression, the government organized a Royal Commission on Youth Employment and the Apprenticeship System. The report of the Commission is an interesting document for what it does and does not say with regard to the employment of girls and boys. The Commission was concerned with the entire area of youth employment and unemployment, education, training and apprenticeships. Not surprisingly, the bulk of the report was clearly focused on the future of boys in the world of paid work. Although the report described the centre of its concern as 'youth', which it defined as 'any young person between the ages of 14 and 25 years', it went on to talk almost entirely of training boys, finding employment for boys, organizing apprenticeships for boys, etc. (*Report of the Royal Commission on Youth Employment and the Apprenticeship System*, 1938, pp. vi–vii).

The report did make one specific recommendation for girls when it noted that there was no provision for domestic science in any of the technical schools, only provision for dressmaking and millinery; it recommended that 'instruction in domestic science be included in the technical curriculum' (*Report of the Royal Commission on Youth Employment and the Apprenticeship System*, 1938, p. xxxi). (A new course in hairdressing had just been established with outside funds). The Superintendent of Technical Education, in evidence to the Commission, commented:

> Many girls leave school with a limited knowledge gained in the domestic science centre. . . From both the domestic and the employment point of view it is desirable that the technical schools should be equipped so that they could continue the work of the domestic science centres and give the girls who have left school

> and older women the benefit of such training. It is agreed that many young women must in future become domestic workers, and that the status of such work should be raised by a systematic course of training.... In such a course the following could be incorporated: Cookery (elementary, advanced and invalid); hygiene; housewifery; science; physiology; laundry work, etc. (*Report of the Royal Commission on Youth Employment and the Apprenticeship System*, 1938, p. xxvi)

In one short section the report directly tackled the controversial issue of female employment. It began by pointing out that 'in spite of the general impression to the contrary, there has not been a world-wide invasion of the labour market by women in the twentieth century'. Instead, women had moved from the traditional occupations of women, in particular agriculture and domestic service, to occupations with better conditions, such as light industry, commerce, the civil service and the professions. The report stated that

> Women are in the main employed in avocations to which they are particularly adapted. In some industries ... a lighter touch is required, or a more deft operation of some machine is necessary and it will be found that for the most part women preponderate.... I may cite the case of machinists working on adding and computing machines. This type of work is of a tedious and monotonous nature, and is essentially sedentary, and it was found that men would not stick to the uninteresting and, after a while, mechanical process of working a machine, especially as that particular line of work offers little or no prospect of advancement.... The fact is that males generally show no inclination to take up these classes of work. In the teaching profession, too, this is the case. The Department has difficulty in obtaining men teachers. Yet here is a profession in which discrimination in wages for a similar class of work is actively practised to the extent that on an average the male receives approximately one-fourth more than the female. (*Report of the Royal Commission on Youth Employment and the Apprenticeship System*, 1938, pp. lxii–lxiv)

The report argued that there was no point in trying to force women out of the workforce, because in the main they were in occupations which suited their 'delicate movements' or 'temperament'. Thus while they did not oppose women being in paid work, they did see the issue quite clearly in terms of essential differences between the sexes. In particular, women, unlike men, were better able to tolerate monotonous, tedious, sedentary and uninteresting jobs with no future in them.

Another example of 'appropriate' occupations for boys and girls from the same era in public schooling can be found in a highly promoted booklet issued by the Education Department in Western Australia in 1936 and used for many years afterwards. Entitled *A Guide to Occupations for Boys and Girls*, the document was a reasonably comprehensive review of available employment opportunites in Western Australia at the time. What is most striking from the perspective of the underlying ideology regarding male and female roles was the very limited nature of the jobs available to girls compared with boys (see Table 1.2).

Much changed in Australia over the next thirty years but not, apparently, the perceived 'appropriate' occupational futures for boys and girls; yet the contradictions for the state began to become more apparent, in particular, the tension between the academic achievement goal of schooling for *all* students and the home and motherhood 'destiny' of female students. This can be seen by looking at some of the reports on education produced in the 1960s.

For example, the Dettman Report of 1969, *Secondary Education in Western Australia*, discussed secondary school reorganization (Education Department, Western Australia, 1969). It stated broad humanistic aims for education, although it did reintroduce the notion of pre-vocational subjects partially as a response to the rising secondary retention rates. It also came out against streaming based on general intelligence. With regard to the specific education of boys and girls it noted with some concern: 'While it is usual for the most capable students to follow the academic course, some elect to take the general course. This is particularly the case in relation to some girls taking the commercial course' (Education Department, Western Australia, 1969, pp. 40–1). In another area the report commented with favour on the innovation of work experience programs, and cited the example of one metropolitan high school which succeeded in gaining significant work experience for its students. It is hard not to observe that the occupational categories considered appropriate for boys and girls in 1936 would still seem relevant in 1969 (see Table 1.3).

The Dettman Report also stressed the importance of pastoral care, guidance and the 'inculcation of the moral values upon which our society rests'. An important role for the school, given the demise of the family which was at least partially due to mothers as well as fathers going out of the home to work, was character training.

Table 1.2 Occupations for Boys and Girls, Education Department, Western Australia, 1936

Level of education	Boys	Girls
Employment for those who leave primary school	Shop and warehouse assistants, factory hands; agricultural work; Government Railway Department; Royal Australian Navy	Shop and warehouse assistants; factory hands; waitresses; cooks; domestic service; laundry work
Employment for those with junior technical course	*Skilled trades — apprenticeships*: Building trades — bricklaying, stone masonry, plastering, carpentry and joinery, plumbing, sheet metalwork, painting and decorating; Engineering trades — fitters and turners, pattern makers, welders, electricians, motor mechanics, brass finishers, blacksmiths, boilermaking, moulding, coach building, government railway workshops, postal service, junior mechanics; Household supplies, food, clothing — breadmaking, pastry cooking, butchering, tailoring; Furniture trades — cabinet making, wood-turning, upholstery chair and frame making; Printing trades — hand composing, machine composing, letter press machining; Others — hairdressing, saddlery and harness-making, jewellery and watchmaking, shipwrighting and boat building.	*Skilled trades — apprenticeships*: order tailoring; factory tailoring; dressmaking and millinery; printing and book-binding; photography; beauty parlour and hairdressing
Employment for those with junior high school course	Commonwealth Public Service — junior officers, clerical division, telegraph messengers; State Civil Service — junior clerks; Government Railways — junior clerks; Police Department — cadets; Commonwealth Defence Forces — commissioned officer; Mining industry — (+ School of Mines course) assayer, mine surveyor, geologist, electrician, draughtsman; Others — banks; insurance firms; municipalities; commercial institutions; general clerical work	Commonwealth Public Service — telephonists, female assistants, typists; State Civil Service — junior typists, junior machinists; Nursing; General clerical work
Employment for those with high school course (most occupations require further tertiary study)	[Sex not specified as above but discussion is in terms of 'boys', except for teaching] Professional occupations — professional accountancy; architecture; dentistry; engineering; journalism; law; medicine; pharmacy; surveying; veterinary science. Teaching — government schools, non-government schools.	

Table 1.3 Occupational Categories Appropriate for Girls and Boys on Work Experience Programs, 1969

Boys	Girls
Cabinet making — furniture factory	General office work — steel distributor
Storeman/dispatch — plywood distributor	General office work — cement tile manufacturer
Factory hand/delivery — laundry service	General office work — machinery firm
Fettling — diecasting factory	Book-binding — printing firm
Metal machining — general engineering works	Shop assistant — chemist
Bowser attendant/lube attendant — service station	Shop assistant — drapers
Motor body building — body works	Shop assistant — chain store
Sheetmetal working — sheet metal fabricators	Telephonist/receptionist — vehicle distributor
Battery building — battery factory	Factory hand — chicken hatchery
Butcher — retail butcher shop	
Electrical maintenance — industrial electrical service	
Storeman — paint manufacturer	
Process worker/storeman — aluminium extrusion plant	
Motor mechanic — stationary engine distributor	

Source: Education Department, Western Australia (1969, p. 48).

> In current society, however, with so many homes where both parents go to work, where many children are unsupervised for an appreciable time after school, and where many homes seem to be affected by a diversity of factors harmful to children, the school must assume more and more responsibility in the field of character training (Education Department, Western Australia, 1969, pp. 72–3)

The views of students themselves were also beginning to provoke as many questions as answers. A survey of secondary school students with regard to their vocational aspirations was carried out by the Education Department in Western Australia in 1973. The *Education Circular* reported those results with a discussion of the merits of vocational versus general education. The varying sex differences in the data were also noted. However, one of the interesting aspects of the figures is not only the obvious sex-role stereotyping, for example, of girls in category C, but overall the large number of girls *wanting* to pursue categories A and B in relation to the relatively small number of women in those kinds of jobs at that time (see Table 1.4). The article's own question is relevant: 'But does this mean that schools should cater for these varying interests?' (Education Department, Western Australia, August 1974, p. 218).

Table 1.4 Vocational Aspiration of Secondary School Students, 1974

Occupational category	Males	Females
A Doctor, professor, lawyer, accountant, clergyman, architect, etc.	940 (38%)	528 (23%)
B Business owner, farmer, contractor, etc.	320 (14%)	85 (5%)
C Teacher, lecturer, social worker, etc.	303 (13%)	1 013 (42%)
D Insurance salesman, real estate salesman, government department clerk, bank teller, etc.	182 (9%)	274 (11%)
E Electrician, hairdresser, mechanic, baker, etc.	483 (20%)	428 (17%)
F Truck driver, labourer, machinist, etc.	150 (6%)	52 (2%)
Total number	2 528	2 480
Total percentage	100%	100%

Source: Adapted from Education Department, Western Australia (1974, p. 218).

By 1975 discrimination against girls and women in Australian schools was becoming an area of much vocal concern in many states. Women teachers and teachers' unions were mounting an increasingly high profile campaign (Porter, 1985). In Western Australia a Committee on Sexist Discrimination was formed to look into discrimination against males or females in the state education system. Among the areas considered was the subject and course choice by students. In their report the Committee noted that it was still the case that girls at Year 8 took home economics and boys manual arts, and that further, because of prerequisites and teacher attitudes, most students continued to take the traditional subjects in their high school options. One important consequence of this was that the 'practical' areas at the secondary level involved girls doing home economics, which had limited employment possibilities in the 1970s, and business education courses geared to a narrow range of occupations, while the boys, through manual arts, were able to do a large range of pre-vocational options (Education Department, Western Australia, 1976, pp. 42–7).

The report was also critical of the vocational guidance resources in use in Western Australian schools, and pointed out that in 1975 there were 14,121 students in pre-apprenticeships and apprenticeships and that less than 6 per cent of these were girls, nine-tenths of whom were in hairdressing, while the boys were in sixty-four different kinds of jobs. It was not unlikely, they argued, that there was a link between the occupational choices made by girls and the options and information provided in schools. The report made a number of recommendations to the Minister regarding possible changes in Education Department policy (Education Department, Western Australia, 1976, p. 55).

In 1981 the Research Branch of the Western Australian Education Department investigated the relationship between sex and subject choice in more detail (Brown, 1982; Brown and Fitzpatrick, 1981). Their conclusions were straightforward:

> In Western Australia, the patterns of enrolment of boys and girls in both tertiary admissions and general elective subjects in high schools have not changed since the early 1970s. Marked sex differences in enrolments are evident at Year 8 level, and intensify through secondary school. More girls still enrol in home economics, typing and language areas; more boys enrol in mathematics, technology and science-oriented subjects. (Brown, 1982, p. 1)

The reasons for the persistence of these sex differences in subject choice in the schools in their study were seen to be:

1 the constraints of what was actually available after schools timetable for 'majority' interests;
2 the social isolation felt by students who chose an option thought to be more suitable for the opposite sex;
3 the discouragement of some teacher counsellors because of their concern for what they saw as the well-being of the students, or their pragmatism in vocational guidance, or the shortage of resources, or their clear value positions;
4 the different background and experiences of boys and girls in relation to these subjects.

By the 1980s state Education Departments around Australia were beginning to become responsive to a variety of social forces with regard to equality of opportunity for girls and women in education. The most clearcut indicators of changes in official ideology in this regard were the statements on policy from the various Director-Generals' offices in most states. In Western Australia 'Equality in Education with Particular Reference to Women and Girls' was released in May 1980. This statement announced that the 'Education Department supports the concept of equality of opportunity through education.' The Department also acknowledged that female teachers 'have a right to work and to have equal pay, and to have equal access to all benefits and opportunities.' However, they did note that there were 'social and family pressures which make equality for women difficult to achieve' (Education Department, Western Australia, July 1980, p. 197).

The Working Conditions of Women Teachers and Counter-Hegemony. Attitudes towards women teachers are extremely important because they clearly denote what are considered appropriate life-styles for adult women — and hence implicitly the direction schools should be guiding girls — and because of the direct potential influence of women teachers as role models for the girls themselves. One area where the attitude of the schooling authorities has been clear has been in the simple numbers of females and males in the teaching ranks. In the early years of this century it was common for Australian state Education Departments regularly to lament the lack of men in teaching and the need to improve conditions to attract the 'best men'. For example, in 1909 the problems seen to be associated with too few male teachers included the following: that women could not manage older children, especially boys; that women had to specialize in infant teaching, which meant there were not enough teachers in the upper grades; that there were accommodation problems in country areas for women; and that women could not teach agriculture to boys in rural areas (Education Department, Western Australia, 1909).

By 1915, after the beginning of World War I, the problem worsened. The principal of the sole teachers' college in Western Australia discussed why it was so hard to attract men, and concluded that it related to the following aspects: fewer boys remained at school until age 18; boys did not show the same interest in teaching as girls; there were more prospects for advancement in other professions for men; the entrance examination rejected more men than women; and women did better at the examinations at the college. Furthermore, 'women students have been noted for their fine bearing and gentle ways, their intellectual capacity and their ability in both lecture room and school.' Women also did better in the practice schools, and the principal concluded: 'but it must be remembered that women at the age of studentship, say from 18 to 21, as a rule are more adaptable, find more interest in teaching problems, and more readily get in touch with children than young men of the same age' (Education Department, Western Australia, 1915, p. 94). These comments were made in the context of complaining about the *lack* of men. It would seem that whatever the superior accomplishments of women teachers, they were not desired, at least in large numbers, by the state Education Departments.

Other 'problems' identified with too may female teachers were claimed to include: women lacked the confidence to teach older students;

the 'education of future manhood' should not be left to women; women did not want promotion; schools in mining and timber towns needed men; science work would suffer; sport would suffer; discipline would suffer; women were happy with low salaries and so depressed the going rate; women would resign and serve less time; women could not handle responsibility; women could not handle power; women caused unemployment.

These arguments regarding too few male teachers continued until the mid-1950s, by which time there were actually more male than female teachers, and some Education Departments began to discuss the issue of too few *women* teachers, which it described as creating 'organizational problems', e.g. the staffing of primary schools, the teaching of home economics and needlework, etc.

Another area where the attitude of the Australian state Education Departments towards men and women comes out clearly is in the concessions given male teachers during and after the two world wars. This is particularly important in the context of the development of the state education bureaucracy. For example, during World War I in a section of the Western Australian annual report for 1920 which stressed how the requirements for entry to the teaching profession had *risen* considerably in recent years, and how permanency could *only* be obtained through a *course* of professional training, the Education Department also observed that some consideration needed to be given to the male teachers who served on active duty. It noted that many of them had been in the middle of courses which would have entitled them to a higher classification, and that years spent in the service made it difficult to prepare for departmental examinations. Nevertheless, none should be disadvantaged by their service. Thus, 'provided that the teachers in question show, within a reasonable time, that they possess the necessary teaching skill and power of control, they will be advanced in classification without undergoing the usual examination' (Education Department, Western Australia, 1922, p. 8). The Department also commented on how well the returned servicemen were doing as a result of their experiences. 'The years as soldiers gave new experience, new ideals, and new feelings entirely, which have all tended to broaden the men's outlook and to sharpen their initiative and resource' (Education Department, Western Australia, 1920, p. 50).

During World War II a long list of concessions was made by the state Education Departments to male teachers on duty including such items as the payment of superannuation contributions, the granting of long-service leave, Christmas pay, overseas service counting as qualifying for promotion, permanency maintained, assistants to go to headteacher lists, consideration given to promotion to inspectorships, military service taken as equal to teaching service for all promotions, various waiving of regulations for women marrying servicemen (*WA Teachers' Journal*, 8 November 1941, pp. 141–2). However, for those *women* teachers who also responded to what was an urgent call for both male and female volunteers from Military Headquarters, the Western Australian Minister informed them that they must resign their positions and hence receive no long-service leave, superannuation pay or any other benefits. The teachers' union protested about this, but to no avail (*WA Teachers' Journal*, 3 December 1941, p. 160).

During both wars the state Education Departments typically commented on how efficient and effective the women teachers were and how patriotic it had been for the married women 'on supply' to come to the aid of the state. However, after the wars the 'temporaries' were let go as soon as possible. It is obvious from the annual reports that during wartime women teachers were considered competent to handle all the areas they were considered incompetent to handle at other times. It is also interesting to note the extent to which the Education Departments were willing to go to adjust to men's service to the country in terms of military duty, when compared with the perceived difficulties in adjusting to women's service to the country in terms of marrying and bearing and raising children.

The area in which we can see most clearly the ideology of the family held by the state Education Departments is the 'equal pay' issue. Equal pay for male and female teachers doing the same job was a very early plank of all teachers' unions. In Western Australia from 1917 until 1971, when it was finally implemented, equal pay was a major and continuous issue for discussion in the organ of the teachers' union, the *WA Teachers' Journal*. It is impossible to trace the complexity of this issue in this short chapter where only a few important aspects will be mentioned.

The crux of the issue was the extent to which the basis for wages was seen as the 'family wage'. This basis was introduced into Australia in the so-called Harvester judgment handed down in the Commonwealth Arbitration Court in 1907. The 'family wage' is based on the concept that a man must earn enough to support a wife and children as well as himself, with normal needs in an average community. As it was assumed that women did not have dependents and that 'family wage' was based on this 'need', as well as personal efficiency in doing the jobs, 'The imposing edifice of a "family wage" was to bar the progress of women's pay rates for over half a century' (Ryan and Conlon, 1975, p. 91).

In 1920 the Western Australian Education Department firmly stated this issue for teachers:

> The vexed question of the relation between men's and women's salaries has received careful consideration. In the abstract, the claim that equal pay should be given for equal work seems just. But our present economic system is based on the family, and in every trade or profession a man's pay must be such that he is enabled to support a wife and family, and so provide for the bringing up of the next generation. (Education Department, Western Australia, 1920, p. 9)

The first major confrontation in Western Australia on this issue was the combined public services strike in 1920, which lasted twenty days. As women teachers were in the considerable majority in the teachers' union, and as it was their salaries which were a particular grievance, it was very much women who supported this militant action. In May 1920 the women of the union executive published 'The Women's Manifesto' in the *WA Teachers' Journal*, urging women to support the executive in whatever action was necessary. They said in part:

> We women teachers have realised for some time past that our services were not being rated at their proper value. During the war all financial claims were waived . . . £25,000 has recently been spent in a partial re-adjustment of salaries . . . . Practically the whole of this has been given to male assistants and head teachers . . . except in the lowest grades, and then only in niggardly fashion, the women teachers as a body received nothing. Our indignation at the injustice of it is natural, but the remedy is in our own hands. Seventy per cent of the teachers of this State are women — we have an overwhelming majority. If we combine to give the Executive our wholehearted support our just claim must be recognized . . . . (*WA Teachers' Journal*, 10 May 1920, p. 41)

The strike was well supported and initially appeared to have won its goals: interim salary relief, similar treatment of both sexes and the establishment of the Public Service Appeal Board. However, the Western Australian Education Department soon reneged on the similar treatment of the sexes, and the equal pay case brought to the newly established Appeal Board was heard, and subsequently cast out on the grounds that it was an 'abstract question'.

The union argued that, basically, women teachers were doing the same work as men teachers, that the majority of positions were interchangeable, that where they were not interchangeable they were of equal responsibility and standard, and that during the war the women had done all the jobs so well, in fact, that they evoked the congratulations of the Director and the Minister. The Minister argued, in opposition, that because of the 'economic' factor men had to support families and thus needed higher wages, that if there were more money available he would prefer to raise men's salaries to attract more men into teaching, and that equal pay was against public policy because it could discourage marriage (see the *WA Teachers' Journal*, 10 December 1920–10 February 1921).

The Western Australian Teachers' Union then persisted with deputations to Ministers on equal pay after resolutions of annual conferences in very nearly every year until the change of policy in 1965. The union was accompanied on a number of occasions by representatives of a large number of other women's organizations. By the 1930s the cause of married women teachers not being able to gain permanency was also a standard subject of deputation. In the 1940s the issue of promotion, and in particular women as heads of schools, began to be pushed. In 1968 accouchement leave was granted. Equal pay came in stages by 1971. Married women were allowed on permanent staff in 1972. 1972 also saw the first woman principal of a co-educational senior high school in Western Australia. The Director-General's policy statement on equal opportunity was issued in 1980. A Superintendent was appointed and an Equal Opportunity Unit established shortly thereafter.

There is little doubt that the women in the Western Australian Teachers' Union were active and instrumental in these achievements. In all Australian states women teachers, working particularly from teacher union bases, have played a major role in counter-hegemonic struggles within education. John Negus, President of the Western Australian Union in 1982, commented after the annual conference on the strength of the 'anti-sexism lobby' within the union: 'One other, not so obvious, feature of Conference which bears remarking upon is the rise of the women's movement or the equal opportunity lobby as a real force in teacher politics' (*Western Teacher*, 10 September 1982, p. 6).

Conclusion

This brief historical examination of the 'official' ideology about the family held by an Australian state Education Department (Western Australia) illustrates various aspects of the nature of the relationship of state, family and workplace in education. First, it is apparent that the Western Australian Education Department had a view of the proper form of the family, that the family was seen as a most important institution in society, and that the Department viewed its function as partially to train children to fit into their appropriate future roles within the family as well as the workplace, and to treat female and male teachers within the same frame of reference. It is also clear that family roles were sex-specific, and that they represented traditional nineteenth century romantic notions of home and hearth, class-based notions about the appropriate forms of working-class families, and class-based understandings of suitable occupations for boys and girls.

This is perhaps not surprising. What is interesting, however, is that there was at various times resistance to the official view, that the Education Department perceived it as such, and attempted to deal with it — though primarily by pushing their own view more strongly or more consistently. Thus the resistance by parents to laundry work in the household management curriculum was dealt with by introducing compulsion. The resistance by female teachers to sewing was sanctioned by reductions in pay and attempts to make it a compulsory subject in the teacher training institution. The preference by female students and their parents for the commercial over the domestic course was lamented publicly for years. In this case, although they could ensure that all girls did some domestic subjects, given their other commitment to freedom of choice and to the academic curriculum, they could not formally insist that all girls did the 'appropriate' course.

Although arguments for the expansion of secondary education were initially couched entirely in terms of the needs of boys and, in particular, the educational waste to both 'the boy and the nation', they moved very quickly during World War I to begin to include efficiency in the competition between nations, and the need for an educated populace in a democracy. After World War II there was an increasing consciousness of Australia as a nation, combined with a view of schooling as serving the state by promoting a better kind of society. Social mobility achieved through the education system in the form of academic achievement also became a stronger feature, as did notions of individualism and the use of education to further the development of individual potential.

It is in these notions — democracy, preparing citizens for a better society, meritocracy, the development of individual potential — that contradictions began to emerge with regard to sex-specific education for boys and girls. Girls should be trained for efficiency in the home, yet they should develop their individual potential. Girls should do domestic courses to prepare for their inevitable destiny as wives and mothers, yet commercial and professional courses were open to them. Girls would only 'end up' in the home, yet secondary schooling should be compulsory and the content should be primarily academic. Girls would be financially dependent upon husbands, yet training for remunerative work was important. Girls of high academic ability should do tertiary study where possible, yet they should eventually retire from the workforce to be good homemakers. Girls should aspire to marriage, yet once this was achieved they should forfeit their right to paid employment, or, if not, should accept that there would be no concessions for family life. These were the kinds of contradictory messages about the family, the economy and the role of the state in education which were increasingly evident in Australian schools in the last eighty years.

Finally, it is also evident that for a long time there have been utopian ideas regarding the role of women and counter-hegemony forces at work in the area of education. They have been well represented by women in the teachers' unions, and they have been, while not entirely successful, sufficiently successful to have moderated much of the rhetoric and some of the practices in schools which have historically disadvantaged girls and women teachers. Women teachers have been the force for considerable change in education, and, while they have been influenced by the recent upsurge in the general women's movement which has been active since the late 1960s, they have also been part of a long and continuous history in education in Australia of battling for equal pay, rights for married women and promotional opportunities. Betsy Wearing makes this point, in her study of the ideology of motherhood, when she points out that some women have been able to question that ideology of motherhood and the family: 'I refer to middle-class professional women who have acted in this movement as bearers of utopian ideas which transcend the existing social order, challenge existing gender and class structures and relationships or power and reveal as ideological prevailing "taken-for-granted" beliefs about gender relationships and roles' (Wearing, 1984, p. 27).

These examples of hegemony, contradictions, resistance and counter-hegemony have also enabled us to see how the state — and its education system — has been an arena of social struggle for interlinked gender and class issues. That it is also the prize itself is apparent in the case of gender issues in education.

References

Althusser, L. (1971) *Lenin and Philosophy*, London, New Left Books.

Anyon, J. (1983) 'Intersections of class and gender: Accommodation and resistance by working class and affluent females to contradictory sex-role ideology', *Journal of Education*, 16, 1, pp. 25–48.

Apple, M.W. (1982) 'Work, gender and teaching', manuscript prepared for *Teachers' College Record*.

Apple, M.W. (1988) *Teachers and Texts: A Political Economy of Class and Gender Relations in Education*, New York and London, Routledge.

Arnot, M. (1982) 'Male hegemony, social class and women's education', *Journal of Education*, 164, 1, pp. 64–89.

Barrett, M. (1980) *Woman's Oppression Today: Problems in Marxist Feminist Analysis*, London, Verso.

Bates, R. (1983) *Educational Administration and the Management of Knowledge* (ESA841 Theory and Practice in Educational Administration), Deakin University, Vic.

Bernstein, B. (1971) 'On the classification and framing of educational knowledge', in Young, M. (Ed.), *Knowledge and Control*, London, Collier-Macmillan, pp. 47–69.

Bourdieu, P. and Passeron, J.C. (1977) *Reproduction in Education, Society and Culture*, London, Sage.

Bowles, S. and Gintis, H. (1976) *Schooling in Capitalist America*, New York, Harper and Row.

Bowles, S. and Gintis, H. (1981) 'Education as a site of contradictions in the reproduction of the capital-labor relationship: Second thoughts on the "correspondence principle"', *Economic and Industrial Democracy*, 2, 2, May.

Brown, S. (1982) 'The lines of least resistance: Factors affecting sex differences in subject choice in lower secondary schools', paper presented at the Women in Education Conference, Perth, WA, April.

Brown, S. and Fitzpatrick, J. (1981) 'Girls, boys and subject choice', Discussion paper no. 11, Education Department, Perth, WA.

Carnoy, M. and Levin, H. (1985) *Schooling and Work in the Democratic State*, Stanford, Calif., Stanford University Press.

Connell, R.W. (1983) *Which Way Is Up? Essays on Sex, Class and Culture*, Sydney, George Allen and Unwin.

Connell, R.W., Ashenden, D.J., Kessler, S. and Dowsett, G.W. (1982) *Making the Difference: Schools, Families and Social Division*, Sydney, George Allen and Unwin.

David, M.E. (1980) *The State, the Family and Education*, London, Routledge and Kegan Paul.

Deem, R. (1978) *Women and Schooling*, London and Boston, Routledge and Kegan Paul.

Dettman Report, *see* Education Department, Western Australia (1969).

Education Department, Western Australia (1900) *Education Circular*.

Education Department, Western Australia (1901) *Education Circular*.

Education Department, Western Australia (1906) *Annual Report*.

Education Department, Western Australia (1908) *Annual Report*.

Education Department, Western Australia (1909) *Annual Report*.

Education Department, Western Australia (1910) *Annual Report*.

Education Department, Western Australia (1914) *Annual Report*.

Education Department, Western Australia (1915) *Annual Report*.

Education Department, Western Australia (1917) *Annual Report*.

Education Department, Western Australia (1920) *Annual Report*.

Education Department, Western Australia (1922) *Annual Report*.

Education Department, Western Australia (1936) *A Guide to Occupations for Boys and Girls*.

EDUCATION DEPARTMENT, WESTERN AUSTRALIA (1969) *Secondary Education in Western Australia*, Perth (Dettman Report).

EDUCATION DEPARTMENT, WESTERN AUSTRALIA (1974) *Education Circular*, August.

EDUCATION DEPARTMENT, WESTERN AUSTRALIA (1976) *Males and Females in the State Education System of Western Australia: A Report to the Minister for Education*, Perth, July.

EDUCATION DEPARTMENT, WESTERN AUSTRALIA (1980) *Education Circular*, July.

EISENSTEIN, Z.R. (1978) *Capitalist Patriarchy and the Case for Socialist Feminism*, New York, Monthly Review Press.

FERGUSON, K. (1984) *The Feminist Case against Bureaucracy*, Philadelphia, Pa., Temple University Press.

GILLIGAN, C. (1982) *In a Different Voice: Psychological Theory and Women's Development*, Cambridge, Mass, Harvard University Press.

GIROUX, H. (1981) 'Hegemony, resistance and the paradox of educational reform', *Interchange*, 2, 2–3, pp. 3–26.

GRAMSCI, A. (1971) *Selections from Prison Notebooks*, New York, International Publishers.

HARTMANN, H. (1981) 'The unhappy marriage of Marxism and feminism: Towards a more progressive union', in SARGENT, L. (Ed.), *Women and Revolution*, Boston, Mass., South End Press.

KANTOR, R.M. (1977) *Men and Women of the Corporation*, New York, Basic Books.

KELLY, J. (1979) 'The doubled vision of feminist theory: A postscript to the "Women and Power" Conference', *Feminist Studies*, 5, 1, Spring, pp. 216–27.

KUHN, A. and WOLPE, A.M. (Eds) (1978) *Feminism and Materialism: Women and the Modes of Production*, London, Routledge and Kegan Paul.

MCROBBIE, A. and MCCABE, T. (Eds) (1981) *Feminism for Girls*, London and Boston, Routledge and Kegan Paul.

MATTHEWS, J.J. (1984) *Good and Mad Women: The Historical Construction of Femininity in Twentieth Century Australia*, North Sydney, George Allen and Unwin.

PORTER, P.H. (1983) 'The state, the family and education: Ideology, reproduction and resistance in Western Australia, 1900–1929', *Australian Journal of Education*, 27, 2, pp. 121–36.

PORTER, P.H. (1985) 'Social policy, education and women in Australia', in BALDOCK, C. and CASS, B. (Eds), *Women, Social Policy and the State in Australia*, Sydney, George Allen and Unwin.

Report of the Royal Commission on Youth Employment and the Apprenticeship System, Perth, 1938.

RYAN, E. and CONLON, A. (1975) *Gentle Invaders: Australian Women at Work 1788–1974*, Sydney, Thomas Nelson.

SPENDER, D. (1982) *Invisible Women: The Schooling Scandal*, London, Writers and Readers Publishing Cooperative Society and Chameleon Editorial Group.

TYACK, D.B. (1974) *The One Best System: A History of American Urban Education*, Cambridge, Mass., Harvard University Press.

WA Teachers' Journal (1920), 10 May.

WA Teachers' Journal (1920–21), 10 December–10 February.

WA Teachers' Journal (1941), 8 November and 3 December.

WEARING, R. (1984) *The Ideology of Motherhood: A Study of Sydney Suburban Mothers*, Sydney, George Allen and Unwin.

WEBER, M. [1904] (1958) *The Protestant Ethic and the Spirit of Capitalism*, New York, Charles Scribner's Sons.

WEILER, KATHLEEN (1988) *Women Teaching for Change: Gender, Class and Power*, South Hadley, Mass.: Bergin and Garvey.

Western Teacher (1982), 10 September.

WILLIS, P. (1977) *Learning to Labour: How Working Class Kids Get Working Class Jobs*, Farnborough, Saxon House.

WOLPE, A.M. (1978) 'Education and the sexual division of labor', in KUHN, A. and WOLPE, A.M. (Eds), *Feminism and Materialism: Women and Modes of Production*, London, Routledge and Kegan Paul.

YOUNG, M.F.D. (Ed.) (1971) *Knowledge and Control: New Directions for the Sociology of Education*, London, Collier-Macmillan.

Chapter 2

Corporatism, Democracy and Teacher Unions in Victorian Education

Jill Blackmore

This chapter analyzes the changing relationships between teacher unions and the state in educational policy-making in the state of Victoria, Australia, since the 1970s. It is argued that teacher union participation in policy and decision-making at all administrative levels indicates an ongoing process of democratization: a process exemplified by the focus on schools as the unit of decision-making. But the involvement of teacher unions in policy and decision-making has come to reflect an increasing tension between the apparent democratization and devolution of educational decision-making at the local level and the increasingly institutionalized position of teacher unions within a framework of 'corporatism'; a political formation which facilitated greater central control of decision-making within education during the 1980s. The notion of corporatism is valid here as an analytic tool to illustrate the connections between liberal democracies and the 'incorporation' of political interest groups by the state into the decision-making process. An example is the Economic Accord of 1983 by which peak union leaders, representatives of large business and the Australian Federal Labor Government established a wages and prices agreement which had become a central tenet of government economic policy by 1989. The issue addressed here is how teacher unions fit within this corporatist framework and its accompanying discourses. The analysis focuses on the Victorian situation, which although unique in its particular historical formation of corporatist tendencies, still displays features of corporatism critical to understanding the politics of education nationally and internationally.

As Hyslop (1988) argues, the political and ideological position of the state in its relationship to teacher trade unions and other social movements (e.g. parent organizations) has been ignored by theorists in industrial relations and only more recently seen as a site for investigation by educational theorists (Bowles and Gintis, 1976). This is a consequence of viewing industrial relations as an administrative 'problem' and the emphasis upon the voluntaristic nature of industrial relations and social movements (environmentalism, women's movement) (Hyslop, 1988, p. 53). Corporatist theory goes some way towards remedying this deficiency. Corporatism has been variously defined. More orthodox adherents to corporatist theory argue that corporatism is a strategy, a method of interest representation, or a mode of policy-making in which the state is a neutral, mediating instrument (Cawson, 1983; Crouch and Heller, 1983).

Underlying particular theories of corporatism lie different political theories of the state which inform interpretations of the association of 'voluntarist' organizations such as trade unions, professional associations and voluntary organizations to the state. In liberal theories of political pluralism, democratic process is seen to be brought about by the voluntary involvement of union, business and other interest group representatives. 'Interests' are seen to be concrete and unproblematic; represented in institutional formations such as parents' and citizens' organizations and unions. In this manner the neutral state effectively mediates between legitimate and competing social and political interests in order to produce a harmonious accord about the distribution of limited resources in the public interest. The intervention of the state is legitimized by an appeal to national unity and socio-economic consensus, a necessary strategy to meet the demands of industrial concentration, technological development, increased international competition and declining profits (Hyslop, 1988, p. 58). It has also been argued that such intervention is based on the principle of equity of representation of interests. It is exemplified in the incomes policy in Great Britain and in the Economic Accord of 1983 in Australia and the apparent agreement on wage justice it produced. It was through this Accord that in Australia during the 1980s the public interest (civil) was equated to a favourable balance of payments (economic), and radical intervention on the part of the government was justified by the equation of the public interest to maintaining the Accord (a position exemplified in the unprecedented alliance between employer airlines and the Federal Labor Government against the pilots' strike in 1989).

But a liberal 'pluralist' interpretation of the 'incorporation' of interest groups into the political processes is inadequate because of the assumption of the neutrality of the state and the acceptance of élite democratic theory implicit to it. This chapter adopts the radical perspective of Panitch (1981), who links the growth of the corporatist state since the 1970s as a by-product, and essential element, of a crisis in capital accumulation. Panitch's interpretation is radical in that he depicts corporatism as a form of capitalist social-political organization, a specific conjuncture of class relations and only one facet of a social formation whereby capital displays power over labour (Hyslop, 1988, p. 62). According to Panitch, corporatism is 'a political structure within advanced capitalism which integrates organised socioeconomic producer groups through a system of representation and co-operative mutual interaction at the leadership level and of mobilisation and control at the mass level' (Panitch, 1977, p. 62). Panitch's approach emphasizes the 'fallacious pretence of egalitarianism in the corporate organisation of society' (Panitch, 1981, p. 23).

At the same time corporatism (based upon consent or implicit voluntarism) is a more subtle alternative to coercion in responding to the crisis of legitimation and accumulation in capitalism. Corporatist theory takes up some of the Gramscian argument regarding the significance of ideology as a powerful hegemonic force to gain the cooperation of the masses to maintain particularly powerful interests. Gramsci's conceptualization of how state power is maintained through a 'hegemony of consent' is most appropriate in this respect. In Jessop's words:

> ... hegemony involves the successful mobilisation and reproduction of the 'active consent' of dominated groups by the ruling class through their exercise of intellectual, moral and political leadership.... For the maintenance of hegemony involves taking systematic account of popular interests and demands, shifting position and making compromises on secondary issues (without however, sacrificing essential interests) and organising this support for the attainment of national goals which serve the fundamental long-run interests of the dominant group ... hegemony is crystallised and mediated through a complex system of ideological (or hegemonic) apparatuses located throughout the social formation. But the practice of hegemony is nonetheless concentrated in the sphere of the civil society or so called 'private' organisations, such as the Church, trade unions, schools, the mass media or political parties. (Jessop, 1982, pp. 148–9)

Furthermore, the lack of neutrality of the state is most evident, Wexler and Grabiner argue, in the link between 'corporatism' (the representation of élite interests) and an emergent form of civil and economic administration — that of corporate management. In the latter the spirit of corporatism is evident while the 'authority remains with the employer, it is *he* who still controls. But those who are controlled are taken into *his* confidence, their views are solicited and so the control, by becoming less of an imposition, is made to operate more effectively (and legitimately)' (Wexler and Grabiner, 1986, p. 16, emphasis added). The use of the generic 'he' not only gives a true rendition of the association of masculinity with authority invested in both the state and the peak organizations but is also symbolic of the male dominance of the process of incorporation itself. Women's interests are represented by men (e.g. in the unions and political party organizations), and any claims by women to be represented as a separate legitimate interest are perceived as being particularistic rather than universalistic, therefore not in the national interest or the common good. It also highlights the irony that the state has, through its policies, ideology and different forms of legislation (e.g. equal opportunity), provided a means of women's integration into the economy while simultaneously supporting the hierarchical and gendered division of labour; it has 'continued to limit women's power and influences in the public sphere through the structure and policies of the corporatist system' (Borchorst and Siim, in Sassoon, 1987, p. 135).

Any discussion of corporatism, therefore, requires a theory of the state which accounts for its relationship to voluntarist or 'private' organizations such as trade unions. In this sense Gramsci's emphasis on the organic relations between the governmental apparatus and civil society is critical. Specific institutions are treated not merely as the technical apparatus of government. Rather, he 'relates them to their social bases and stresses the ways in which their functions and effects are influenced by their links to the economic system and civil society' (Jessop, 1982, p. 146). He gives precedence to class relations over the specificity of institutional structures of the state, and stresses the modalities of state power in particular periods. Within this conceptual framework this chapter is concerned with how the structure and ideology of the corporate state relate to educational governance, and in particular how the hegemony of consent has been constructed and maintained.

Corporatism and Educational Governance

How and why does corporatism feature in educational governance? Wexler and Grabiner, in an analysis of corporate formation in education in the USA, argue that corporatism is evident in the sectoral reorganization of education in America which has been dominated by a Rightist discourse of reform (Wexler and Grabiner, 1986). The crisis in capitalism has led to a focus on education as the solution to national economic ills as exemplified in the various reports on public education following *A Nation at Risk* (1983). At the same time, while the influence of the Right is undoubted, they depict a primary contradiction in the Rightist social movement which is reflected in the educational discourse for reorganization of public education. One is the *language of the market* (laissez faire, individual freedom and commodification of social relations) and the other is the *language of morality* (social integration, minimizing diversity, restoring the patriarchal family). While this contradiction can be attributed to different class factions and social groups, the importance of corporatism as a social form is 'that it surpasses or supersedes these contradictions with a higher and less democratic form of capitalism' and thereby resolves this particular contradiction, at least in the short term, through temporary political alliances over specific issues (as in the case of the anti-abortion lobby in the USA) (Wexler and Grabiner, 1986, pp. 14–16). While such an alliance is often shortlived because of the implicit often oppositional consequences of each political position — that of the language of the market in education is privatization, which is premised upon freedom of choice, whereas that of the language of morality is censorship, which implies restricting freedom of choice — it still controls the educational debate.

Similar conservative political formations are emerging in Australia. Johnston defines three distinct conservative discourses which have joined in opposing the progressivist education of the 1970s: the religious fundamentalists, who see radical influences as undermining Christian morality and social order; the cultural élitists, who perceive the principle of egalitarianism as a leveller and reducing educational standards; and the technocratic stance, which asserts that the young are inadequately equipped by education with the skills, knowledge and attitudes necessary for work. He argues that in Australia, underlying the new conservatism and economic doctrine, is 'the notion that social market values provide the moral basis for the good society and a step towards the resolution of the crisis. . . . Government and administrative issues are transposed into questions of individual responsibility, self reliance and freedom of individual choice' (Johnston, 1981, p. 10). The language of the market in the Australian context is antithetical to the language of equality and social justice embedded in the traditions of welfare capitalism and the rallying cry of the educational progressivists.

A common administrative resolution for such contradictions at a superficial level is one of encouraging decentralization towards school-based decision-making, while maintaining hegemonic control by the state through centralizing mechanisms as legitimated by an ideology focusing on accountability, standards and evaluation. The administrative form in Australia has been to establish consultation processes with the various educational interest groups (parent, teacher and business organizations). In this way corporatism appears to meet the demands of all legitimate interests. Given this theoretical starting point, it suggests why the justfication for restructuring education throughout Australia since the early 1980s has exploited the rhetoric of voluntaristic 'participation' (whether of parent or teacher interest groups) in response to a perceived educational crisis (as indicated by 'falling standards and productivity') which produced two apparently antithetical administrative formations and discourses — those of school-based decision-making and corporate management. This tension has been most evident in Australia since 1985. There has been an overt shift in state government reports on education, such as *The Quality of Teachers* (Swan Report, 1985) in New South Wales, *Towards the 1990's* in the Northern Territory (1987) and *Better Schools* in Western Australia (1986), *School Renewal in NSW* (Scott Report, 1989) and the Cox Report in South Australia (1989), towards the notion of schools as the units of collaborative and community-based decision-making better to meet the needs of the local market and produce more equitable outcomes. At the same time this discourse has been juxtaposed to a push towards a corporate management framework which is essentially hierarchical and efficiency-driven. There have been similar contradictory tendencies in the UK with the Baker Education Act (1988) and in New Zealand in *Tomorrow's Schools* towards the more extreme cases of self-managing schools and national curriculum and standardized assessment.

In Victoria the relationship between teachers and their state government employer on the surface would appear to offer a contrast to the tendencies described above. The Victorian situation was unique, even in the Australian system, in the decade prior to 1986: first, because of the high level of teacher union activism in educational policy-making; second, due to the extent to which the policy of devolution and decentralization was developed, espoused and implemented in schools and regions as the basis of 'democratic reform' (The Ministry of Education, *Ministerial Papers*, 1983–85). This 'democratization' of decision-making structures was exemplified by the growth of representative policy committees at regional and central levels, as well as school-based decision-making in all areas of policy such as curriculum, assessment and resource allocation (Blackmore and Spaull, 1987). Teachers and parents on school councils in Victoria have been increasingly carrying out what has traditionally been perceived as administrative work (decision-making on policy and the distribution of resources) due to rapid structural reforms which have occurred in many Australian states towards more decentralized school governance. The thrust of the Victorian Labor Government's *Ministerial Papers* (1983–85) on school-based decision-making, curriculum, school councils and school improvement was towards school self-evaluation and community participation rather than top-down accountability. This perspective has been reinforced by the trend towards the 'co-option' of individual teacher activists, generally executive level unionists, into the state bureaucracy as policy-makers, consultants and administrators, as well as the representation of teacher unions on all policy committees at central, regional and school levels. It is a trend replicated to a lesser extent among parent organizations. Furthermore, this process of 'incorporation' of both individuals and unions has been couched in terms of democratic participation.

At the same time, since 1986 Victoria has felt the centralizing thrust of corporate management, as have other Australian states. Increasingly, there has been a shift in policy emanating from a revamped 'lean and mean' Ministry of Education as staff at the centre and regions have been relocated to schools, the director has become executive manager, principals are perceived as line managers and Regional Directors have become regional managers. Furthermore, teacher career restructuring is being framed by corporate management principles. Current teacher award restructuring proposals look to increasing 'productivity' through performance objectives, advanced skill teachers and reduction of influence of teachers on local committee systems in favour of greater control to the principal (*Education Victoria*, October 1989). The teacher career restructure proposal of October 1989, as other modifications of the system, reflects a convergence with the other states towards close adherence to the practices and principles of corporate management.

It is here that 'corporatism' as a political formation and strategy takes on a new meaning. The incorporation of teachers (both individually and collectively) into the decision-making process in a liberal democratic state has effected the 'quieting' of oppositional discourses in education. The following account of the impact on teachers' administrative activities of a radical restructuring in the state of Victoria, Australia, since 1979, emphasizes the changing relationship between teacher unions and the state. This section leads on to discussion of how the creation of new administrative arenas (school-based committee systems, regional boards and consultative committees), which had the potential to democratize educational governance, has also led to the co-option of teacher interests into the dominant perspective of the state Labor Government, often to the detriment of teacher interests. The term 'arenas' refers to particular situations in which teachers and the bureaucracy, parents and teachers, parents and the bureaucracy interact for the purpose of decision-making, because it is here that the 'administration of resources' is contested and negotiated among the various cultural interests (parents, teachers, educational bureaucrats). Finally, the third section deals with how the strategy of corporatism facilitates the state's 'steering capacity' to control and divert oppositional discourses and thus effectively to quiet reform. In so doing, the discourse shifts towards the imposition of different agendas and the practice of a 'management pedagogy' rather than a 'critical' pedagogy in the name of the dual corporate managerialist objectives of efficiency and effectiveness.

Victorian Background

In Victoria the state system of education (which provides schooling for approximately 70 per cent of the student population) has undergone rapid and radical reform since 1979. Historically, Australian state governments, being constitutionally responsible for primary and secondary education, have administered through highly centralized Education Departments, each under the control of a Director-General of Education directly responsible to the elected political Minister. Interest groups (parent and teacher associations, political parties, business) have traditionally attempted to influence the direction of government educational policy indirectly through submissions, informal consultation and, in the case of unions, directly through militant action since the mid-1960s. The relationship between teacher unions and the Education Department has been ill defined, with industrial conditions mediated through an 'independent' Teachers Tribunal until 1983. At the same time there has been a constant union-Departmental connection, as evidenced by the presence of senior Departmental officers who have been former teacher union activists. In the 1980s this became more overt, when the state Labor Government recruited union leaders as ministerial advisers and policy-makers, thus effectively institutionalizing a long association between teachers and the Labor Party (Tanner, 1983).

In 1968 the Victorian Secondary Teachers Association (VSTA) and Technical Teacher Union of Victoria (TTUV), the more militant of the three Victorian teacher unions (the third being the primary Victorian Teachers Union (VTU)), took the initiative for reform. Their largely successful agenda included reform of teacher assessment, improved teaching conditions (size of classes, face-to-face hours of teaching, salaries), establishment of minimal recruitment and teaching qualifications, reduced staff-student ratios and alternative modes of school-based curriculum and assessment. The union objective of 'equality of educational opportunity' matched the philosophy of the newly elected Federal Labor Government in 1972, which established the Schools Commission chaired by Peter Karmel. The Commission's first report, the Interim Report, encapsulated much of the Labor Party and teacher union rhetoric of participation and school-based decision-making. At the same time ideas of participation and community involvement were being implemented in community and alternative schools scattered about the state (Johnston, 1983; Fitzgerald *et al.*, 1977). This collaborative activity was further promoted by the Schools Commission's expectation that participatory processes be an element of any programs funded by grants from the Commonwealth and demands from parent organizations and representatives on policy bodies for a greater say in educational decision-making (Commonwealth Schools Commission, 1983, pp. 203–9). From a different perspective, conventional administrative literature and empirical research also claimed that school-based participative decision-making resulted in schools being more responsive to community needs, and a greater commitment by teachers involved in making the decisions (Blackmore, 1986; Conway, 1984; Imber, 1983). Thus the push for greater participation in decision-making has mixed origins and motivations. While teachers envisaged that it would increase their professional autonomy, the Labor push came from a concern for workplace democracy. The Education Department saw participative decision-making as a means of managerial control, while parents saw it as reducing bureaucratic unresponsiveness and maladministration and as making claim to their legitimate rights.

During the 1970s the trend within the large state educational bureaucracies was towards administrative decentralization, partly to divert increased teacher/departmental conflict away from the centre to the regions and partly to increase efficiency since bureaucratic processes had become so unwieldy. In Victoria this took the form of administrative decentralization into regions in 1974, and the broadening of representation on School Councils to include teachers and students in 1976. The Victorian Liberal Government in 1979 adopted the recommendations of a private management consultancy (*PA Report*) to continue the administrative restructuring towards decentralization. Policy formulation was to be at the centre, coordination of resources by the regions and implementation at the school level (Macpherson, 1983). But it was the newly elected Victorian Labor Government in 1982 which took the policy of decentralization to its logical conclusion with the devolution of not only administrative but also all policy-making responsibility to the schools.

Teacher unions had taken unprecedented political action in supporting the election of the Labor Government in 1982. Secondary teachers had traditionally promoted a collaborative decision-making process in schools, primarily to gain increased *teacher* control of the workplace, but were still ambivalent regarding parent involvement on what they regarded as matters of 'professional expertise' — policy and educational issues (Blackmore and Spaull, 1987). Furthermore, since 1983 school principals in technical, high and primary schools had been locally selected by representative panels appointed by the local school council of each school. The powers of school councils have been greatly extended into all policy areas of curriculum, school administration and finance. In addition, the State Board of Education was established as an advisory body to the Minister for Education, and regional boards similarly to advise the new regional directors. All such bodies were to be representative of all educational interests based on the premise that decisions should be made by those who are most affected — teachers, parents and students, and would thus be more effective (Watkins, 1988; Chapman, 1986b). Participative and collaborative decision-making was a key concept in the Labor Government's manifesto of educational reform laid down in the six *Ministerial Papers* (1982–85) on curriculum, school improvement, school councils, regional boards, program budgeting, and participatory decision-making structures.

During the same period (1982–85) the industrial relationship between the teaching service and their employers was radically altered due to changing structural, political and professional relationships. A major source of conflict between the teaching service and its employer was the Teachers Tribunal, established in 1948 by a Labor government in an attempt to improve the status of teachers by setting up an independent mediator on working conditions and salaries. The profusion of bodies influencing teachers' conditions led to confusion over who was the 'employer', the Department or the Tribunal, until the Tribunal was replaced by a Teaching Service Conciliation and Arbitration Commission in 1983. Victoria also differs from other states in that the Education Department fully integrated industrial relations into its employer role (Spaull and Hince, 1986, p. 120). Since 1982, in the absence of mechanisms by which to resolve disputes, industrial agreements, in which each union has separately negotiated a log of claims directly with the Minister, laid down staffing guidelines, teaching conditions and, most importantly, prescribed school-based administrative and curriculum committees to be elected from the teaching staff. School principals are now expected to inform, consult and be influenced by both teacher and parent interests through this new school-based 'committee system' of decision-making, which in most instances has significant impact upon teaching conditions, administrative structures and processes, curriculum policy and, one may suggest, pedagogical practice.

Teacher unions have also been actively incorporated into other policy-making committees at the central level and on the regional boards (Deakin University, 1985). Individual teacher unionists, many of them long-term activists in curriculum and school reform and improvement, have become the new breed of public servants influencing and forming policy through the advisory State Board, the revamped Victorian Curriculum and Assessment Board, the Curriculum Branch and the School Improvement Program. The common expectation, therefore, since 1983 has been for both union and parent association representation on critical policy committees at the centre, region and school levels of administration.

However, these inroads of teachers as active decision-makers into the traditional hierarchical administration of schools and educational bureaucracy have been progressively undermined by worsening economic conditions requiring budgetary constraint. The Labor governments at both federal and state levels have been pressured to become 'economistic' in their approaches to welfare and education in their determination to create an image of being economically responsible. Since 1979 the formerly proactive role of the teacher unions in determining the agenda of reform has been subsumed under a more conservative governmental reform agenda of corporate management which was common to all political parties by the mid-1980s. Rationalization and efficiency are the central governmental objectives. At the same time, while facing a real salary decline relative to others with similar training, teachers have been expected to take up greater extracurricular responsibilities within the committee system. While some teachers have gained through the managerialist approach, others have lost. As Seddon points out, the 'intensification of teaching commonly entails a deskilling in the core processes of curriculum, pedagogy and evaluation, and reskilling in technical and managerial procedures' (Seddon, 1988, p. 1).

The three major teacher unions have come to assume a more reactive position despite their alliance with, and electoral support of, the Victorian Labor Government in 1982. This reactive stance is significantly moving towards a more confrontationist stance as the implications of recent policy directions have become clear. Control of education has moved out of the hands of the 'professional administrators' into the hands of corporate managers, politicians and non-educationally trained administrators in this search for the elusive goals of managerial efficiency and effectiveness. This move in the locus of power was initiated during the period 1979–83 under Liberal and then Labor governments, when the role of the Director-General was increasingly circumvented by ministerial control (Badcock, 1988). Traditional power bases within the departmental bureaucracy were further undermined with the three administrative divisions of technical, high and primary schools being combined into a single

Schools Division under a General Manager and a Corporate Management Group comprised of the General and Regional Managers (formerly Regional Directors). The push towards corporate efficiency led to a further restructure at the centre of the Ministry in 1987–89 with the dispersal of many of the centrally-based administrators, consultants and policy-makers back into the regions and schools and recurrent 'refining' of the corporate divisions at the centre. Many of those individuals recruited into the central policy and planning during the early phases of administrative restructuring and the formulation and implementation of new post-compulsory curriculum and certification policies are now 'relocated' to the newly amalgamated regions and schools, while those remaining within the Ministry are faced with full-blown corporate managerialism in the form of performance appraisal, particularly of middle level managers in the regions and the centre and increasingly of principals in schools.

At the same time that there is apparently increased administrative devolution to schools, the process of centralization for economic accountability and efficiency has intensified rather than dissipated, with program budgeting acting as a key element in the maintenance of close control of programs at regional and school levels. Corporate managerial rhetoric has been symbolized in the renaming of key administrative personnel as managers and recurrent attempts to distinguish between principals as line managers with particular corporate responsibilities and the rest of the teaching force (*VSTA News*, 9, 26, 7 September 1988, p. 3; see also Ministry of Education proposed Career Restructure, October 1989). The professional status of teachers as decision-makers has been further eroded with the return to more traditional hierarchical notions of leadership which reinvest the formal role of the principal with greater control. Professional development courses are now aimed at promoting school-based 'leadership' and 'improvement', with the principal as the focus of line management rather than the centre of a collaborative process. Two contradictory elements have therefore coexisted in the discourse of reform since the early 1980s: on the one hand, a push towards school-based decision-making and democratization of policy-making which was community-based and premised upon principles of collaboration and participation; on the other hand, the demand for increased economic accountability and governmental control of educational finance as indicated by greater 'productivity'. These contradictions have to some extent been temporarily and partially reconciled through the corporatist strategies of the state and federal Labor governments as exemplified in particular policy documents on curriculum and administration emanating from the now 'incorporated' federal Schools Commission, the Victorian

State Board of Education, the Victorian Ministry of Education (e.g. the *Ministerial Papers*) and agreements on teacher career restructuring (*The Age*, March 1990, p. 3).

Decentralization and devolution, therefore, have not been unproblematic for the unions both organizationally and politically. Likewise, participation has been a two-edged sword. The earlier decentralization into regions in 1974 had forced the unions to reorganize on similar bureaucratic lines, although their early successes against inspection as a means of teacher assessment (1968–72) had depended largely upon branch activity, unity and initiative (Blackmore and Spaull, 1987). The incorporation of teacher union representation into the policy-making process, and the restructuring of the regions and the Ministry since 1983 again forced union organizations to respond, since union representation is required on all major committees, e.g. Implementation of Agreement, committees on school closure and rationalization procedures, Regional Boards, and Fields of Study Committees to develop new course guidelines for the new Victorian Certificate of Education for post-compulsory education at Years 11 and 12. Apart from stretching central and branch resources and personnel to the limit, union executives have centralized the decision-making process within the unions with the promotion of a single log of claims, thus moving policy initiatives and action away from the branches. The single log of claims negotiated at the centre and embodied in the Industrial Agreements (1983–85) established baseline conditions for all schools in the state. While encouraging industrial peace, they have also institutionalized inflexibility. These formulae have, while generally protecting all schools from unfavourable conditions, acted to the detriment of rank and file union activity in specific schools where union branches had won better conditions, by the standardization of conditions. Union representation on all committees has added further stress for teachers already preoccupied with the demands of school site amalgamations and the development of new fields of post-compulsory curriculum and modes of assessment. There is a widening rift between the Labor Government and schools, as there continues to be the expectation that teachers' voluntary participation should continue while their material and professional conditions are undermined in terms of increased work hours and performance indicators. Participatory decision-making has made increased demands on all unionists' and teachers' energy and time, and, one could argue, increased accountability of teachers to both their clients and the bureaucracy.

The extent to which this apparent democratization of decision-making has benefitted teachers and students is contestable, in terms of favourable outcomes and increased participation by previously excluded groups. The question remains: how do corporatism and democracy 'fit together' as processes of decision-making?

Democracy and Corporatism

A new element in the relationship between teacher organizations and the state has emerged since the early 1970s. The decline in national economic productivity since the mid-1970s has forced a new 'settlement' in a mood of rapprochement between organized labour and governments which has been less confrontational, with a tendency towards increased worker participation in organizational decision-making. Howe attributes this to the need for capital to renegotiate the post-war compromise between labour, monopoly capital and the state. As a consequence of the capitalist crisis of the 1980s, since capital is unable to uphold its side of the bargain in terms of maintaining the material well-being of the workers in return for industrial peace, two conflicting strategies have emerged. The first is a process of incorporating labour into a new and more sophisticated form of compromise and agreement; the second is a direct attack on all unions (as exemplified by the New Right). These are not necessarily mutually exclusive, and are maintained concurrently (Howe, 1986, p. 2). The move towards corporatism has taken two forms, according to Howe: one directed towards economic nationalism; the other towards joint economic planning premised upon the assumption that the quality of life of workers will be insured and productivity increased, in return for labour's passivity. Thus bargaining between labour, government, business and the 'community' means each side 'attempts to represent the general public interest and abandon its special interests' in the search for a compromise (Howe, 1986, p. 13). This form of economic democracy, Howe contends, involves pluralist assumptions about the nature of capitalist society. It assumes both capital and labour benefit in a non-adversarial relationship, while allowing underlying unequal relations of production and gender to remain unchallenged.

There are significant implications for labour (and teachers as workers) in this analysis. The first is that the emphasis on neutral and technical aspects (increasing productivity, training, etc.) depoliticizes the economic sphere. The second is that economic rights become political rights. In this way the right for free choice in the market is equated to political rights, but not necessarily responsibilities. Finally, there is an assumption that such activity is for the common good, i.e. assumes a homogeneous workplace, whereas in fact the workplace is highly class, race and gender-biased. It assumes that the peak organizations can negotiate and determine what is 'in the national interest' on behalf of specific constituencies. According to Triado:

> Not only are the substantive ends of public policy (economic growth, industry competitiveness and restructuring, high technology etc.) simply assumed to coincide with the 'common good', but key functional groups are identified as embodying the capacity for achieving such ends. The minimum requirement of a democratic society is the safeguarding of the negative liberties (vote in elections). The exercise of positive freedoms (to participate in decision-making processes) however falls upon particular groups, classes and individuals within all existing democracies. Such inequalities were justified by liberal pluralists through their market-theoretical assumptions of free competition between interest groups. Under corporatist arrangements, the problem is compounded; formalised, functional participation by some groups on public policy making brings into sharper relief how privileged participation of some can be justified. Clearly it cannot, and this is why the 'logic' of democracy implies its radicalisation; that is, positive fredoms must be generalised. (Triado, 1984, pp. 44–5)

But, as Howe points out, there is an inherent contradiction in corporatism in that it works only to the extent that the incorporated leadership is seen as legitimate by its constituents. While incorporation requires that the leadership be 'sufficiently insulated from the mass pressures', such isolation from the mass base means the leadership loses its legitimacy. If the leadership is well integrated into its constituency, then corporate planning will be undermined because it is forced to accommodate to workers' demands (Howe, 1986, p. 15). In the Victorian educational context, disillusionment regarding the union leadership is evident among rank and file teacher unionists, who feel powerless as issues of amalgamation, district provision and career restructuring are negotiated away from the chalkface and between union officials and the Ministry (Blackmore and Spaull, 1987; *Victorian Teacher*, October 1989). In this way the union leadership is losing its legitimacy as the negotiator for teachers confronted with the consequences of such decisions in terms of the intensification of their labour at the workface.

Two questions are pertinent here. First, to what extent does this incorporation process function to exclude competing interpretations concerning the ends of a particular activity, given this concern for consensus?

Second, how can those needs which do not come within the scope of the 'corporations' be organized, represented and educated? These questions raise issues of class, race and gender. Can middle-class women, for example, represent working-class or Aboriginal women? It was an issue raised by the 'unrepresented' in the economic summit of the federal Labor Party in 1983, when the Economic Accord was negotiated between 'key' leaders and peak organizations representing the unions, business and the government. Working-class women, migrants, the poor and welfare recipients were all 'represented' by a single welfare delegate. Lack of representation of those groups outside the corporatist structure ultimately results in the 'marginalization of vital areas of social life', particularly when the objective is consensus. There is little recognition of difference in needs and objectives. In that sense it is difficult to perceive of corporatism as a progressive development for labour or less organized social groups. Not surprisingly, some Marxists view social democratic corporatism as replacing the tradition of liberal democracy as a capitalistic means of controlling economic conflict (Encel, 1979, pp. 37–43).

This point is developed by Triado. In analyzing the relationship between liberal democracies and corporatism in the capitalist system, Triado first perceives inherent tensions between the functional characteristics of corporatism and the normative dimensions of democracy. He argues that 'corporate' representation is denied to certain groups and classes without corporate status, and narrows the scope of political activity in conformity with the given social order. Second, he suggests that the current move towards corporatism must be contextualized within the crisis of capitalism because it is a response to the problem of governability in increasingly complex situations and administrative overload. Corporatism is a strategic solution, an instrumental means of going about public policy formation within a liberal democracy as a form of political rationality premised upon consensus which is, in fact, increasingly distanced from more participatory democratic expectations (Triado, 1984, p. 37).

> Corporatism furnishes the institutional means to mediate the demands of *functional* interest groups . . . with the aim of developing an administrative *consensus* over resource allocation, investment planning, industry restructuring, the introduction of high technology, economic performance, full employment, wage levels, price controls, and various policies to augment the 'social wage', all pursued with the aid of certain ideological and cultural accoutrements stressing the overriding 'national interest'. (Triado, 1984, p. 40)

Offe perceives it as a shift in political rationality from demand management to supply side restructuring (Offe, 1975). This is the consequence of a shift from state intervention on a long-term basis towards increased politicization on a daily basis. It is a shift which is increasingly evident as the educational bureaucrats are faced with producing new policies to meet the demands of Ministers concerned with the immediate retention of power rather than longer-term outcomes, e.g. social equality. It is particularly evident in recent policy-making in education at both state and federal levels where short-term economic pragmatism dominates long-term social concerns such as social justice, and best exemplified in Australia by the restructuring of tertiary education as laid out in *Higher Education: A Policy Statement* (1988) to meet the immediate economic needs of a failing industrial and manufacturing sector and a balance of payments deficit.

Democracy, therefore, in the corporatist mode is not pursued in the normative sense of 'classical democracy' or, as Pateman calls it, positive participatory forms of democracy, but rather the élite notions of representative democracy or 'negative' participation (Pateman, 1970), although the rhetoric continues to confuse the difference (Blackmore, 1987). Crouch and Heller (1983), in referring to the European context during the 1970s, argue that the incorporation of the unions by governments allows unions to be manoeuvred into acting as instruments of mobilization and integration of workers towards governmental ends. The consensus mode of conflict resolution which accompanies this incorporation in a period of economic crisis and conflict leads to the increasing division between membership and leaders of unions. This form of inclusion of union leaders in decision-making diverts attention from more significant trends in the economy relating to the accumulation of capital and creates tensions within the union organization. Increasing bureaucratization and top-down policy decisions by union leaders enforced through this new corporatism conflict with the union rhetoric of democratization of decision-making (Ozga and Lawn, 1981, p. 23). Corporatism, therefore, raises issues of representativeness and the nature of *participatory* democracy both at the macro-political level (e.g. the economic summit) and the micro-organizational level (e.g. educational and union bureaucracies) (Blackmore and Spaull, 1987; Watkins, 1988).

Dilemmas Confronting Teacher Unions at the Organizational Level

As already suggested, corporatism has had significant impact, first, on the organization of the teacher unions, in terms of both organizational structure and the relationship between union bureaucrats and rank and file. Second, it has had an impact on ways in which unions formulate their strategies. Finally, it raises issues of representativeness and democratic process.

In the union bureaucracies, for example, Hyman depicts a historical dichotomy in the relationship between union leadership (union officials) and the rank and file which has romanticized the practices of what occurs on the shop floor. Meanwhile, 'trade union bureaucrat' has become a term of deprecation, representing union officials as scapegoats for the contradictions which are inherent in the nature of trade unionism within a capitalist system (Hyman, 1979, pp. 54–5). Hyman argues that union officials, although generally more progressive than their constituents, frequently appear to perform a conservative role in periods of membership struggle and activism. This is because of the contradictions inherent in their ongoing mediating role between employers and unions; this favours sustaining an accommodative rather than a confrontationist relationship with employers and the state, given the current non-revolutionary stance of unionism together with the union officials' self-interest to maintain an image of professional competence in collective bargaining in a corporatist system. Rank and file teachers, therefore, perceive that their conditions are being whittled away by various conservative settlements negotiated by their representatives.

This is not to suggest that those at the chalkface are necessarily more progressive. Trade union consciousness interrelates intimately with material and ideological influences. This means that the politics of trade unionism constitutes a totality often '*resistant* to major strategies of radicalisation and democratisation' at its very source (Hyman, 1979, p. 63). This phenomenon is exemplified in the institutionalized dominance of males in unions in general and the continuing lack of representation of women's interests in the upper echelons of teacher union organizations despite their numerical advantage. Male dominated union organizations tend to work to exclude women within the occupation from the possession of managerial skills and power (Blackmore, 1987). It is an issue currently being addressed by peak union officials in Australia who have now recognized that the participation of women, of whom over 50 per cent are in the workplace, is the key to future union power. Hence the representation of women in the upper echelons of union organizations must occur in order not to alienate further the rank and file (S. Crean, Australian Council of Trade Unions Congress, October 1989). Whether the presence of women in the union leadership will lead to the legitimation of women's interests (e.g. child care) remains to be seen.

Second, teacher unions have altered their strategies under the dominant consensus mode of operation of corporatism. Historically, there has been a tension regarding the strategic collective activities of teachers between professionalism and unionism. They have been associated with mutually exclusive behaviours. This professional/union dichotomy has been theoretically undermined by Ginsburg *et al.* (1980) as being an ideological construct which appears increasingly to have lost meaning in current organizational and political contexts and with the changing relationship between the state and teacher unions (see also Blackmore, 1987). Lawn depicts ongoing tensions between professional and union strategies in a series of historical case studies of teacher union activities in Portugal, the USA, England, Scotland, Sweden and France. By contextualizing teacher activities in each instance it can be seen that the ideology of professionalism on the one hand creates a teacher identity and culture, but on the other in periods of economic crisis professionalism has contradictory meanings. While it can be useful for teachers in combatting run-down of the service, it can also be used to constrain teachers taking militant action (Lawn, 1985, p. 4). As stressed by Gramsci, 'ideologies are neither free floating nor merely reflections of the dominant class. The dominant ideologies are always the product of struggle' (quoted in Sarup, 1984, p. 142). Hence the ideology of professionalism may unintentionally distort, 'misrecognize, mask or incorrectly grasp the primary workings of institutions' (Ginsburg *et al.*, 1980, p. 193).

Larson defines professionalization as 'the attempt to translate one order of scarce resources — special knowledge and skills — into another — social and economic rewards' (Larson, 1977, p. xvii). Although the élite professions seek institutional privileges which, once attained, steer them towards relatively 'traditional' intellectual functions, the need to defend these privileges as well as the immersion of professionals in everyday life, counteract this tendency (Larson, 1977, p. xv). Thus the ideology of professionalism may serve to further interests within occupations (doctors over nurses) or between occupations when it is used to control teachers who, in attempting to gain the same control over their workplace as doctors, are said to be acting 'unprofessionally' since collective union activity is viewed as antithetical to the individualistic characteristics of professionals.

Thus teachers' collective action as unionists has sat uncomfortably beside an ideology of professionalism characterized by notions of service, expertise and skills, collegial loyalty and accountability, applied research, individual ethics and male values (Ozga and Lawn, 1981; Ginsburg *et al.*, 1980). While the ideology of teacher professionalism would, on the surface, appear to have brought progressive change in education, or at least for teachers, investigations of specific instances illustrate how at particular times it has not (Grace, 1978, 1985). As Ginsburg points out, it is necessary to look at why and how teachers 'take up the concept of professionalism in their commonsense accounts of the situation' (Ginsburg *et al.*, 1980, p. 195). The position of teachers in this regard is not clear. As Wright argues, teachers are caught in a contradictory position in perpetuating and reproducing the intellectual hegemony of the middle class while undergoing deskilling of their labour as workers (Wright, 1982). Wright's notion of the contradictory position of teachers would seem to 'fit' apparent teacher behaviours with teachers enjoying some degree of status and occupational benefits from being 'professionals', while on the other hand taking militant action as their only strategy to pursue what they perceived were educational goals.

In practice the union/professional dichotomy is rapidly disintegrating. Teacher unions have recently affiliated with trade union organizations, the peak body being the ACTU, and education has been conceded to be included in the federal conciliation and arbitration system with a 1987 decision that teaching is an industry (Spaull and Hince, 1986). As Tipton points out, such a decision removes past paradoxes in theory. *Educational* institutions have been largely perceived as places for the production and transmission of knowledge, they

> had never been explored because of the habit of treating them as part and parcel of the process of social stratification. But looking at them as places of work is another matter ... although the study of educational organisations as workplaces has been bedevilled by the tyranny of taxonomies in organisational analysis, the intellectual isolation of the study of organisations, as the management orientation of educational administration as a field. (Tipton, 1985, p. 36)

The recognition that teachers are educational workers has particular significance in Victoria in the form of the Industrial Agreements. At the school level another aspect of the impact of the Industrial Agreements from 1983 onwards has been the significant reduction in industrial conflict. This has encouraged over 85 per cent of all Victorian teachers to join their respective unions (Spaull and Hince, 1986, p. 54). Thus the incorporation of teachers, and more specifically union members, into the decision-making structures of schools, has made the union/professional dichotomy less relevant and meaningful. Historically, Victorian union organizations have been the source of much of the pedagogical and political debate, and union issues have become educational issues and vice versa, whether in policy or practice, regarding curriculum, school organization, administration or pedagogy (Blackmore and Spaull, 1987). Not all teachers belong to unions but, it is argued here, union activity and involvement in educational policy-making significantly affect the work situation of all teachers, influence perceptions of what teachers do, as well as create a culture of professionalism and collectivism. More particularly, recent studies of the impact of administrative restructuring and school-based decision-making upon the respective activities, responsibilities and relationships of principals, teachers and parents in these administrative arenas have indicated significant changes in how school administration is to be perceived. Teachers are equally active in administration through the committee system (school-based administrative and curriculum committees, school councils) and involved with policy-making, just as principals are now expected to become advocates for their schools programs, promoters of curriculum change, facilitators of democratic practices and professional development, communicators, arbitrators between community interests, and sensitive to interpersonal relations (Chapman, 1986a, 1986b, pp. 50–5). Such involvement by teachers and parents sets up different expectations as to how decisions can be influenced when participation as a strategy is undermined by the new management imperatives.

It is questionable as to what extent this apparent democratization has influenced administrative practices, and in what way the incorporation of teachers on these representative bodies has affected the capacity of teachers to influence policy and improve school practice. Ironically, teacher union incorporation by the government at the *centre* has led to an apparent 'co-option' of unionists at the *school* level in decisions. This is problematic in a time of worsening conditions with the closure and amalgamation of schools, few promotional or financial incentives available to teachers during a period of declining enrolments, fiscal constraint imposed from the centre, and contestation over limited resources between state and private schools and within schools. Not surprisingly, union membership disillusionment with its leaders has increased as the Education Ministry's rhetoric of devolution, collaborative decision-making, participation and process orientation has been subsumed by that of corporate management promoting instrumental ends of efficiency and effectiveness. The power of the corporate management discourse over the participatory/community discourse is symbolized by the changing position of the principal, who is both responsible to the Ministry through the line management structure for finance and to the school council representing the community on policy. This ambiguity in accountability is highlighted in Watkins' study of regional boards and relevant to discussion of school committee systems. Watkins argues:

> the rhetoric advocating the transfer of power and decision-making from the centre to the schools was not reflected in the organisational procedures and structures which were set up. The reality underlying the rhetoric was a concern for corporate management emphasising central control and accountability to an all-powerful government through the Minister. In such an organisational reality power and authority flowed down from the Minister to the centre and through the regions to the schools. Essentially, discretionary power remained firmly entrenched in the centre. (Watkins, 1988, p. 1)

Thus the process of incorporation has reduced the use of past effective strategies in that opposition to decisions in any of the administrative arenas is seen to be against 'democratic process'.

Third and finally, the issue of 'representativeness' is highly problematic. The regional boards, which are composed of elected parent representatives of a geographical area and nominated teacher and bureaucratic group representatives, provide an appropriate example. While the notion of community is central to the *Ministerial Papers*, it assumes different meanings in different contexts and discourses. At a time when the government is establishing structures to facilitate participation, therefore, a contradiction exists between the political construct of organizations (teacher unions, parent organizations and schools) and the citizenship model of community. Watkins elucidates this: 'in the political scenario all the members of the adult community participate in the election of government. In organisations the general scenario is that autocratic and unequal power prevails' (Watkins, 1988, p. 7). The representation of teacher unions and parent organisations has a specific, well defined constituency and agenda, as do ministerial representatives, but not so the generally elected parent representatives. Furthermore, while teachers claim their right to participate (or be represented) in decision-making in the positive sense, they often simultaneously offer to the students the negative right of 'being represented', just as élite democracies protect the right of 'being represented'. This relates closely to Triado's notion that negative democratic participation is critical to corporatism in a liberal democracy. At the same time the interests of 'community' reduce to the interests of the 'state', as representing community. Teachers are again caught in a contradictory position *vis-à-vis* the community and within the democratic process.

In considering 'the relationship between representatives and their constituents; the responsiveness of representatives to their constituency, and the linkages between the two groups on policy matters, it must be remembered that they are working within the parameters of Government guidelines' (Watkins, 1988, p. 3). Whether individuals on committees actively represent interests, not merely in terms of a particular action or practice, but as a totality reflecting the overall organization and practices of those participating is also critical. Watkins uses Pitkin's distinction between descriptive and substantive representation, the former 'being someone', while the latter requires 'doing something' (Watkins, 1988, p. 5). He concludes that the boards are largely representational rather than participatory forms of democracy in which representation is a 'public, institutionalised way of involving many people and groups whilst benefitting the centre by distancing the state government from difficult decisions.' Likewise, schools may have clear structures and guidelines regarding committees and decision-making processes, but these are still in tension with the normative, positive dimensions of participation. At the macro level he concludes: 'In fact, by establishing a more decentralised administrative decision-making structure the state government can strengthen central control through indirect means while still appearing to hold on to its long standing ideological commitment to devolution and decentralisation' (Watkins, 1988, p. 18). Thus teacher interests are equally committed in order to maintain their own professional legitimacy and interests but are constrained by the way the state establishes the guidelines and controls the discourse and debate within its framework of corporate management and fiscal constraint.

The Quieting of Oppositional Discourse

Corporatism, therefore, is not merely a process or set of structures. The power of the corporatist ideology lies in its capability to capture the discourse of educational reform in the name of consensus. The trend towards the representation of teacher, student and parent interests in the name of democratic process has, in many specific instances of reform, worked to the detriment of teachers in schools because it 'quietens' the more radical and oppositional discourses. This is best understood as a consequence of the tension between the expectations of a more positive version of participatory democracy set up in the Victorian *Ministerial Papers* as well as the historical development of union involvement in participatory democratic forms in the early years of the Labor Government, and the representative and élitist character of the democratic process implicit in corporatism. Several dilemmas confront teacher unions.

First, the implications of the 'incorporation' of teachers' unions in Victoria by the state government since 1983 have only begun to surface, as in the partnership between the National Union of Teachers and the local educational authorities during the 1970s in the UK and the close relationship between the state and the FEN in France (Lawn, 1985). By advocating participation for its educative value as well as the promotion of specific group interests, previously radical and oppositional stances have been 'quietened' by their incorporation into the decision-making process, which has in turn smothered their criticism of the wider political agenda of corporate management espoused and practised by conservative governments (Johnston, 1981).

Second, at the school level the paradox in Victoria is that because of the emphasis on the decision-making *process* and *consensus* as the desired outcome, the involvement of all interested parties in communities in school closures, amalgamations and system rationalization has favoured governmental intervention when agreement is not reached, thus allowing the imposition of the state's own desired outcome, which can be summarized as reduced expenditure through system rationalization. Teachers are committed to the democratic decision-making process; therefore, if the outcome of that process is in doubt due to an inability to gain consensus, the state intervenes as the arbiter. Thus, while the process of decision-making appears to be participative and democratic, it often produces unfavourable and undemocratic outcomes. In the search for consensus process is privileged by the Ministry over any debate over substantive issues and what are desirable outcomes for the local community as opposed to the interests of 'the state'. To maintain a particular position without concession in this search for consensus and thus apparently impede democratic process is to be perceived as doctrinaire and confrontational. The effect is to produce incremental change at the superficial level. Likewise, within this consensus framework teacher union executives have been accused by the rank and file members of cooperating in decisions with politically conservative and educationally detrimental outcomes (Blackmore, 1986). An analysis of the current contestation between the discourses of corporate management and participatory decision-making offers some explanation as to how, when teacher unions emerge from apparent successes on specific educational issues such as representation on policy-making committees or curriculum reform, it is at a cost. Participatory democracy thus becomes a rhetorical ploy, co-existent with more élitist notions of representative democracy embedded in the very decision-making *structures* and *processes* of corporatism.

Control is also maintained by more subtle and indirect means. Pusey argues that control over education should not be confused as control over concrete and specific aspects of curriculum or decision-making structures, e.g. standardized curricula, legal constraints, external examinations. A proliferation of specific controls creates more unmanageably complex coordination problems for governments. What governments want is *less* complexity and more *governability*; a generalized form of control in the sense used by Habermas as a 'steering capacity' which facilitates increasing the use of power by producing voluntary compliance and involvement (Pusey, 1981, p. 9). Corporatism, with its rhetoric of participation of vested interests and consultation, provides a rationale which appeals to the commonsense democratic notion of participation as a good. It therefore provides a basis for such voluntarism. It is basically an ideological rather than a bureaucratic device, a mechanism of indirect technical control of educational practice. Control can be equally more subtly effected through agreement upon educational procedures such as evaluation and curriculum packages, criterion referenced instruments, modular content and consensus decision-making procedures (as in the Victorian Certificate of Education) rather than direct, concrete intrusion by inspectors and supervisors (Pusey, 1981, p. 10). Current moves towards state-wide curriculum and assessment guidelines in Victoria, and national guidelines, act in the 'steering capacity' suggested by Habermas: in directing and determining the agendas, without concern for the specifics. Meanwhile, the steering capacity is maintained through the collaborative decision-making process which has been subsumed into important elements of corporate management.

The consequences of the state 'steering' towards technicist solutions and the scientization of politics according to Pusey are, first, to debase educational practice through the 'inculcation and expectation that technical formations of issues problems and facts ... are ipso facto more authoritative than ordinary non-professional understanding'; second, to demoralize educational practice by fostering a problem-solving inventiveness which assumes that tinkering with manipulable variables will lead to a solution, a process to which human values are irrelevant. Finally, it devalues common speech and experience, the common cultural 'resources', by imposing a false construct or 'artificial' technical language which restricts discourse to predefined issues (Pusey, 1981, pp. 12–13). Ultimately, therefore, the process of 'incorporation' undermines the essential benefits of participation of non-experts, e.g. parents and students, which could offer a more transformative perception of teaching and administration. It changes the emphasis in the teaching/learning process away from a critical pedagogy to what Aronowitz and Giroux call a 'management pedagogy' in which 'teachers are relegated to instrumental tasks that limits the possibilities for oppositional discourse and social practices. Pedagogy in this case, is reduced to the implementation of taxonomies that subordinate knowledge to forms of methodological reification, whilst theories of teaching are increasingly technicised and standardised in the interest of efficiency and the management and control of discrete forms of knowledge' (Aronowitz and Giroux, 1985, p. 24). The central question of learning is a management problem; that is, how to allocate resources to produce the maximum number of certified students within a designated time at minimal cost. Such management pedagogies ignore questions regarding cultural specificity, teacher judgment and how student experiences and histories relate to the learning process. They embody a mode of teacher control in which the payoff for the school system is the good public relations made possible as school administrators 'provide technical solutions to the complex economic, social and political problems that plague their schools. Simultaneously, they invoke the tenets of accountability as indicators of success' (Aronowitz and Giroux, 1985, pp. 28–9). In this way the state redirects, diverts or transforms the potentially emancipatory discourses upon which policy is premised into a managerial-technicist model; the discourse of corporate managerialism has effectively captured the key words of 'consultation', 'process' and 'devolution'.

Another way in which the state maintains its steering capacity is through the tension between centralizing and decentralizing forms of government. State government reports in general have assumed the rhetoric of administrative decentralization and school-based decision-making merely to disguise increased central demands for more efficient use of diminishing resources, thus passing the onus on to local decision-makers to make the difficult resource allocation and equity decisions. What is clear is that a particular version of technically oriented, supposedly value-free corporate managerialism is implicit in the structures and that this has become conventional administrative wisdom, regardless of partisan politics. Ryan persuasively argues that the utilization of arguments of rational administration, cost-cutting efficiency and quality education which inform state policies does not yield 'good' policy, only managerially 'correct' policy and inevitably conservative educational outcomes (Ryan, 1984, p. 33). Thus the incorporation of teacher unions in the name of consensus and democracy at all levels of this process has produced the same controlling effect as do the more overt managerialist mechanisms controlling teachers in the USA and the United Kingdom (teacher competency testing, performance-based assessment and teacher education programs, and inspectorial 'visitations'). Teacher unions are expected to negotiate on issues which are determined within the technicist model of education; the boundaries of change are limited largely to non-educative, managerialist issues.

Finally, Giroux talks about how corporatism (the political strategy) enables the discourse to be centred on particular notions of production (central to corporate managerialism) which have an impact on teachers' work conditions.

> Another important aspect of the discourse of production is that it points the way in which labour is objectively constructed; that is, it provides an analysis of the conditions under which people work and the political importance of these conditions is either limiting or enabling of what educators can do. This issue is especially important for analysing the critical possibilities that exist for public school teachers and students within specific conditions of labor to act and be treated as intellectuals. Quite simply, if teachers and students are subject to conditions of overcrowding, lack of time to work collectively in a creative fashion, or are subject to rules and regulations that disempower them, the technical and social conditions of labour have to be understood and addressed as part of the discourse of reform and struggle. (Giroux, 1985, p. 138)

This is critical given the current implications of the restructuring of teacher career paths and the renegotiation of the educational settlement surrounding the new post-compulsory 'comprehensive curriculum' which is requiring another round of school reorganization in the early 1990s. Teachers' voluntary involvement in the committee systems is being ignored, while their conditions of work are being eroded under new career structures based upon productivity gains.

Apple also points out that discourses can both serve to reproduce conservative agendas of reform and bear the seeds of oppositional discourses and practice (Apple, 1984). Consequently, policy within the corporatist framework often represents ideologically and educationally contradictory notions. This is most evident in the production of recent documents from the representative body, the Victorian State Board of Education. The State Board is a good example of 'corporatism' in that it has representatives from the state, Catholic parochial and independent private school systems, from teacher unions, business, universities, parent organizations and educational bureaucrats. Furthermore, many of the permanent staff are former teacher union executives. It is a body comprised of 'representatives' of various peak organizations and key community interests. This Board, which has a research and policy advisory function, has increasingly come to operate within parameters of the dominant managerialist discourse of efficiency and effectiveness rather than act as an independent authority. Thus its most recent working papers concentrate on the role of the principal, monitoring of schools, literacy, performance indicators and accountability. In turn, these are ambiguously linked to radical concepts of social justice, equity and disadvantage (e.g. 'An Odd Couple? Social Justice and Performance Indicators', Social Justice Standing Committee, 1988).

Likewise, debates on curriculum reform at state and federal levels, in which teacher unions are actively involved, indicate two oppositional discourses. One reflects the nationalistic urges of 'competitive economies', the other the pluralistic nature of a multicultural society. The former calls for instrumental solutions promised by the hard sciences, the latter a recognition of the significance of values. The nationalistic, competitive economy theme is represented in the central guidelines of the common curriculum of the Victorian Certificate of Education to be introduced fully by 1992; the pluralistic/cultural theme is to be represented by facilitating the diversity of school structures and pedagogies accompanied by the sympathetic environments which offer a comprehensive curriculum. Giroux is justifiably critical of the 'pedagogy of normative pluralism' which on the one hand recognizes the existence of racial, gender, ethnic and other types of conflict among different groups but on the other searches for a 'common culture' of curriculum which is ideologically dishonest.

Recapturing the Centre Stage

There are possibilities for recapturing the discourse of reform. An oppositional discourse which frames different priorities and policy responses can emerge at any particular instance. In practical terms it requires that individuals and groups, for example, recognize the slippage in the rhetoric between participatory and representative forms of democracy and act upon the principles of the first. Watkins cites the example of how a school closure decision by the Ministry of Education was reversed after active campaigning by parents, teachers and students through the legitimate processes and structures which already existed (Watkins, 1988). In a sense such action was exploiting those corporatist elements which had previously acted as constraints.

Such a political strategy requires substantive issues of content and outcomes to be taken up in the various administrative arenas in which decisions are made. Curriculum, for example, is contested and negotiated at all levels and in various arenas in which teachers as individuals and unionists have involvement — in school councils, in subject committees and state authorities such as the Victorian Curriculum and Assessment

Board (VCAB). In these committees the opportunity exists to communicate the ways in which knowledge is historically and socially constructed in ways which benefit certain groups and exclude others. This means reversing the priorities from the managerialist use of technicist solutions to those which value the normative dimension of participation, to specifying and understanding the material conditions under which students and teachers work and how these can be altered through collective, as well as individual, action (Giroux, 1985, p. 87). Union representatives have been vocal in maintaining such material conditions, in creating 'enabling contexts' for reform, but have lost out at the ideological level. The democratic discourses have been subverted by managerialism; union representatives have participated in the discourse but not controlled or influenced it. Ultimately, the material conditions have also been undermined, as signified in the current award restructuring of teaching. There is a contradiction in that teachers, steered towards a technicist, positivist view of what constitutes knowledge by educational settlements negotiated in different *administrative* arenas between the educational bureaucracy, politicians, universities, parent and teacher representatives, practise the same control over their students in defining knowledge and classroom practices by moving towards cognitive, non-experiential agendas, particularly through communicative practices.

Other possibilities to reconceptualize the notions of bureaucratic rationality and hierarchy which undermine democratic discourses in schools also lie in the very gendered construction of teaching and administration. Ferguson argues that the dominance of a bureaucratic discourse which permeates everyday existence in schools can be subverted by the 'subjugated knowledges' of women located 'lower down in the hierarchy', marginalized and not fully co-opted into the bureaucratic discourse (Ferguson, 1984, p. 23). A feminist discourse would

> interject into public debate a reformulation of the basic political questions of power and rationality, and can legitimate a concern for community. Feminist discourse can provide a way of thinking and acting that is neither an extension of bureaucratic forms nor a mirror image of them, but rather a genuinely radical voice in opposition.... Change emerges out of people's confrontations with the existing social arrangements; coming up against institutionalised limitations in a personal way, not simply in theory or at a distance, opens the way to resistance. (Ferguson, 1984, p. 29)

But as with other critical discourse from outsiders, a feminist discourse faces the danger of being absorbed, recodified and recolonized by the dominant bureaucratic discourse, unless it is ongoing and critically self-reflective. Feminists have become 'femocrats' within the élite representative structures of corporatism in liberal democracies. Equity is now a major priority in government policies, although often lost in their implementation. The irony is that while women have been able to exploit the liberal ideology of equality to make claims to equal work opportunities in teaching and administration, this same ideology has been utilized by the state to control their militancy and by their male colleagues in the administrative hierarchy to demand conformity to technicist and masculine models of 'leadership' (Blackmore, 1989). What appears as change to benefit women is often subverted by the corporatist process, which does not necessarily produce more equitable outcomes.

In conclusion, it has been argued that the current restructuring in Victoria requires a reconceptualization of democratic process because of the involvement of teachers and teacher unions in everyday administrative decisions in new 'democratic' structures within a corporatist framework. At the same time the apparent democratization of decision-making structures has not necessarily resulted in more democratic decisions with outcomes which reflect a move towards greater social justice, e.g. greater representation of women. It has merely highlighted the contradictions between various ideological elements from which teachers make sense of their everyday practice. In looking at the incorporation of teacher unions into the decision-making processes at all levels of the educational bureaucracy, this chapter has indicated how the nature of corporatism and its associated ideologies of participation and decentralization have effectively quietened the oppositional discourse of the unions. This analysis suggests that it is not sufficient merely to be satisfied with democratic structures and processes, for they can be constraining or enabling. Equally important are the discourses which come to dominate and displace more emancipatory discourses in these new administrative arenas. Democratic process is no guarantee of ethical outcomes, and this is evident in the Victorian situation in which the discourse of educational reform is now dominated by Rightist principles of corporate managerialism which assumes a particularly negative connotation of participation. It is necessary to challenge those situations in which certain discourses centred on key concepts such as efficiency and effectiveness become accepted as 'givens' — in which partial aspects of oppositional discourses are appropriated and assimilated by the dominant discourse and thus take on the force of ideology, as when assessment drives curriculum, standards replace quality, equity is subsumed under efficiency.

Finally, this is not enough unless the possibilities for changing the practices and overall outcomes are ventured once the essential features of conservative discourses are uncovered, displayed, and alternative options are raised. Howe suggests three strategies to rebuild a progressive radical movement which begins with this reconceptualization of teachers' capacity to bring about change: first, the rebuilding of rank and file caucuses and militancy at the branch level; second, developing organizational forms which address conditions of capital's strategies, e.g. the facilities to counter conservative claims; and, finally, facilitating the active participation and leadership of women and minorities in the union movement which allows unions to claim to be truly 'representative and participative' (Howe, 1986).

References

APPLE, M. (1984) 'Conditions of labour, conditions of teaching', *The Review of Education*, Summer, pp. 259–65.

ARONOWITZ, S. and GIROUX, H. (1985) *Education under Siege*, New York, Bergin and Garvey.

BADCOCK, A.M. (1988) *Devolution at a Price: A Review of the Quantity and Quality Controls Relinquished by the Restructured Education Department of Victoria*, Blackburn, Acacia Press.

BLACKMORE, J. (1986) 'Tensions to be resolved in participation and school based decision making', *Educational Administration Review*, 14, 1, pp. 29–47.

BLACKMORE, J. (1987) 'Contradiction and contestion: Theory and ideology in defining teachers' work', paper presented to British Educational Research Association, Manchester, September.

BLACKMORE, J. (1989) 'Reconstructing educational leadership: A feminist perspective', in SMYTH, J. (Ed.), *Critical Perspectives on Educational Leadership*, Lewes, Falmer Press.

BLACKMORE, J. and SPAULL, A. (1987) 'Australian teacher unionism: New directions', in BOYD, W.L. and SMART, D. (Eds), *Education Policy in Australia and America: Comparative Perspectives*, Lewes, Falmer Press.

BORCHORST, A. and SIIM, B. (1987) 'Women and the advanced industrial state: A new kind of patriarchal power?', in SASSOON, A. (Ed.), *Women and the State*, London, Hutchinson.

BOWLES, S. and GINTIS, H. (1976) *Schooling in Capitalist America*, New York, Harper and Row.

CAWSON, A (1983) 'Functional representation and democratic politics. Towards a corporatist democracy?', in DUNCAN, C. (Ed.), *Democratic Theory and Practice*, London, Cambridge University Press.

CHAPMAN, J. (1986a) 'The changing nature of the principalship in a decentralised and devolved system', *Educational Administration Review*, 4, 1, pp. 48–68.

CHAPMAN, J. (1986b) 'Decentralization, devolution and the teacher: Participation by teachers in the decision-making of schools', paper presented to American Education Research Association, San Francisco, Calif.

COMMONWEALTH SCHOOLS COMMISSION (1983) *Annual Report, 1982–3*, Canberra, Commonwealth Government Printing Service.

Conway, J.A. (1984) 'The myth, mystery and mastery of participative decision making in education', *Educational Administration Quarterly*, 20, 3, pp. 11–40.

Crouch, C. and Heller, F. (Eds) (1983) *Organisational Democracy and Political Processes,* London, John Wiley and Sons.

Darling-Hammond, L. (1987) 'Schools for tomorrow's teachers', *Teachers College Record*, 88, 3, pp. 354–365.

Deakin University (1985) *Report on the Restructuring of Victorian Education*, Geelong, Social and Administrative Studies, Deakin University.

Education Victoria, various issues.

Encel, S. (1979) 'The post industrial society and the corporate state', *Australian and New Zealand Journal of Sociology*, 15, 2, pp. 37–43.

Ferguson, K. (1984) *The Feminist Case against Bureaucracy*, Philadelphia, Pa., Temple University Press.

Final Report of the Committee of Enquiry into Education in South Australia: Education and Change in South Australia (1982) (Chairman: Dr J. Keeves) Adelaide, Government Printer.

Fitzgerald, R.T., Musgrave, P.W. and Pettit, D. (1977) *Participation in Schools*, Ringwood, ACER.

Ginsburg, M., Meyenn, R.J. and Miller, H.D.R. (1980) 'Teachers' conception of professionalism and trade unionism: An ideological analysis', in Woods, P. (Ed.), *Teacher Strategies*, London, Croom Helm.

Giroux, H. (1985) 'Critical pedagogy, cultural politics and the discourse of experience', *Boston University Journal of Education*, 167, 2, pp. 22–42.

Grace, G. (1978) *Teachers, Ideology and Control: A Study in Urban Education*, London, Routledge and Kegan Paul.

Grace, G. (1985) 'Judging teachers: The social and political contexts of teacher evaluation', *British Journal of Sociology of Education*, 6, 1, pp. 3–22.

Gramsci, A. (1971) *Prison Notebooks*, Trans Q. Hoare and G. Nowell Smith, New York, International Publishers.

Higher Education: A Policy Statement (1988) circulated by the Hon. J. Dawkins, Minister of Employment and Education.

Howe, C. (1986) 'The politics of class compromise in an international context: Considerations for a new strategy for labour', *Review of Radical Political Economics*, 18, 3, pp. 1–22.

Hyman, R. (1979) 'The politics of workplace trade unionism: Recent tendencies and some problems for theory', *Capital and Class*, 8, pp. 54–67.

Hyslop, A.G. (1988) 'Trade unions and the state since 1945: Corporatism and hegemony', *International Journal of Sociology and Social Policy*, 8, 1, pp. 53–91.

Imber, M. (1983) 'Increased decision-making involvement for teachers: Ethical and practical considerations', *Journal of Educational Thought*, 17, 1, pp. 36–42.

Jessop, B. (1982) *The Capitalist State, Marxist Theories and Methods*, Oxford, Martin Robertson.

Johnston, K. (1981) 'The production of conservative discourses', *Discourse*, 2, 1, pp. 1–13.

Johnston, K. (1983) '"A discourse for all seasons"? An ideological analysis of the Schools Commission reports, 1973–81', *Australian Journal of Education*, 27, 1, pp. 17–32.

Lange, D. (1988) *Tomorrow's Schools: The Reform of Education Administration in New Zealand*, Wellington, Government Printer.

LARSON, M.S. (1977) *The Rise of Professionalism: A Sociological Analysis*, Berkeley, Calif., University of California Press.

LAWN, M. (Ed.) (1985) *The Politics of Teacher Unionism: International Perspectives*, London, Croom Helm.

MACPHERSON, M. (1983) 'An analysis of some current events in educational administration in Victoria', unpublished paper, Monash University.

MINISTER OF EDUCATION, VICTORIA (1985) *Ministerial Papers 1–6*, Melbourne, Victorian Government Printer.

OFFE, C. (1985) *Disorganized Capitalism: Contemporary Transformations of Work and Politics*, Cambridge, Polity Press.

OZGA, J. and LAWN, M. (1981) *Teachers, Professionalism and Class*, Lewes, Falmer Press.

PANITCH, L. (1977) 'The development of corporatism in liberal democracies', *Comparative Political Studies*, 10, 1, pp. 61–91.

PANITCH, L. (1981) 'Trade unions and the capitalist state', *New Left Review*, 125, pp. 21–43.

PATEMAN, C. (1970) *Participation and Democratic Theory*, Cambridge, Cambridge University Press.

PUSEY, M. (1981) 'How will governments strive to control education in the 1980s?' *Discourse*, 1, 2, pp. 9–17.

RAMSAY, H. (1983) 'Evolution or cycle? Worker participation in the 1970s and 1980s', in CROUCH, C. and HELLER, F. (Eds), *Organizational Democracy and Political Processes*, London, John Wiley and Sons.

RYAN, B. (1984) 'Education and change in South Australia: An unhappy alliance', *Discourse*, 5, 2, pp. 23–35.

SALLIS, J. (1988) *Schools, Parents and Governors: A New Approach to Accountability*, London, Routledge.

SARUP, M. (1984) *Marxism/Structuralism/Education*, Lewes, Falmer Press.

SCOTT, B. (1989) *Schools Renewal: A Strategy to Revitalize Schools within the NSW State Education System*, Sydney, Management Review Unit, Department of Education.

SEDDON, T. (1988) 'Teachers' work: Past and present', paper presented to the Australian and New Zealand History of Education Society, Canberra.

SOCIAL JUSTICE STANDING COMMITTEE (1988) 'An Odd Couple? Social Justice and Performance Indicators', *Working Paper No. 3*, Melbourne, State Board of Education.

SPAULL, A. and HINCE, K. (1986) *Industrial Relations and State Education in Australia*, Ringwood, Australian Educational Press.

TANNER, L. (1983) 'The policy formulation process of an Australian political party in opposition. A case study of the Australian Labor Party's School Commission proposal', in PALMER, I. (Ed.), *Melbourne Studies in Education, 1983*, Melbourne, Melbourne University Press.

TIPTON, B. (1974) 'The hidden side of teaching: The teachers' unions', *London Educational Review*, 3, 2, pp. 20–30.

TIPTON, B.F.A. (1985) 'Educational organisations as workplaces', *British Journal of Sociology of Education*, 6, 1, pp. 35–45.

TRIADO, J. (1984) 'Corporatism, democracy and modernity', *Thesis Eleven*, 9, pp. 33–51.

Victorian Teacher, various issues.

VSTA News, various issues.

Watkins, P. (1988) 'Representative democracy in a regional board of education', *International Journal of Educational Management*, 2, 1, pp. 18–25.

Watkins, P. (forthcoming) 'Devolving educational administration in Victoria: Tensions in the role and selection of the principal', *Journal of Educational Administration*.

Wexler, P. and Grabiner, G. (1986) 'The education question: America during the crisis', in Sharp, R. (Ed.), *Capitalist Crisis and Schooling: Comparative Studies in the Politics of Education*, South Melbourne, Macmillan.

Wright, E.O. (1982) 'Class boundaries and contradictory class locations', in Giddens, A. and Held, D. (Eds), *Classes, Power and Conflict*, Berkeley, Calif., University of California Press.

Chapter 3

Reform Programs and the Culture of Schools

David Dawkins

Two major refom programs were a central feature of the Australian education system in the 1980s: in 1980–83 came the Transition from School to Work Program (referred to here as the Transition Education Program), which was replaced in 1983–87 by its successor, the Participation and Equity Program (the PEP program). This chapter discusses the implementation of the first of these 'grand slam' programs in schools in the state of Victoria, emphasizing the importance of the cultural context of educational sites for education reform. It is argued that significant features of the cultural context of educational sites where the program functioned facilitated either the contestation or reproduction of cultural hegemony in education.

The evaluation studies of both programs make it clear that, in the state of Victoria at least, and most likely elsewhere as well, the small groups of designers of the programs at the political centre in Canberra were unable to impose on teachers their own interpretation of the program. Indeed, despite the political origins of each program, they were open to interpretation. As one would expect, since teachers do not share homogeneous views, there was much equivocation about the aims and conduct of the programs. Nevertheless, under the direction of the educators who took control, both programs were judged in Victoria to have been avenues for significant reform; the Transition Education Program was credited with initiating significant curriculum reform (Kemmis *et al.*, 1983) and the PEP program with pedagogical reform (Rizvi and Kemmis, 1987). But to what extent did they engage in the contestation of cultural hegemony? And to what extent did the programs engage with teachers not directly involved with them? On the first question the evaluation studies of both programs are mute; on the second it is clear that the views espoused by the programs were not 'well articulated or widely shared by

Victorian teachers'. The discussion which follows focuses on school project activities within the Transition Education Program, since that is where data are most familiar to the author, but the report of the PEP program (Rizvi and Kemmis, 1987) also reads with great familiarity.

For a full discussion of the conduct of the two programs and of their effect on educational practices readers should consult the evaluation reports by Kemmis *et al.* (1983) and Rizvi and Kemmis (1987) respectively. The concern of this chapter is to consider how educational programs which are supposed to improve the life chances of individuals do not seem to have made much difference in the long term.

The study from which this paper is derived (Dawkins, 1986a) was itself a re-examination of data collected in the course of the evaluation of the Transition Education Program. That evaluation research, which began in 1981, provided a rare opportunity to observe the development and implementation of a major educational reform program from policy-making level through administrative processes to its conduct at the school classroom level. The data and publications of the program gathered in the course of the evaluation were later subjected to further analysis using the method of immanent critique advocated by critical theory (Adorno, 1969; Horkheimer, 1937; Habermas, 1972; Held, 1980; Giroux, 1983a; Brodkey, 1987), which requires claims made for the program to be compared with actual practices. In this process a deconstruction of the master narratives of the program subjected to reassessment the statements of its aims to improve education in general and the position of students 'at risk' in particular (they were considered to be at risk of attaining only poor educational achievement, and thus becoming unemployable), and statements of its achievements in curriculum reform.

This re-examination of the data from the Transition Education Program evaluation was prompted by my dissatisfaction with the nature of its discourse. This is not to question the validity of the evaluation, but merely to say that there were questions which remained unasked by the evaluation, much less answered, because they lay outside the brief, which was essentially to provide a commentary on its processes and internal relationships. In terms of program achievements the evaluation was primarily concerned with aspects of curriculum reform, which may have been adequate for the task commissioned by the state government, but was inadequate as a mechanism for social critique. It commented on curriculum reform to the extent that this made schoolwork more engaging for students or was more attuned to employment opportunities, but was mute on questions about reforms likely to effect a general improvement in the life chances of students through the contestation of cultural hegemony in education. This suggested that the data be reconsidered via a deconstruction of the program narratives in a quest to find answers to these questions.

This chapter provides a condensed account of parts of that re-examination of the program data, but before presenting that account three side issues require brief comment: first, curriculum studies; second, the nature of cultural hegemony; and third, the political influences which gave direction to the Transition Education and PEP programs.

Curriculum Studies and Cultural Factors

Only in the most tenuous way was the link between curriculum and sociocultural factors drawn to the reader's attention in the Transition Education Program report. Questioning the motives of the unstated political agenda and social implications of the program tended to be confined to its periphery, finding expression in project discussion papers and professional fora (e.g. Emmett, 1981; Hammond, 1981; Dawkins, 1982a; Reilly, 1982c). It was this proclivity towards program processes to the exclusion of sociocultural questions which prompted my re-examination of the data, with a particular concern to consider why the program either contested or reproduced the conditions of cultural hegemony in education.

Contemporaneous with the preparation of the evaluation report, Lundgren (1983) had criticized curriculum studies as being unlikely to produce a critique of the education system. This, he argued, occurs because the fundamental concerns of such studies are what pupils *do* rather than how educational systems and curricula themselves provide constraints or possibilities for change. There remains a sustained criticism that the conceptualization of curriculum is often separated from socio-cultural context (see Cornbleth, 1988; Goodson, 1988; Giroux, 1990).

Giroux (1983b) offered an even more antagonistic view, arguing that the absence of any serious attempt at social critique in curriculum studies is not merely an oversight but is, while not being conspiratorial, in collaboration with cultural hegemony in society. Dale (1982) also argued that the ideological component of education is simply ignored by curriculum studies and educational processes are treated as though they are quarantined from mainstream culture, thus permitting the redefinition of political activity within education: 'Political questions are bracketed out and replaced by questions about processes of decision-making; politics are reduced to administration. The focus is on the machinery, rather than on what powers it, or how and where it is directed' (1982, p. 129).

The Transition Education Program evaluation report, too, focused on the internal politics of the program and its curriculum reform achievements for a rather specialized sample of students, but ignored the place of the program in the wider social context, and did so quite 'naturally' because of its curriculum orientation. How the view has evolved that curriculum studies 'naturally' focus on the internal politics of education to the exclusion of wider sociopolitical influences of culture, because that is seen as its fundamental task, has been touched on by Carr and Kemmis (1983).

It is against this 'naturalness' that some writers have protested. Apple (1982) and Codd (1984) argue that commonsense knowledge structures mass consciousness in ways that mask existing power relations in society. Giroux (1983b) argues that commonsense understanding must itself be subjected to analysis, for the 'naturally' given commonsense understanding of educational discourse is itself a soical construct. He has in mind Gramsci's point that even everyday discourse should be subject to critical analysis because this will make clear the underlying interests that exist to support cultural hegemony.

Cultural Hegemony in Education

Gramsci (1971) maintained that in society there exists a 'civil' (i.e. cultural) hegemony which is indistinguishable from, but similar in effect to, the coercive authority of the state. He argues that there are two major superstructural levels of society: the 'civil' or 'private' level and the 'political' or 'state' level. At the first level the dominant social groups exercise an indirect hegemonic control throughout society, while at the second level the state exercises direct juridical domination. Thus he contrasts the power of the ruling classes to rule through subtle non-coercive processes that allow them to do so with the 'consent' of the ruled classes with the coercive juridical power of the state to govern. The 'consent' permitting the ruling class to rule is '"historically" caused by the prestige (and consequent confidence) which the dominant group enjoys because of its position and function in the world of production' (1971, p. 12). However, cultural hegemony is not just a matter of relative structural locations within society, for individuals are not merely differentially located in society but learn to deal with one another according to their relative locations. He argues that, by providing one context for learning functions appropriate to one's location in society, the education system forms part of the state apparatus by which cultural hegemony is maintained.

The concept of cultural hegemony has frequently been employed, but often with an undefined and taken-for-granted meaning (e.g. Paulson, 1971; Branson and Miller, 1979; Dwyer *et al.*, 1984). Connell (1977), however, engages with the concept to suggest the need to extend it to take account of the stability apparent in industrial societies, which have a well-developed working class. Most importantly, he distinguishes cultural hegemony as a *situation* rather than a system of total control. He argues that differing degrees of hegemony may be imposed because different situations employ a variety of mechanisms by which the dominant manage subordinate groups. In this sense hegemony cannot be conceptualized as a fixed condition, for its manifestation will vary from one situation to the next. He also argues that even in the most oppressive situations (his example is Nazi Germany) cultural hegemony never achieves the condition of total control, and thus the further importance of defining cultural hegemony as a situation is that to do so is to assert that it does not confer absolute power. Thus he can say,

> In defining hegemony as a situation, I wanted to stress its historically contingent character; or to put it in plainer English, the fact that cultural control can be opposed, weakened, and overcome. It may be difficult, but it is possible. In an analysis of hegemony there should always be a consideration of counter-hegemonic activity. (Connell, 1977, p. 220)

Thus we should expect to find manifestations of cultural hegemony throughout education systems, and at the same time to observe these to be faced with contestation from counter-hegemonic opposition.

Given this, and notwithstanding the conclusion of the Transition Education Program evaluation that significant curriculum reform was achieved, it will be argued here that the program has done little to redress conditions in the education system which enhance the reproduction of social inequality and the maintenance of cultural hegemony. Furthermore, one reason why counter-hegemonic contestation occurred with quite varied manifestations, and only in certain sections of the program and not throughout, and why it had little overall impact on cultural hegemony in education, is to be found in the nature of the cultural context of educational sites. But first, a note on the political rather than educational influences which significantly shaped this program and its successor.

The Politics of Educational Programs

The Transition Education Program was born of economic crisis, the details of which have been elaborated elsewhere (Dawkins, 1986b). Here the argument is restated briefly.

The federal government, a coalition of conservative parties, had come to power in November 1975 after orchestrating a constitutional coup which saw the reformist Labor Government dismissed by the Governor-General, and the conservative opposition installed as a 'caretaker' government until elections could be held, at which it was 'returned' to office with a substantial majority. Their election campaign (adopting the slogan 'Turn on the Lights') focused on the issue of economic management; indeed, they sought legitimacy for the constitutional crisis generated by their blockage of supply bills in the Senate by arguing this to be the only responsible course of action in view of Labor's economic mismanagement. Thus the onus lay with the new government to demonstrate its own competence, but, having won office on the grounds of superior ability to manage the nation's economy, in 1979 they were faced with a worsening situation. Moreover, the crisis for the government was not merely to do with the economy; it was also a crisis of legitimacy. It was a situation displaying all the crisis tendencies of advanced capitalism proposed by Habermas (1976): crisis in the economy leading to rationality crisis in politics and legitimation/motivation crisis in social institutions.

Rationality crisis developed as the government adopted a number of ad hoc measures to salvage its reputation. One of these was to shift blame by attributing youth unemployment to the 'failure' of the state education system. In this it was aided by its allies in the media. Typical examples were articles in *The Bulletin* headlined 'A wasteland where there should be knowledge' (8 September 1979) and 'Why teachers aren't what they used to be' (25 December 1979), attacking state education while at the same time assuring the more affluent and business-community segments of their audience that the private education system, substantially occupied by those readers' own children, was much superior. The main features of this attack on education have been detailed by Windschuttle (1979) and Foley (1981). Much of the attack was quite spurious and based upon circular validation between press and politicians. In this process statements by politicians attacking state education as deficient would be reported in the press, and subsequently the same statements, now accorded factual status by publication, would be reproduced by politicians as supporting evidence in further attacks, often by the same government parliamentarians who had initially generated them (Teese, 1981).

But, by being too successful at shifting blame away from themselves and onto the education system, they were hoist by their own petard. Though the arguments may have been spurious and circular, nevertheless they touched a responsive nerve in Australian society, and there was a growing concern about the content and pedagogy of state school education as parents and pupils worried about jobs and careers in the face of shrinking opportunities. This loss of confidence in the state education system was one of the contributing factors to the beginnings of a drift of students away from the state system and into private schools (see White, 1987; Ashenden, 1989), which was pointed to by the government when mounting further attacks as 'hard' evidence of the failure of the state system. The loss of confidence was also seen in another response, in this case by youth, for it could be argued that the dramatic increase in unemployment among the 15–17-year-olds (who by virtue of being unemployed had clearly rejected their option of staying at school) was more than an indicator of fewer job vacancies; it was also an indication that many young people saw no relevance in further schooling, preferring the dole queue and what little hope existed of finding a job to further education as an avenue into employment. The government, by seeking to divert criticism away from the state-administrative system and towards the education system, had contributed to its own legitimation crisis.

Ostensibly, the Transition Education Program was introduced to 'improve' the state education system by overcoming problems which were claimed to aggravate, if not exactly be the cause of, youth unemployment. As might be expected in view of the events outlined above, it was greeted with considerable cynicism from teachers in the state system (see Kemmis *et al.*, 1983). That such cynicism was not unfounded may be gauged by the fact that the program was announced in conjunction with the Government's parliamentary response to the Williams Report (1979); indeed, the very first indication that the program was to be established was contained in the ministerial statement on that report.

The Williams Report was essentially a workforce planning document which took a conservative view of education. It afforded particular support for the view that the education system needed to be more aligned to the requirements of industry, on ideological grounds equating the education process with the supply of trained labour. Its emphasis on labour supply and fiscal control contrasted sharply with the Karmel Report (1973), commissioned by the previous government, which placed emphasis on equal participation in education and argued that schools should not be influenced by marketplace values on individual talents (for a comparison see Freeland and Sharp, 1981; Young, 1981). It is interesting to observe how these two reports, prepared by committees having privileges and securities assuring their independence, could be so different in emphasis; their emphases accorded well with those of the respective commissioning governments.

When the announcement of the Transition Education Program is seen in the context of a legitimation crisis and in conjunction with the Williams Report, it is evident that the program had at least two clear, but unstated, political objectives: one, to align education more closely with the economic and political strategies of the government; two, to restore confidence in the state education system, and by the same token to help restore legitimation for the government.

The program was supposed to run for five years from the beginning of 1980, but it did not survive a change of government. Labor came back into office in March 1983, and the PEP program was announced in August that year. The transition to the new program began in January 1984.

Unlike the Transition Education Program, which had its origins in legitimation crisis and meritocracy, the PEP program was derived from egalitarian philosophies. Rizvi and Kemmis (1987) trace its development to the political ideology of the Labor Party. Pointing to earlier debates on education pulished in *Labor Essays* of 1982 and 1983, they highlight two contributions as representing the ideological source of the program. From the first of these they note Bennett's (1982) insistence 'that it was possible for schools to intervene in the processes of reproduction, and that schools could "make a difference" in altering patterns of power distributed within Australian society' (Rizvi and Kemmis, 1987, p. 53). As the second source they regard the paper by Dawkins and Costello in the following year (1983) to have built on Bennett's propositions:

> Dawkins and Costello thus faced the considerable challenge of devising a framework for educational policy that simultaneously responded to the problems of economic decline and unemployment, the continuing State Aid (to private schools) issue, the need for educational systems to serve diverse objectives and a pluralistic community, and the promotion of the objective of equality of educational opportunity. What emerged later as the Participation and Equity Program can be viewed as the practical resolution of these competing political demands. (Rizvi and Kemmis, 1987, p. 53).

If the major political objectives of the program were to achieve participation and equity in education, then the results of the Victorian evaluation study suggest that it did lead to greater pedagogical democracy and access to education. However, this opinion needs to be viewed with caution. The program, like its predecessor, was curtailed, in this case by a cut in funding just nine months after schools in Victoria received their first funds. The justification for this on the part of the Prime Minister, viz. that the program had been so successful that its effort could be reduced, was rejected by program staff as sheer 'sophistry'. The curtailment of the program was part of a general reduction of resource allocation, not only to education but to all social budgets, at a time when commentators (e.g. *The Bulletin*, 25 April 1989; Raskall, 1987) were noting an increase in the transfer of wealth to the wealthy as Labor displayed an increasing tendency to desert its traditional platform and adopt policies more to be expected from its rivals for office, gradually adjusting its social welfare program to the needs of party *realpolitik*. It should also be noted that the early stages of the PEP program were developed without any input by the Labor economists who came later to dominate party policy. Since then, there has been an acceleration of the drift to the Right (Kenway, 1990), whereby the education budget has been severely pared over several years and schools' efforts directed to achieve instrumental objectives of which the architects of the Transition Education Program would have been proud. This has been done under the ministerial direction of the same Dawkins who, with Costello, shaped the underlying ideology of PEP, albeit in a quite different role.

The rhetoric surrounding both of these programs was replete with unimpeachable statements about improving the quality (however defined) of education and the life chances of individual students. Yet, despite the declamatory language, it is clear that the Transition Education Program was born of crisis, and it displayed every sign that it was a hastily conceived, ad hoc program. The proposition that it had been carefully worked out at a joint meeting of state government ministers and departmental advisors (*Commonwealth Record*, 19–25 November 1979:1783) is at odds with much of the informal data and sits uneasily alongside later developments which saw several states (including some governed by the same political party which spawned it) threaten to withdraw from the program because of dissatisfaction with Commonwealth guidelines. The program was closely tailored to the élitist meritocratic emphasis of party policy, and the demise of the program came with a change in policy as government changed hands. Once again, rhetorical probity suffused statements outlining the new program, reflecting the declared philosophy of the new governing party. However, the divergence between the two, as with policies in many areas, seems to have been rhetorical rather than of fundamental difference.

The question confronting us here is that of how cultural hegemony dominating social relationships in wider society is maintained via the education system. Cultural hegemony, it was noted earlier, is a process whereby individuals' actions are limited according to what seems possible to them. These possibilities are particularly revealed in gender and class relationships, and these two areas will be the foci of discussion.

In Search of Affirmative Action

One of the most surprising features of the Transition Education Program report is its treatment of affirmative action. There is a certain irony in the fact that only just over two of its 273 pages are devoted to the issue, especially since one of the points made in this brief space is that throughout the program affirmative action had low visibility. But more importantly, what it has to say is rather contradictory, and requires explanation.

On one hand the report notes that the program displayed little initiative in specifically addressing the issue of affirmative action: 'The vast majority of projects have girls as half of their intake yet it is left to projects dealing *exclusively* with girls to formally *address* their presence in Transition education' (Kemmis *et al.*, 1983, p. 136; original emphasis). This is further underlined when it is realized that projects exclusively for girls amounted to 4 per cent of all projects in 1981 and 5.1 per cent in 1982. The contradiction arises because, on the other hand, the report speaks of an 'equal opportunities lobby', describing it as 'most articulate and effective in directing a significant share of the transition resources to the needs of a specific interest group' (p. 73). The development of projects representing 4 and 5.1 per cent of program activities in the respective periods hardly rates as grabbing a significant share of the resources, nor do these figures conjure up the vision of an articulate and effective group of lobbyists. Why then is there this contradiction? Why was it possible for the evaluation study to identify a feminist 'lobby' formidable enough to have been able to divert 'significant' resources to their own cause, when the evidence is that they were unable to stimulate more than a minimal effort at school project level?

There can be no doubt that women did have an articulate, vociferous, even formidable presence in the Transition Education Program, but only within the program's secretariat. This was because the program secretariat was governed by cultural norms and values which supported feminist ideology in general, and the need for affirmative action within the program in particular. Furthermore, the low visibility of girls' projects was because the same was not true of project sites within schools.

Let us first consider the cultural context at secretariat level. The discourse and literature of affirmative action within the secretariat were highly visible. There was a conspicuous use of gender-neutral pronouns; women's issues were a constant feature on meeting agenda; sexist remarks were rare, usually made by outsiders, and never was their articulator permitted to escape unscathed; program guidelines, the major 'product' of the secretariat, emphasized affirmative action for girls; the newsletter, *Transition News*, gave prominence to reports of girls' projects in most issues. Evidence concerning the structure, procedures and literature of the secretariat indicates that the 'women's lobby' was not only very active, but also was faced with little or no opposition. This strongly suggests a cultural context which nurtured (as taken for granted) an awareness of counter-sexist affirmative action.

The cultural context within which policy/administrative activities took place was not specially engineered for the program. It was the product of the collective cultural baggage brought in by personnel joining the secretariat, who tended to be people committed to egalitarian ideologies, including gender equality. Thus the Transition Education Program report is quite accurate in identifying an ideological commitment within the secretariat, and saying that this was a manifestation of a developing feminist consciousness within education in general, arguing that it,

> indicates the degree to which feminist ideology has been influential within the field of education, and the extent to which the contestation over women's issues over the last decade has produced numbers of politically experienced people, with common objectives and experience in collaborative action in the pursuit of systematic change. (1983, p. 73)

The authors of the report suggested that there was a concentration of such women within the secretariat, but only acknowledged this phenomenon as a political presence, as an articulate and effective women's lobby. The report neglected to recognize that the effectiveness of affirmative action within the secretariat owed as much to the cultural context as did its failure at the school project level. When we turn our attention to school-based projects, we find that teachers there worked within quite a different cultural context.

Although there is evidence of greater participation in education by girls (Branson and Miller, 1979; Connell *et al.*, 1982; Jones, 1982; Dwyer *et al.*, 1984; Kenway and Willis, 1986; Wilson and Wyn, 1987), it has been argued that the changes have been disappointing and piecemeal, and that changes in participation have not been matched by improvements in equity. Yeats (1990) emphasizes the importance of the 'cultural understandings of teachers' in achieving real change and improvement for girls in education. Concurring with this, my argument is that although the Transition Education and PEP programs did achieve considerable changes in curriculum and pedagogy in schools, including changes to do with affirmative action for the improvement of girls' education, these changes rarely made any difference in terms of contesting patriarchal hegemony in schools. To put this argument in detail, I will consider some projects for girls from the Transition Education Program, and argue that the cultural understandings of teachers, or what I call the cultural context of educational sites, was a crucial factor.

Contesting Patriarchal Hegemony in the Culture of Schools

Most program activities at the school level were, as one would expect given the objectives of the program, geared towards providing work 'experience' for their youthful clientele. However, the overall effect of this was negative. Besides being a way of shaping students' behaviour to suit employer values and channelling students into occupations as a quasi-employment agency (Watkins, 1980; Cole, 1981; Dawkins, 1982b, 1983a), the vast majority of projects provided work 'experience' along gender-specific lines. Undoubtedly, this occurred to a large extent to meet the socialized expectations of students, but one would expect an education reform program in the 1980s to be very conscious of the need to broaden the options available, not only for girls but for boys too. From the guidelines developed and the newsletters disseminated by the secretariat, it was clear that this consciousness was very evident within the decision-making structure of the program. But at school project level it was a different matter, for, as already noted, even the program evaluation commented that it was left to those few projects designed exclusively for girls to address these issues. Even then, some projects for girls reproduced rather than contested patriarchal hegemony. For instance, a project (Cramer, 1982) in a state institution substantially occupied by state wards or similar rather than offenders (over a two-month period only eight of 576 girls admitted were there as a result of criminal offences), did little to contest patriarchal hegemony. It was a project dominated by psychological and vocational counselling techniques, with an overwhelming emphasis on learning to *cope* with aspects of patriarchal hegemony rather than *contesting* it. (The internal discourse of the project, of course, did not describe the situation in these terms. It included no concept of hegemony;

there was no hint of recognition that cultural hegemony exists, but instead social relations were perceived in pathological *vis-à-vis* 'normal' terms.) At the same time it was essentially a work experience project in which the 'skills' training was almost entirely confined to traditionally domestic work roles.

That was an extreme example. It was also outside the sphere of influence of the secretariat, because by virtue of its being in a state institution it was only funded, and not supervised by, the program administration. Another project, however, this time at a school and within the control of administrative guidelines, provides a further example. Although regarded as an exemplary project by program administrators and exclusively for girls, it failed to contest cultural hegemony. This was a textiles project (Dawkins, 1983b) which was favourably regarded, since it adopted an innovative 'alternative' curriculum, engaged the interest of students who would otherwise have been problematic, and provided training which might help them find a job on leaving school. It was what had formerly been a needlework class that had, under the aegis of the program, been developed into a spinning and weaving group, thus giving the girls wider range and more autonomy in developing their craft, and provided options for craft oriented careers.

This project did engage the interest of its students. For example, one girl who under a more promising employment market most probably would have left school, succinctly summed up her attitude to school by saying, 'I hate school, but I'd hate being unemployed more', but then went on to say how much she enjoyed the textiles project. However, by no stretch of the imagination could it be regarded as counter-hegemonic affirmative action. The teacher who initiated the project deserves full credit for thinking in terms of improving the curriculum area she was responsible for at the school, and she was successful to the extent that it became an 'alternative' project for 'low achieving' girls that was categorized as exemplary in the secretariat's opinion (because it was an avenue for 'alternative' curriculum development and exclusively for girls). But in reality the textiles project was little more than a streaming mechanism; it was a means by which the school coped with 'low achieving' girls by dumping them into a submerged stream flowing beneath the general school curriculum. By doing this, the project can only be regarded as having restricted their choices even further. While the same girls might self-select themselves into this stream even if a wider choice were available, this does not justify the practice. In real terms the cultural context of the school led to the establishment of a substream, and to the identification and designation of students as 'low achievers' who would enter it.

Two further examples indicate the importance of the cultural context of schools in the contestation of patriarchal hegemony. The first was a cluster project involving six schools from working-class suburbs with substantial numbers of immigrant families (Reilly, 1982a). The main administrative reason for the funding approval of this project was that it was thought to be one leading to the improvement of employment opportunities for girls attending the schools, thus satisfying the aims and requirements of the government's program. But there were other reasons.

One of the originators of the project said that her motive in proposing it was the desire to see the women on staff be prepared to stand up for girls who were victims of a 'dreadful system'. The desire to change what some women perceived to be undesirable features of the school (low regard for females, sexual harassment, and a bias towards a traditionally male work oriented curriculum) was a major motivating force behind the project. It was thought necessary because,

> Male colleagues contributed to the difficulties of women by reinforcing these unacceptable attitudes. They used physical intimidation to control students. Men who didn't use it openly, didn't have to spell it out.... Young inexperienced women newly appointed to the school cop the full impact of the students' low regard for females. To deal with this problem women adopt a variety of strategies.... To quote a colleague: 'Being female in this school is a bit like working with a permanent disability. It can be done, but it is an extra, and in this case unnecessary, burden....' The young, inexperienced and attractive women faced particular difficulties.... Then towards the end of 1980, two new young teachers were assaulted in the classroom by male students. The young women were both shocked and upset by these events. I was appalled to learn that the battle.... had gone one step further.... Moreover one of the students involved in these incidents was a boy I had seen grabbing a girl on the backside when she was queuing in the canteen. She was unable to deal with him but he went away embarrassed when I tackled him. It occurred to me that for every incident I saw there were probably several more serious ones that I didn't see. I checked with two Year 11 girls. Again I was appalled. A small number of boys were causing the girls serious problems by harassing them sexually in the yard during recess breaks. The harassment of the girls varied from bottom pinching, grabbing of passing girls to indecent exposure. (BRUSEC, 1983)

The project eventually organized considerable effort in combatting inequalities, disadvantage and harassment suffered by girls within the culture that has been described. But what is of great interest is the degree to which project personnel were helped or hindered in their efforts by their teacher colleagues at the schools, and what this suggests about the cultural context of schools.

The cultures of the six schools, for women, at best constituted a highly discriminatory infringement of civil rights and at worst facilitated outright assult. That was the common and taken-for-granted cultural context of schooling for the female population of the schools. The women proposing the project, therefore, were functioning within an entirely different cultural context from the women in the secretariat. Instead of the warmly supportive context within which the secretariat proposed policy initiatives for affirmative action, they were obliged to work within, and indeed attempt to change, a hostile culture.

The case study reports staff resistance to the project from the beginning: a principal who publicly criticized the submission; staff resistance to a project worker addressing parents about employment prospects for girls on the grounds that this was 'sexist' and 'discriminatory' because little of this was done for boys; claims of 'reverse discrimination'; further claims (sounding more like complaints) that women had for the first time used the power structure in an organized manner. Responding to this, the project workers decided as a first step to commence a campaign to change staff attitudes, seeing this as the key factor in changing the school experience of girls. They may not have described this in terms of culture or counter-hegemonic action, but that is what it was. They were engaged in more than opposing specific sexist practices; they had begun to contest patriarchal hegemony embedded within the culture context of the schools.

Resistance often came from staff who, while acknowledging the existence of sexist discrimination in a general sense (e.g. textbook material, classroom and staffroom discourse, playground and sportsground behaviour, sexual harassment, career prospects for women teachers seeking senior appointments as much as for female students seeking first jobs, etc.), became defensive about suggestions that what they too were engaged in might also contribute to sexism. The circulation of reports highlighting girls' problems with mathmatics, for instance, became a confrontationist situation.

> It became a very personal thing of saying this is what happens and some of the maths teachers saying 'It doesn't happen here',

> and 'It's not my experience'. A 'your word against mine' situation ... confronting maths teachers (or others) with research showing that sexist teaching styles are widespread met similar problems whenever tried in BRUSEC schools. In many cases, the applicability of external research to particular schools or classrooms ... were rejected. (Reilly, 1982a, p. 53)

In this we see the hegemonic influence of the cultural context; the taken-for-granted assumption that what *we* do is perfectly 'natural', is done without malice, and often with the best of intentions, and therefore not discriminatory. Teachers may not deliberately engage in discriminatory behaviour, but through the subtle influence of culture internalized by virtue of their social and gender location, they may well contribute to cultural hegemony in schooling. This project, by aiming to change teacher attitudes (consciousness raising if you like), was an attempt to change the cultural context of the six schools. In doing so, it was contesting cultural hegemony in education.

The project can be accorded some measure of success. The case study records that within the first six months the project was publicly recognized in the six schools, school policies on a number of practices were changed, and a variety of curriculum changes was introduced. The legitimacy of the concept of equal opportunity was accepted by a growing number of teachers.

Another project for girls (Robinson and Dawkins, 1983) provides a useful comparison to the one above. In many ways it was a very similar project, particularly in that from the program administration's viewpoint it was considered to be successful in achieving its aims. Like the first, it was a cluster project based on several schools. It also had a coordinating project worker who, with staff from each school, formed an organizing committee to act as the action research facilitator for the project. However, it did not achieve the type of success enjoyed by the BRUSEC project. In the terms set by program guidelines it was a success; in terms of contesting patriarchal hegemony it was a failure.

The project was established to supplement another program which had been set up by the Schools Commission, designed to encourage girls to widen their options by considering careers in traditionally male-dominated jobs. Planned as a counter-measure to growing unemployment in an industrial area, the project had as its main goal the production of a book exploring career options to be used by the Schools Commission program. The idea came from the girls themselves who had been drawn from the schools and had elected to join as a group to develop a project of their own design. (The group had been formed towards the end of a funding period as a means of utilizing surplus funds which would otherwise be returned to central treasury.) The book was intended to provide information about a range of options open to girls, suggesting what they could take on as work 'experience' while still at school and also as future careers. It was to provide descriptions of traditionally male-dominated jobs which could be undertaken by girls, what tasks and experiences might be expected, and a discussion of male worker reactions to their presence. (Since it is not to my purpose here, I will avoid the debate about the value of directing girls into menially subordinate and unpleasant male occupations which have become available largely as the result of shortages due to the upward mobility of Australian-born, as distinct from immigrant, males.)

Located deep within rural Victoria, the schools were set in a highly industrialized area surrounded by farmlands. The main industries are coal mining and power generation, these being supplemented by light manufacturing and service industries. It is in these supplementary industries of manufacturing and service that most girls have traditionally found jobs as an interlude between school and marriage, while some have sought jobs in professions often requiring them to move to the state capital (e.g. teaching and nursing). Changing cultural norms and economic circumstances disrupted the traditional patterns, creating greater problems of unemployment for girls than for boys in the region.

Although the case study credits the project with modest success in producing the book and a degree of attitudinal change among the girls involved, it reveals that there was little gain in changing the attitudes of teachers from the schools. Perhaps this was inevitable, given that it was a hastily organized project devised to soak up loose funds and that it was product oriented rather than geared towards changing attitudes. There are two notable differences between this project and the one previously discussed. First, instead of operating within the schools' culture it drew the girls from their various school sites to join as a separate group; and second, the whole intention of the project was remote from and, as a consequence, misunderstood by schools' staff.

While the idea to produce a book came from the girls, the underlying intention of the program staff who proposed the project was to provide a situation that would give the girls experience in exercising autonomy and initiative. This it clearly did, for in devising the idea and the processes to carry it to completion it provided precisely the experiences intended. However, being task oriented, the project gradually took on the characteristics of an extracurricular activity. From the viewpoint of the schools' staff it was difficult for them to become interested, much less engaged, with a project which was not seen as their own. It was seen as unrelated to their own work and external to their own concerns.

Support for the project was minimal because it was imposed upon, rather than coming from, the four participating schools; consequently, there was only token commitment. Teachers found the idea hard to grapple with, difficult to fit into any curriculum context, and were unsure of what was expected. So mild was the interest it generated that teachers outside the project failed to comprehend its aims, even key contact persons in schools. One such person pointed to 'heaps and heaps' of information produced more professionally and attractively than this book. But the book was never intended to compete with commercial publications. It was a product which could be used, but the product was incidental to the real objective of the project, viz. to provide the girls with an exercise in autonomous decision-making.

What may be learnt from this project? There was evidence that it was a desirable project because of restricted career options for girls due not only to the nature of local industry and the state of the economy, but also because their options were constrained by conventional linkages between gender, education and employment. These linkages were reinforced by the nature of the education available at the schools, which was delivered in a cultural context facilitating patriarchal hegemony. It may be true that some girls did benefit from the project by learning to act with autonomy and to exercise initiative. It may be that they did produce a book which illustrated wider career options for girls. It may also be that, individually, they did consolidate the learning about career options for themselves in traditionally male-dominated occupations. But as far as the schools were concerned, and as far as any girls who did not participate in this or the Schools Commission programs were concerned, it had little or no effect. In particular, in terms of the contestation of patriarchal hegemony embedded within the culture of the schools, it might as well never have happened. For the teachers and girls outside the project, and succeeding cohorts of girls passing through the schools, nothing had changed.

Contesting Hegemonic Work Orientations in the Culture of Schools

Schools, as a major legitimizing institution in society, support the hierarchic division of labour by justifying the separation of students into streams which supply the workforce with a mix of labour appropriate to the hierarchically structured employment market. In Victoria, finding the 'proper mix' of mental and manual skills had been institutionalized in the 1950s into a three-tier system of secondary schooling, viz. private schools, high schools, technical schools. Some (e.g. Gilmour and Lansbury, 1978) more accurately argue that there are five school levels: élite private (almost entirely church-aligned, mainly Protestant, but including Catholic and Jewish), élite government high, parochial Catholic, standard government high, government technical. Three-sector analyses (e.g. Anderson and Vevoorn, 1983) illustrate the bias within this system which enables élite groups to use private schools to gain privileged access to tertiary courses and occupations, but the usefulness of five-sector analyses (e.g. Praetz, 1983) is that they highlight the gross differences existing within state school education. While many of the differences existing between high and technical schools have been corrected, noting such differences has been made more difficult through recent moves by the state government to collapse the high and technical categories into one division within the Ministry of Education. These moves were for a while thwarted because of fears by technical school teachers that they might lose their more favourable pay and conditions than those of high school teachers, but the proposal has been enhanced by the decision (in 1989) to call all state secondary schools 'secondary colleges', thus equalizing the terminology at least, and through award restructuring.

The organization of schools and curricula into a hierarchy which suits the needs of a labour market stratified to serve ruling class interests has always been a feature of the Australian education system. Lawrey (1972) traces the legitimated institutionalization of this to the Fink Royal Commission of 1899. Thomas (1980), Taylor (1983) and Maddock (1983) all argue that the poor selection of school and subjects, even though this often constitutes the only choice available in working-class schools, eliminates working-class students in a system that ostensibly provides open access to higher occupational categories. This notion of self-selection may carry implications of class deficiency, but Connell *et al.* (1982) argue that this elimination is an effect of the subtle influence of cultural hegemony in education, which channels youth into making decisions that effectively reduce their options and life chances.

> The effect of the hegemony of the academic curriculum within mass secondary education, then, is not to *obliterate* ideas and practices which grow out of working-class needs and experience. It is to disorganize and fragment them; and at the same time it produces resistance to the imposition of academic curriculum. In

> so doing it is both part and paradigm of the operation of class hegemony in Australian life. (1982, p. 126; original emphasis)

Recognizing the separation of school curricula along the lines of a mental/manual dichotomy, the Transition Education report argued (Kemmis *et al.*, 1983, pp. 85f) that this was part of a wider sociopolitical process, and went on to claim that the dichotomy was accentuated within the program. This was no less a claim than that the program had acted to promote the reproduction of unequal social relations. However, a shortcoming of this argument in the report was that, by implication, it suggested that the streaming of students in the program was merely an unfair instrumental function (thus reflecting the same process within the wider education system), but failed to go further and recognize this instrumental function as an expression of cultural hegemony in education. Quite realistically, it presents a picture of educators having to cope with an immediate problem, viz. what to do with low achieving youth, and doing so without regard to the sociopolitics of their solutions. But these actions are precisely the commonsense patterns of behaviour referred to previously, by which cultural hegemony is maintained. Common sense tells us that the immediate problem (in this case 'low achieving' youth in danger of becoming unemployable) has to be dealt with, and there are long established practices which serve as a guide in doing so; it tells us that the aim of the Transition Education Program is to assist youth in the transition from school to work, but does not tell us to question the structuring of work relations; it tells us that program evaluations are intended to comment on how well objectives are achieved, but not that we should engage in ideology critique.

The report (going beyond its evaluation brief) drew attention to the fact that the education system is geared towards a hierarchically structured workforce, pointing out that the dichotomy of the curriculum serves the interests of the labour market, and beyond that the interests of a stratified society (which we here recognize to be the interests of the ruling class). But why this should be so, and under what conditions one finds oppositional behaviour counteracting it, was never a question for the evaluation. Although the report makes reference to some projects which did contest and oust the dichotomy, the explanation for this was to suggest that it was a consequence of the adoption of a socially critical approach to the school curriculum (see Kemmis, Cole and Suggett, 1983). However, it failed to suggest why those particular schools came to adopt the socially critical capacity to contest the mental/manual dichotomy, nor why the bulk of projects were not like them.

Two Construction Projects

Two projects are particularly appropriate to our discussion. Both were engaged in large-scale construction activities as their distinctively manual component. The first (Reilly, 1982b) can be said to have broken the mental/manual dichotomy, and thus to have contested the cultural hegemony of work relations; the second (Dawkins, 1983b) can be said to have reproduced the mental/manual dichotomy, consequently reinforcing the cultural hegemony of work relations.

The first of these projects was unique in that it was the only project of the entire Transition Education Program recorded as having involved students in the submission planning process. It was focused on physically demanding and potentially dangerous work, but integrated this with mental tasks done in the 'classroom', even to the extent of planning. It grew out of the need to recover recreational space at the school which had been used for site offices and materials stockpiling when a part of the school was under construction. A normal school response to this situation would be for a request for minor works, viz. the construction of a 'playground', to be forwarded to the Department (now Ministry) of Education. In due time, possibly several years, the request would find its way to the top of the priority list and a Public Works Department crew would arrive and construct the facility along conventional standardized lines. In this school, however, a nucleus of teachers proposed that the grounds reconstruction should be planned cooperatively by students and teachers with advice from external consultants (this came via the Architects-in-Schools scheme, a combined initiative of the Royal Australian Institute of Architects and the Department of Education) and funded as a project of the Transition Education Program.

The project was not merely a landscaping exercise nor just an activity organized around the school's manual skills curriculum. It was both of these and more; it was experience-based learning which integrated mental and manual tasks, as shown by this vignette from the case study:

> Frank worked with Bruce in the yard on the problem. . . . Bruce: 'Do the same with this figure which is the internal radius. Then you have the volume of that part of the shell and you'll know how much concrete you've got. . . . This is the inside radius and this is the outside radius. Take one from the other and you'll have the volume'. Frank: 'I was trying to figure out the dome and how much concrete has to go inside the dome to make the outer shell. I used a formula. I got the formula from the Maths teacher but I

> did the calculations. Now Bruce wants me to do another one to figure out the thickness, we'll know how much money we'll need.... Now you know what it's used for, all these figures ...' (Reilly, 1982b, p. 31)

Mental 'academic' work became intrinsically interesting when linked to manual goals which endowed it with the sense of hard reality, in contrast to the conventional academic curriculum. This point was made by an art teacher who, describing the production of a scale model of the grounds plan to show the location and effect of a structure constructed of heavy power poles, emphasized the level of student engagement with the task: 'Model making in schools usually means necrophilia — techniques of yesterday tried out for situations yesterday. The models in there are try-outs for situations which exist in the yard and which are solved' (p. 35). The same feeling that work associated with the grounds reconstruction project attracted more serious participation than conventional classroom work was expressed by students, one of whom added a telling comment on classroom management:

> John: 'Students are going to think more seriously about building than listening.' Gino: 'Because if they're out there, they're going to think that teachers and everybody depends on them. In class it's different because the teachers wouldn't really care if you didn't do the work as long as you don't disturb anyone.' (p. 35)

Reilly argued in his case study of the project that the dichotomy between mental and manual curricula had been overcome by the integration of the two in meeting project objectives, and at program level it was regarded as a fine example of innovative, experience-based, 'alternative' curriculum reform. It also contested internalized concepts of hegemonic work relations transmitted by the culture of schools. It did this by providing students with evidence from their own experience that mental work was not abstractly remote from manual practices, nor was it beyond their own individual capacities. It provided the experience of success for students who, in the normal course of school events, would have regarded mental work as 'boring' or themselves as not sufficiently 'brainy' (cf. Connell, 1977).

The integration of the manifestly manual project with mental academic curricula was not universal, nor, as one might expect, did all the teachers participate. When Frank and Bruce worked out their calculations for the concrete pour, they had to get the formula from the maths teacher because project activities had not been integrated with the school mathmatics program. That the need to know particular formulae at times specific to the requirements of the progress in grounds reconstruction did not synchronize with the progressive steps of maths education provides some insight into the way conventional notions about knowledge dominate classroom practices. It also indicates that the conventional academic curriculum constrained the project. Nevertheless, there was a high level of integration between the project and the school curriculum; and there was wide support from the staff.

The grounds reconstruction project provided a sharp contrast to another project for the construction of a bushwalking track (Dawkins, 1983b). There were some obvious similarities between the two projects: both were organized around construction work; both aimed to develop transferable work skills; and both claimed to integrate school curricula with project work. An examination of the project proposals suggests that the only substantive difference between the two was the nature of the construction task. There were, however, considerable differences.

The construction of the track project required the creation of a 200-kilometre walking track. About sixty kilometres of that were along a beach, which required no work other than to establish campsites; but the other 140 kilometres were hard work; so hard that the project was frequently likened, with deliberate unkindness, to the construction of the Great Wall of China. There were two kinds of tasks. The most elaborate was the construction of campsites (erection of toilet blocks, water storage, fireplaces), fences and stiles (simple post and rail construction) and walkways over swampy ground. The other was the simple (but far from easy) slashing and clearing of bushland.

Despite claims to the contrary made in the school proposal and program literature, there was only the most tenuous link between the construction task and the school curriculum. The only parts of the school curriculum to mesh with the project were those labelled 'work experience' and 'character development'. Even then it was difficult to describe this as integration. For instance, it was only in the last week of each term that students engaged in track work, and then it was offered as an alternative choice to spending the week in school doing private study or a week of conventional work experience located in industry. From the staff viewpoint it was a low priority task used to mop up loose students; from the student viewpoint it was also a low priority task that was tedious but useful for escaping less desirable options. Character development was deemed to occur when students used the track recreationally in bushcraft exercises, i.e. in quite an extracurricular activity.

There was considerable division among teachers about the project. The case study reported that little thought had been put into linking the project with the school curriculum, and few teachers engaged in any project-related work. The major impression to be gained by an outsider was that any educational potential of the project seemed to have escaped the notice of teachers, and that there were abrasive relations between many teachers not involved with 'the track' and certain key personalities in the school who enjoyed bushwalking and who 'owned' the project. For instance, one teacher who tried to use the track project as the basis for an English assignment resentfully claimed that the work he had assigned the students was 'cancelled' by another teacher in charge of track work (who then counter-claimed that the assignment was inappropriate at that stage of the track construction).

The track project was perceived to be outside the main concerns of the school, to be 'the baby' of the principal and a few staff members, and directed towards recreational rather than educational uses. It had no substantive link to the school curriculum, and its tasks consisted of labouring, some simple carpentry and the assembling of components for campsites and walkways supplied in construction kits predesigned and prepared by the National Parks Service. The most elaborate tasks required no more skill than was required for conventional manual subjects (woodwork and metalwork) taught at the school, and many tasks (slashing, clearing and trench digging) required far simpler 'skills'. Furthermore, many students were alienated by the project. They regarded themselves as engaged in no more than providing a convenient source of free labour. They felt themselves conscripted, even though track work was a voluntary choice made from three options. Under these circumstances the unquestionably manual emphasis of the project became completely divorced from any mental activity. If anything, the project reinforced notions of manual work having low status and little reward within the social structure of the school, and by extension within society at large, and was regarded as the unenviable lot of those whose fate it was to be born lacking the 'brains' for success at mental, 'academic' pursuits. In doing this, the track project merely reflected an already existing hierarchic division of mental and manual subjects within the school curriculum.

There was no deliberate policy of discrimination functioning at the school. On the contrary, teachers acted with the best of intentions and wishing only good fortune for their students, but the ideological underpinnings of the mental/manual dichotomy were deeply embedded within the cultural context of the school. The hierarchic division of the standard curriculum into mental and manual streams, with a third stream of transition education projects comprising an even lower level, was part of the taken-for-granted context of schooling which required no explanation, no thought even, because that was the 'natural' way things are.

The textiles project mentioned earlier also illustrates this. That project for girls was set within the same school. As far as the program secretariat was concerned, the textiles project was the main component of the Transition Education project at the school; the track was regarded as a minor, incidental, part. Within the school, however, while most staff appeared to be quite uninformed about either aspect of the project, it was difficult to get the principal and other key personnel to talk about Transition Education in any other way than to speak of the track.

Why should this be so? In the terms of the Transition Education Program itself the textiles project was regarded as successful, far more so than the track project. It engaged the interest of its students; it was related to the conventional school curriculum; it transmitted useful skills to the girls, which held out some promise, however slim, of the possibility of future employment. From the viewpoint of the program secretariat it was an exemplary project. In contrast, the track project provoked mutinous grumblings from its students; it was perceived by all as extracurricular; it provided the students with no employable skills. So why should it have enjoyed such favour within the school? Several possible answers come to mind. Coinciding with the interests of key personalities, it enjoyed favoured treatment; textiles was a girls' project and thus rendered invisible; the track was a project on a grand scale involving community figures, thus warranting greater attention; textiles was a small project submerged from view under the flow of school activity; and so on. All views can be supported by evidence in the case study interviews.

What does this say about the culture of the school? It suggests that this school was like most others, viz. a place where education is viewed in straightforward meritocratic terms, where inequality and disadvantage are understood as individual social deficiencies, and where teachers coped as best they could with a situation thus defined and did so in commonsense ways. Thus 'the problem' was considered to be one of engaging students' interest in school for the few years they would be there, students who were unsuccessful at the conventional academic curriculum, were in school against their preferred wishes, and probably would have left school if it were not for the prospect of unemployment. That is precisely how many teachers and students described the situation.

Now compare that with the cultural context of the grounds project school. Situated in one of the most multicultural urban industrial areas in Australia, the most common form of employment among parents was as process workers in factories. The social composition (consciously working-class, displaying characteristic features of economic vulnerability, union awareness and a certain class solidarity despite the diversity of ethnic origins) was relatively homogeneous. The staff was also remarkably homogeneous in composition, being largely comprised of teachers who had made a conscious decision to teach in the school. This, it seems, was either because of similar working-class origins or for ideological reasons. The school had a history of teachers with a high degree of interest and activity concerning the trade union movement and teacher unions. They displayed a close similarity to Grace's finding that 'the teaching group within inner-city schools now contains articulate members who resist, in various ways, what they take to be the undesirable features of state education' (1978, p. 216). In practical terms this was manifested in a cultural context which rejected meritocratic views of education and rejected deficit notions of student 'failure'. Consequently, the grounds project was not introduced into the school as a vehicle for coping with 'underachieving' and difficult students. The staff may not have described the situation in terms of cultural hegemony, nor even thought of what they were doing as contesting cultural hegemony, but that is what they were doing.

Cultural Context and the Contestation of Hegemony in Education

These examples show how perceptions of the social world and the functions of education can vary from site to site. Forms of education vary according to perceptions of what constitutes a problem and what solutions are appropriate. At one school the problem was defined as that of engaging the interest of 'low achieving', disaffected students. The solutions, an invisible textiles project for girls and a 'character building' construction project, interposed a hegemony of gender and occupational roles. At another school the problem was couched in terms of counteracting conditions of inequality, and the solution was to introduce a whole-school-based project which attempted to restrict the imposition of a mental/manual dichotomy, which may be described as an attempt to contest the cultural hegemony of occupational roles.

Two projects for girls also provided a contrast. At one site the project staff attempted to change teacher attitudes in a consciousness raising exercise, and, to the extent that they were successful, they were contesting cultural definitions which supported patriarchal hegemony. At the other site the project had less success because it focused on a specific activity rather than aiming to change the cultural context of the schools, thereby doing nothing to contest patriarchal hegemony at the school sites.

It should be emphasized that this argument does not imply any judgment about educational competence. It is not suggested that 'bad' teachers used the program, either innocently or deliberately, to impose disadvantage on some students by reproducing the conditions of cultural hegemony, any more than it is suggested that 'good' teachers used the program to redress inequality by contesting the conditions of cultural hegemony. However, it is suggested that teachers function with the same taken-for-granted views of the world that we find in other sections of society, and that these views contribute to the cultural context of school sites, which facilitate either the reproduction or the contestation of cultural hegemony.

The conclusion to be drawn from these examples is that the contestation of cultural hegemony in education is not simply a function of curriculum reform. The program provided many examples of innovative curriculum reform which engaged the interest of students, while at the same time reproducing the conditions of cultural hegemony, most notably in vocationally oriented projects within the technical and further education sector. However, examples also indicate that under the right circumstances projects did more than provide engaging curriculum reform, and did in fact contest cultural hegemony. The significant factor in determining whether or not curriculum innovation led to the reproduction or contestation of cultural hegemony was the shared cultural context of the project site; what, in the evaluation report, was alluded to as the 'perception of the learning site'.

The 'perception of the learning site' suggested that the adoption of innovative and alternative styles of curriculum was a function of the school community's educational perceptiveness. From the curriculum theory approach of the evaluation it was suggested that the 'perception of the learning site' either permitted the adoption of innovative curriculum which was judged to be successful in the Transition Education Program's terms (it was interesting, developed skills and held some hope of future employment) or else constrained projects to adopt conventional approaches judged to be less effective in a purely educational sense (streaming devices which channelled 'non-academic' students into projects enabling the school to cope with their presence).

Such a view is too superficial. Although the 'perception of the learning site' did influence the development of projects as outlined above, to think only in terms of perceptions of curriculum innovation and pedagogical techniques, and merely to note their varying capacity to engage the interest of problem students, is to think in terms of form and not substance. A closer analysis reveals that while projects did indeed develop new forms which were attractive and interesting to students, this was often insufficient to improve the life chances of students. For that to happen, the cultural hegemony internalized through the experiences of teachers and students had to be contested, but before this could happen the cultural context of the educational site had to be one in which there was some awareness of social disadvantage, even if this did not happen to be couched in terms of hegemonic social relations.

There can be no contestation of what is not perceived, which is why projects either reproduced or contested cultural hegemony not according to some educational notion of the 'perception of the learning site', but by the degree to which the cultural context of the learning site defined the students as, on the one hand, 'at risk', the hapless victims of an ineffective education system and/or their own personal deficiencies, or else, on the other hand, as the victims of social inequalities, of hegemonic social relations.

Implications

To say that educational reform which really improves the life chances of individuals cannot come by government decree is to state the obvious, as the Transition Education and PEP programs have demonstrated. Both programs did, however, indicate that teachers can 'capture' the grand slam programs and use them to work towards improving the life chances of students by contesting cultural hegemony in education. This suggests that education policy should be taken out of the hands of politicians, for, quite apart from the fact that both programs were overshadowed by unstated political agenda, the extent of debate generated by the two programs from secretariat through to school level should give us confidence in the professional ability of educators to develop school-based policies, a matter to which the major political parties in Australia pay lip-service without actually devolving any but the most inconsequential power.

We also need to know more about the cultural contexts of educational sites, for if, as argued here, the cultural context of educational sites is crucial to the contestation of cultural hegemony in education, then we need to know much more about the culture of schools. In the case of affirmative action the projects which contested patriarchal hegemony were those where teachers in charge not only had a consciousness of gender inequality, but also worked to make that consciousness a part of the collective cultural context of the schools where they worked. Similarly, the contestation or reproduction of the cultural hegemony manifested in the mental/manual dichotomy of school curricula was a function of attitudes towards social inequality in the cultural context of school sites.

That is precisely what one would expect, because teachers are not homogeneous. They, too, come from different social contexts, and even if we were to suppose that most are from the working classes, they may very well identify with quite different class values, as studies of upward social mobility have indicated. It would be interesting, therefore, to know more about the culturally diverse values of teachers. An understanding of the culture of schools is crucial for any success in improving life chances for hegemonically disadvantaged social groups.

There is a wide variety of other factors which have not been considered here. For instance, why do at least half the teachers I know fit Nias' (1986) description of the teacher as privatized worker? Why do many teachers entertain escape fantasies: the country restaurant, the craft shoppe, the hobby farm? Why do many state school teachers demonstrate a lack of confidence in the education provided by the sector they work within by sending their own children to private schools, and eschew the type of schools in which they teach other people's children? What can we learn from the social demography of teachers? What is the range of professional attitudes, i.e. do many teachers regard their job instrumentally in much the same way as a forklift driver who has to stack so many crates of bicycle parts before the end of the shift, and, if so, why? Why are schools places of such awful internecine strife, quite apart from the domestic and social problems that are transported into the school culture, that many teachers and students desperately wish they were elsewhere? To know more about these matters is to chart the campaign territory for the contestation of cultural hegemony in education.

References

ADORNO, T.W. (1969) 'Scientific experiences of a European scholar in America', in FLEMING, D. and BAILYN, B. (Eds), *The Intellectual Migration*, Cambridge, Mass., Harvard University Press.

ANDERSON, D.S. and VEVOORN, A.E. (1983) *Access to Privilege: Patterns of Participation in Australian Post-Secondary Education*, Canberra, Australian National University Press.

APPLE, M.W. (Ed.) (1982) *Cultural and Economic Reproduction in Education: Essays on Class, Ideology and the State*, Boston, Mass., Routledge and Kegan Paul.

ASHENDEN, D. (1989) *State Aid and the Division of Schooling in Australia*, Geelong, Deakin University Press.

BRANSON, J. and MILLER, D.B. (1979) *Class, Sex and Education in Capitalist Society*, Malvern, Sorrett Publishing.

BRODKEY, L. (1987) 'Writing critical ethnographic narratives', *Anthropology and Education Quarterly*, 18, 2, June, pp. 67–76.

BRUSEC (1983) *Report 1982*, Melbourne, TEAC.

CARR, W. and KEMMIS, S. (1983) *Becoming Critical: Knowing through Action Research*, Geelong, Deakin University Press.

CODD, J.A. (1986) *Philosophy, Common Sense and Action in Educational Administration*, Geelong, Deakin University Press.

COLE, P. (1981) 'Work experience: A critique of current practice and directions for program development', Occasional Paper No. 1, Melbourne, VISE.

CONNELL, R.W. (1977) *Ruling Class, Ruling Culture*, Cambridge, Cambridge University Press.

CONNELL, R.W., ASHENDEN, D.J., KESSLER, S. and DOWSETT, G.W. (1982) *Making the Difference: Schools, Families and Social Division*, Sydney, George Allen and Unwin.

CORNBLETH, C. (1988) 'Curriculum in and out of context', *Journal of Curriculum and Supervision*, 3, 2, pp. 85–96.

CRAMER, B.J. (1982) *Case Study No. 3*, Melbourne, TEAC.

DALE, R. (1982) 'Education and the capitalist state: Contributions and contradictions', in APPLE, M.W. (Ed.), *Cultural and Economic Reproduction in Education*, Boston, Mass., Routledge and Kegan Paul.

DAWKINS, D.M. (1982a) 'Transformation and reproduction: The Transition Education Program in Victoria', in *Educational Research in the 1980s: Collected Papers of the 1982 Annual Conference*, Australian Association for Research in Education, Brisbane, November.

DAWKINS, D.M. (1982b) 'Educating the unemployed: Transition Education in TAFE Colleges in Victoria', paper delivered to the Annual Conference of the Sociological Association of Australia and New Zealand, Sydney, August.

DAWKINS, D.M. (1983a) *Case Study No. 10*, Melbourne, TEAC.

DAWKINS, D.M. (1983b) *Case Study No. 22*, Melbourne, TEAC.

DAWKINS, D.M. (1986a) Contestation and Hegemony in Education Exemplified by the Transition from School to Work Program in Victoria, unpublished doctoral thesis, Deakin University, Geelong.

DAWKINS, D.M. (1986b) *Economics, Politics and Education*, Geelong, Deakin University Press.

DAWKINS, J. and COSTELLO, R. (1983) 'Education: Progress and equality', in REEVES, J. and THOMSON, K. (Eds), *Labor Essays 1983*, Melbourne, Dove Communications.

DWYER, P., WILSON, B. and WOOCK, R. (1984) *Confronting School and Work*, Sydney, George Allen and Unwin.

EMMETT, G. (1981) 'Transition education: The beginning of a new curriculum or nonsense?', *AdVISE*, No. 26, November, pp. 1–2.

FOLEY, J. (1981) 'Media representations: A documentation of strategies employed in the treatment of education by the print media, 1981', in *Melbourne Working Papers*, Melbourne, Melbourne University, Sociology Research Group in Cultural and Educational Studies.

FREELAND, J. and SHARP, R. (1981) 'The Williams Report on Education, Training and Employment: The decline and fall of Karmelot', *Intervention*, 14, pp. 54–79.

GIDDENS, A. (1978) *The Class Structure of the Advanced Societies*, London, Hutchinson.

GILMOUR, P. and LANSBURY, R. (1978) *Ticket to Nowhere: Training and Work in Australia*, Ringwood, Penguin.

GIROUX, H. (1983a) *Critical Theory and Educational Practice*, Geelong, Deakin University Press.

GIROUX, H. (1983b) *Theory and Resistance in Educational Practice*, Geelong, Deakin University Press.

GIROUX, H. (1990) *Curriculum Discourse as Postmodernist Critical Practice*, Geelong, Deakin University Press.

GOODSON, I.F. (1988) *The Making of Curriculum*, Lewes, Falmer Press.

GRACE, G. (1978) *Teachers, Ideology and Control: A Study in Urban Education*, London, Routledge and Kegan Paul.

GRAMSCI, A. (1971) 'The Intellectuals', in HOARE, Q. and SMITH, G.N. (Eds and Trans), *Selections from the Prison Notebooks of Antonio Gramsci*, Southampton, Camelot Press.

HABERMAS, J. (1972) *Knowledge and Human Interests*, London, Heinemann.

HABERMAS, J. (1976) *Legitimation Crisis*, London, Heinemann.

HAMMOND, B. (1981) 'Issues in the identification of students in the transition from school to work in the ACT', Discussion Paper, ACT Schools Authority Transition Education Project.

HELD, D. (1980) *Introduction to Critical Theory*, London, Hutchinson.

HORKHEIMER, M. (1937) 'Traditional and critical theory', in GIROUX, H., *Critical Theory and Educational Practice*, Geelong, Deakin University Press.

JONES, B. (1982) *Sleepers, Wake! Technology and the Future of Work*, Melbourne, Oxford University Press.

KARMEL REPORT (1983) *Schools in Australia: Report of the Interim Committee of the Schools Commission*, Canberra, Australian Government Publishing Service.

KEMMIS, S., COLE, P. and SUGGETT, D. (1983) *Towards the Socially-Critical School*, Melbourne, VISE.

KEMMIS, S., DAWKINS, D.M., BROWN, L., CRAMER, B. and REILLY, T. (1983) *Transition and Reform in the Victorian Transition Education Program*, Melbourne, TEAC.

KENWAY, J. (1990) 'Education and the Right's discursive politics: Private versus state schooling', in BALL, S. (Ed.), *Foucault and Education.*

KENWAY, J. and WILLIS, S. (1986) 'Feminist single-sex educational strategies: Some theoretical flaws and practical fallacies', *Discourse*, 7, 1, pp. 1–30.

LAWREY, J. (1972) 'Understanding Australian education 1901 to 1914', in CLEVERLEY, J. and LAWREY, J. (Eds), *Australian Education in the Twentieth Century*, Melbourne, Longman Australia.

LUNDGREN, U.P. (1983) *Between Hope and Happening: Text and Context in Curriculum*, Geelong, Deakin University Press.

MADDOCK, J. (1983) 'They stream themselves — don't they?', in BROWNE, R.K. and FOSTER, L.E. (Eds), *Sociology of Education*, Melbourne, Macmillan.

NIAS, J. (1986) *Teacher Socialisation*, Geelong, Deakin University Press.

PAULSON, R.G. (1971) 'Educational stratification and cultural hegemony in Peru', *Journal of Developing Areas*, 5, April, pp. 401–15.

PRAETZ, H. (1983) 'Education and employment: Patterns of participation of Victorian 15 – 19 years olds. Working Paper, Melbourne, VISE.

RASKALL, P. (1987) 'Wealth: Who's got it? Who needs it?', *Australian Society*, May.

REILLY, T.J. (1982a) *Case Study No. 7*, Melbourne, TEAC.

REILLY, T.J. (1982b) *Case Study No. 1*, Melbourne, TEAC.

REILLY, T.J. (1982c) 'Transition education: Schooling's new legitimacy', in *Educa-*

tional Research in the 1980s: Collected Papers of the 1982 Annual Conference, Australian Association for Research in Education, Brisbane, November.

RIZVI, F. and KEMMIS, S. (1987) *Dilemmas of Reform: The Participation and Equity Program in Victorian Schools*, Geelong, Deakin Institute for Studies in Education.

ROBINSON, M. and DAWKINS, D.M. (1983) *Case Study No. 17*, Melbourne, TEAC.

TAYLOR, S. (1983) 'School choices and life chances', in BROWNE, R.K. and FOSTER, L.E. (Eds), *Sociology of Education*, Melbourne, Macmillan.

TEESE, R. (1981) 'The social function of private schools', in *Melbourne Working Papers*, Melbourne, Melbourne University.

THOMAS, C. (1980) 'Girls and counter school culture in Melbourne', in *Melbourne Working Papers*, Melbourne, Melbourne University.

WATKINS, P. (1980) 'Curriculum change and the school-work interface: A critical analysis of work experience', *Australian and New Zealand Journal of Sociology*, 16, 2, pp. 37–44.

WHITE, D. (1987) *Education and the State: Federal Involvement in Educational Policy Development*, Geelong, Deakin University Press.

WILSON, B. and WYN, J. (1987) *Shaping Futures: Youth Action for Livelihood*, Sydney, Allen and Unwin.

WINDSCHUTTLE, K. (1979) *Unemployment: A Social and Political Analysis of the Economic Crisis in Australia*, Ringwood, Penguin.

WILLIAMS REPORT (1979) *Education, Training and Employment, Vols 1 and 2: Report of the Committee of Inquiry into Education and Training*, Canberra, Australian Government Publishing Service.

YEATS, L. (1990) *Theory/Practice Dilemmas: Gender, Knowledge and Education*, Geelong, Deakin University Press.

YOUNG, R.E. (1981) 'Progressive and degenerating education policy theories', in YOUNG, R., PUSEY, M. and BATES, R. (Eds), *Australian Educational Policy: Issues and Critique*, Geelong, Deakin University Press.

Chapter 4

Conspicuous Consumption: Class, Gender and Private Schooling

Jane Kenway

This chapter is about social class, gender and education. More specifically, it is about the powerful and privileged class of Perth, Western Australia, the gender regime associated with the culture of that class and types of schooling which this social group consumes. More specifically still, it is about one aspect of the gendered/class culture of this group, that associated with the consumption of goods and services, the use of consumption as a mechanism of social structuring and its implications for the field of education, also a mechanism of social structuring.

This study stands in opposition to conventional ways of viewing the relationship between private schooling and social inequality and it is appropriate, therefore, that it begins with an outline of this dominant position and some of its ideological consequences. The chapter then identifies an alternative and superior way of considering the connections between private schooling, social class and gender, first, by outlining a relational view of social class as it has been applied to the study of private schooling and, second, by discussing the literature which best integrates analyses of class and gender. This prepares the ground for a recognition of the social role of consumption and provides the theoretical framework for the second part of the paper. Here the modes of consumption which are characteristic of the suburban contexts in which Perth's most esteemed private schools are set are shown to be part of the gendered class culture of the clients of these schools. The relationalities which infuse the locale also infuse its inmates' use of schooling, providing a belief that a range of personal intangibles may be purchased through private schools, a translation discourse through which the offerings of the schools are read, and mechanisms for defining 'the self' and 'the other' and thereby a means of achieving social distance and closure. To demonstrate these points, data are drawn from a wider study conducted in and around three of Perth's high status private schools, titled here, for the sake of anonymity, The Ladies School of Perth (LSP), St Jerome's Co-educational College and Perth Boys' Grammar (PBG) (see Kenway, 1987b).

Private Schools and Their Client Class: Contrasting Approaches to Analysis

The Categorical Approach

The most common manner of thinking about the relationship between private schools and the class structure is to consider who are their clients, i.e. whom they serve as parents and whom they produce as ex-students. This way of investigating and describing the social class of private school clients has its roots in theories of social stratification which, historically, have held a dominant position in the sociology of education in Australia. Despite considerable differences in scope, sophistication and intention, work as varied as that of Encel (1970), Hunt (1976), Smolicz and Moody (1978), Carpenter (1985a, 1985b), the *Association of Independent Schools Surveys* (1974, 1975, 1978), Praetz (1983), Radford and Wilkes (1975) and Higley, Deacon and Smart (1979) can be thus categorized. At its simplest, the use of such a perspective in the above work is characterized by an absence of overt theorizing, accompanied by an eagerness to identify male parents according to certain criteria. These tend to be occupation, occupational prestige, income, formal educational achievement, suburban status and so on. The tendency is to chart the population's distribution within the categories and to allocate individuals to a particular stratum. Sometimes this is identified as a class or a status group (e.g. the *AIS Surveys*, 1975, 1978). As the collective work of Smolicz, Carpenter, Hunt, Radford and Wilkes and the AIS surveys reveal, the focus is usually on occupation, the fathers' in particular, although both Carpenter and Smolicz also include that of mothers. The strata identified within the occupational category tend to differ between studies, yet the 'occupational prestige scales' originally devised by Broom, Jones and Zubrzycki (1968) within their multidimensional stratification theory, provide a common conceptual schema.

Given the disparate, ambiguous and somewhat arbitrary nature of this work, it is neither necessary nor fruitful to replicate its findings here. Suffice it to say that the occupations of the parent population of high status private schools tend to be heavily concentrated in professional and managerial categories, parents tend to have achieved higher levels of formal education than have state school parents and they tend to reside in the more expensive and reputable suburbs.

Within this social stratificationist approach the most comprehensive and theoretically informed work on the class of private school clients is that of Encel (1970). He seeks to offer some account of the changing client population of these private schools, to situate this within a broader study of social stratification in Australia as it has evolved since settlement and to draw out the role of private education in 'establishing and perpetuating a hierarchy of social differences' (p. 143). Encel offers his study of power and authority in Australian society as a Weberian analysis based on the dimensions of class, status and power. However, in the case of private schooling his work is more within the conventions of studies of the élite, the 'Who's Who', as he concentrates particularly on that small number of boys' schools which make a distinctive contribution to supplying members of various male élite groups in Australia. Private schools are placed within analyses of the composition of the political, bureaucratic, economic and military élite, and patterns of ownership, kinship networks and social and political alliances are mapped out. Higley, Deacon and Smart (1979) also conducted a study of Australia's élite and made similar points on the role of private schools.

Although more theoretical than the statistical exercise which the studies cited earlier tend to be, Encel's and Higley, Deacon and Smart's work still suffers from a number of the deficiencies of the social stratificationist approach in education and, more broadly, in the field of sociology. While there are variations within it, it is possible to make several general criticisms of this perspective and to note that, although Weber is often regarded as the inspiration of this work, it misses much of what he had to offer to the study of social difference generally (see Wild, 1978; Austin, 1984) and the study of private schools in particular.

The stratificationist perspective as applied to education and private schooling has scarcely acknowledged its theoretical history, let alone engaged in theoretical debate with other perspectives. Stratification theory is concerned with documenting differences of social benefits or goods among adults, usually males. It is concerned to identify what such benefits are, economic, social and/or political, and to rank people according to, say, income differences, status differences and differences of political affiliation and power. The data thus produced are then divided into strata, and groups of individuals are identified as belonging to the same strata if they posses similar social benefits. Thus society is conceived of as 'a series of layers like the strata of a geological succession' (Connell, 1983, p. 87); such layers are sometimes identified as classes, if one considers the economic dimension, or status groups, if one considers the dimension of social esteem. This perspective is best described as a categorical approach to social differences and is concerned primarily with systematically sorting and classifying individuals along and within various dimensions. The research technique associated with social stratification studies is survey research and, as Connell (1977, p. 4) notes, 'the characteristic research problems arise as matters of technique.' Methodological and theoretical debates tend to revolve around the nature and number of the dimensions of stratification, their relationship to each other, and the number of strata within dimensions. Deciding on the boundaries between strata has always been rather arbitrary.

As any number of observers note, the indeterminacy of the gradations and dimensions of the class, power and status hierarchies within stratification theory is one of its many weaknesses. Explaining how or why they came to exist in the first place and how they maintain themselves has seldom been of great concern. In many cases the sociocultural contexts of stratification are ignored altogether. History is often thought of in terms of social mobility or in comparative terms across time. For instance, in the private school literature this perspective will show changes in the class composition of the clients or the expansion and contraction of occupational groups. However, any notion of history, let alone class, *as a process* is missing and so this perspective is unable to account for the ways in which private schools have been, and are, caught up in class formation and relations. Further, as Wild (1974) observes, the complex, subjective, qualitative features of class cultures and consciousness are not amenable to the mode of assessment or description associated with survey research or to a consensus or functionalist notion of society. Complex concepts such as class, status and power are often restricted to individual attributes and remain unrelated to social dynamics. Finally, these studies are not without ideological consequences for the way in which society and social change are viewed. As Connell (1977, p. 33) says: 'If practical conclusions are drawn from them, they are necessarily couched in terms of "inequalities" rather than oppression or exploitation . . . and the implications drawn are for administrative action rather than class mobilization.'

A key feature of this work is methodological individualism; the individual is taken as the primary unit of analysis rather than, say, social structure or social history; individual decisions, activities, motivations and achievements are the focus, rather than the structure of relations between groups. Further, it is pointed out by Austin (1984, pp. 46, 47) that in theory this has the effect of reducing major structural aspects of society to individual attributes and interpreting social change as a consequence of individual will. The tenor of social life is derived from the movement of individuals through the social structure.

While surveys on private school clients, then, provide some beginnings to any quest to understand the private school/social class relationship, they must at best be regarded as an aid to further description of a more qualitative kind and to analyses of a more dynamic and relational nature. Without these they tend to be rather sterile and repetitious, missing what private schools achieve for their clients and what the clients do for the schools.

A Relational Approach

An althernative way in which the class of private school patrons has been studied is that of Connell and his various colleagues. This literature finds its origins in Marxist class theory, particularly the version which may be traced through Lenin, Gramsci and E.P. Thompson. It is useful, therefore, to provide a backdrop for the discussion of their position on private school clients by briefly mentioning something of this theoretical heritage.

Wright (1980) outlines the three basic and essential premises of a Marxist analysis of the class structure, noting, first, that it is relational: 'classes are defined according to their social relation to other classes' (p. 325). Second, it is concerned with the ways in which economic relations are socially organized, and with a focus, third, on production rather than exchange, i.e. it is concerned with the social relations between groups of people within the process of production. Class is regarded as 'a common position within the relations of production' (p. 326). The collectivity of people occupying the 'common position' is often seen as a class 'in itself', people placed in an objective location in a structure of positions. However, defining and classifying the class structure should, as Wright observes, be regarded as one moment of study and analysis, to be superseded by the vastly more complex project of understanding class formation — how people in places become classes 'understood as historically dynamic social forces' (p. 326) which have developed political and ideological forms sufficient to make them conscious of themselves as a class and to interact with others in a class-related manner.

Connell and his various colleagues' work meets the above criteria for a Marxist analysis (see Connell and Irving, 1981). Further, they have constantly indicated how little they are concerned with the moment of categorization, and how much more concerned they are to work with an historical theory of class. According to Connell and Irving (1981), this includes the following: concern with the particularities of time and place in the process of class interaction and formation; recognition of intention and constraint in the lived experience of classes of people. Classes are defined as 'the major social groupings that emerge in the process of social polarization around the labour market created by the property system' (p. 19). They exist in a latent form as a consequence of the labour/capital contradiction in the economy but are formed through a process of mobilization in which a common situation leads people to 'realize their shared experience and develop a language of system or symbols to express it and develop movements and organizations to carry on conflict, to change or defend their situation' (p. 19). Classes form in interaction, conflict and struggle. The study of class is the study of a process, not a category, an 'event', as Thompson argues (1963, 1978).

In discussing the dynamics of the class structure, and in emphasizing the political, cultural and psychological dimensions to class formation, Connell and his colleagues draw extensively on Gramsci. While not ignoring the state as a site for class struggle generating coercion and consent, they tend to be more concerned with those aspects of civil society wherein 'the subordinate class lives its daily life in social forms created by, or consistent with, the interests of the dominant class; and through this daily life acquires beliefs, motives and ways of thinking that serve to perpetuate the power of the dominant class' (Connell and Irving, 1981, p. 20). Although acknowledging the significance of this 'cultural and psychological integration', Connell and Irving are at pains to point out that this does not imply complete co-option of one class by another but rather points to the greater mobilizing force of the dominant class and its capacity to disempower the working class in its attempt at mobilization through, in part, cross-class alliances.

Thus it is clear why Connell is interested in schooling and why, from a ruling class point of view, schooling is to be regarded as an aspect of class mobilization, and also as a means of subduing the working class. Connell *et al.* (1982) are concerned to define whom high status private schools serve and how they do so. How, then, within the terms of a relational historical view of class, are the clients of prestigious private schools labelled? When Connell *et al.* refer to the patron class of these private schools, they call it the 'ruling class'. They are basing the categorization 'not on what people *have* but what people do and under what circumstances' (1982, p. 144), and those they most clearly locate in the ruling class are people who, by virtue of their work, significantly 'shape the lives of others' (p. 144). In drawing, albeit loosely, from Wright's (1976) categorical model of class identification, Connell *el al.* (1982)

include the dimensions authority in the workplace and the mental/manual labour distinction leading to professional authority. Thus their definition of 'ruling class' is somewhat more open than the earlier statement implies, including mainly 'managers, business men [sic] and professionals'.

Certainly, as they see it, those professionals who depend for their class and that of their children upon a particular relationship to knowledge will have a vested interest in education. However, rather than emphasizing the differences between professionals and those more clearly identified as ruling class (those who control and maintain capital accumulation, see Connell, 1977), Connell *et al.* emphasize their 'unity in diversity', claiming that both have 'access to power and privilege and also depend on and contribute to an order which will sustain it' (p. 146). Even so, differences within the ruling class are recognized. As they note, the catchments of private schools 'register' diversity and change within the ruling class, and that 'overcoming their effects by evolving and imposing a common educational practice is a permanent, necessary task of the ruling-class school' (1982, p. 152).

It is evident from the stratification studies cited earlier, and from Connell *et al.*, that high status private schools include among their clients a proportion of people engaged in the sort of work which, even given Connell *et al.*'s loose definition of rulling class, cannot be thus categorized. Given this, how legitimate is it to call them ruling class schools and how, in class terms, does one explain these people's presence in the schools? How, even, does one classify them? One of the most contentious issues within Marxist class analysis concerns how to define the class position and interests of white collar employees, technical experts and less esteemed professional people and middle managers — those who are often called 'the new middle class' (see Abercrombie and Urry, 1983; Wright, 1980). How do Connell *et al.* address this problem, not just with regard to definition, but, more importantly, to the matter of interests? These 'outsiders' they do acknowledge as 'different' within the milieu of the ruling class school, but they refuse to classify them as of another class:

> ... contrary to much popular and academic myth, we are speaking here of a minority, not a majority, of the population. In any event, numbers are not what is really at stake in defining classes. Our basic argument is that Australia's middle managers, humbler professionals, technical experts and small business people do not have the stable interests which characterise both working and ruling class, and lack a developed set of cultural institutions devoted to the expression and defence of fundamentally shared interests. The distinctiveness of the groups commonly and

> loosely referred to as 'middle class' is best appreciated, we believe, as an example of the diversity and conflict which exist within classes. (1982, p. 147)

Thus their emphasis upon process and class relationships allows Connell *et al.* to skirt this issue, while at the same time making the important point that the schools try to express 'what is common in their interests and situation and to subordinate differences and conflicts' (1982, p. 146).

The matters to be addressed in this study are to do with the processes of class mobilization and formation in struggle. Like Connell and his colleagues, I see class groupings as arising out of capitalist property relations and relating to positions in the labour market. My view is that any holistic and adequate view of class must be concerned with the ways in which the labour market and the labour process are organized, the opportunities they permit, the constraints these impose, the means by which people are recruited into, and allocated to, the social division of labour and the economic, cultural, political, ideological and psychological mechanisms by which class relations are reproduced, challenged and changed.

One significant aspect of class formation is the class culture which provides people's class experience and helps to produce their subjectivity. The class culture includes not only the workplace but all the institutions and interactions which 'connect individuals to society' (Hogan, 1982, p. 35) — the school, family, club, suburb, social group and so on. These form the complex web through which a class culture develops its coherence and its predictability, the nature of which will depend very much on the matters outlined above, including the extent and nature of class conflict. It is in the context of a class culture that a class *develops*, produces itself, makes sense of its situation and utilizes its available resources.

The reproduction of classes is brought about by the distributive mechanisms which result in the social division of labour and allocate people therein. Education is obviously a significant mechanism among many. Classes are also reproduced through their relationships with each other, through cultural and ideological processes best enunciated through Gramsci's (1971) notion of hegemony. My focus in other related studies (see Kenway, 1987a, 1987b, 1990) has been on the educational hegemony of high status private schools and on their role in class *relations*, and it is appropriate to make one quick point here concerning the broadly dual character of ideology resting on the matter of difference between 'the self' and 'the other'. Therborn (1980) has called this ego-ideology and alter-ideology. He argues that for dominant groups such a distinction is crucial, the ego-ideology being that which forms the subjectivity of the dominant, and the alter-ideology being that which strives to dominate the formation of 'other' class, race or sex subjects.

This way of thinking is pertinent to these private schools. High status private schools constantly offer a favourable definition of themselves for popular consumption, one claiming to take into account the 'interests' of the *non*-private school community. The alter-ideology is, of necessity, concerned with a hegemonic effect, and must have persuasive force. Connell *et al.* put this problem neatly when they say of private schools,

> ... there is a contradiction between the ruling class's need for class organization and its need to maintain hegemony over other classes.... The more clearly they draw lines and stress social distinction, the more they serve their clients' demands for class identity and the class's need for solidarity. But in so doing they may offend those excluded, create resentment against privilege and erode the hegemony of their clientele in society at large. (1982, pp. 153, 154)

In addition though, users and supporters of the schools promote (and hold) a set of beliefs about themselves and 'the other', i.e. the state system, which is only for internal consumption. Its essence is a sense of the superiority of the insider and the inferiority of the outsider, in terms which would be unacceptable to outsiders. Its audience is strictly internal. The primary focus in this chapter is on this ego-ideology of the private schools, their self-production; on how they define themselves, and others *to themselves*, the tensions and complexities inherent in the definitions and the part they play in producing a class culture with its associated classed and gendered subjectivities. My interest is in the contribution of these schools to a class producing itself, in the way in which the clients use the school and the school works on behalf of the clients and, by extension, the class to help develop a 'class for itself', i.e. collectivities of people conscious of shared interests and oppositions. Specifically, I am concerned with the ways in which people experience this self-production as it becomes part of class production.

Class and Gender

I have talked at some length about class with little reference to gender. In the critical literature on private schooling such a silence was, until recently, not unusual. While some scholars have examined the social role of girls' private schools in the light of feminist theory (e.g. Theobold, 1984, 1986), the intersections between class and gender have, until the last eight years or so, been either glossed over or overlooked entirely. Even now, there exist very few adequate studies of class, gender and private schooling in Australia. Connell, Ashenden, Kessler and Dowset continue to lead a rather limited field in this regard. Given this lack, I will not discuss the limited private school literature. Instead, this section focuses on more general analysis of the relationship of class, gender and education. These days it should go without saying that class and gender are related, and in complex ways. However, as an ever-expanding body of literature demonstrates, how they relate is a matter much disputed, caught up as it is in discussions of the relationship between capitalism and patriarchy, Marxism or socialism and feminism. Also contributing to the complexity of the debate is the range of feminisms and Marxisms brought to bear on the issue (see Kenway, 1987b, Chs 1 and 2). It is neither appropriate nor possible to canvas this field here, so I will simply offer a brief account of some thinking among Marxist-feminist theorists of education.

For Marxist-feminists, capitalism and patriarchy are regarded as two distinguishable sets of power relations, each containing their own histories, contradictions and complexities and ideological and material bases. However, because they are integrated in a dialectial fashion, it is also held that to separate them analytically is difficult if not impossible. As a consequence, both Marxist and other feminist accounts of education are perceived as incomplete. As Arnot (formerly MacDonald) (1982) provides the most concise and developed theoretical statement of this perspective, I shall illustrate this point by drawing from her work. She observes the ways in which class domination under capitalism is supported by male dominance over women in the workplace, the family and in civil society. She also observes that class relations limit and structure gender identities and assist in constructing gender divisions. She notes that the social relations of production are characterized by male dominance over women and fuelled by the biological reproduction of workers in the patriarchal monogamous family. Here the nurturance of children is regarded primarily as women's work, and this is represented culturally as a natural division between the male public sphere of work and the female private sphere of family. Arnot argues that the congruence of these two structures is socially constructed via a bourgeois hegemony which wins men's and women's consent to particular definitions of masculinity and femininity. She recognizes capital and labour, male and female as both social dichotomies and social hierarchies involving 'material and symbolic power' and 'class and sexual struggle' (1981, p. 163). However, she also acknowledges that a coincidence of interests does not mean that each power structure is essential to the other. Rather, she accords them relative autonomy, claiming that changes in one do not necessarily lead to changes in the other.

Barrett (1980) points out that within Marxist feminism a number of lines of argument exist with regard to the relationship between class and gender. However, the line of reasoning which Barrett finds most persuasive is one which argues that women occupy a dual relationship to the class structure: first, a direct relationship as wage labourers or owners of capital; and, second, an indirect relationship mediated by dependence upon the male and his relationship, and by responsibilities for domestic labour and child care. In noting that capitalism constitutes 'the historical context in which gender is now played out' (1980, p. 137), Barrett emphasizes the importance of the moment of separation between home and workplace which accompanied the institution of the wage relation. As she says, this has been accompanied by an ideology incorporated into capitalism and promulgated among both classes of men that domestic labour and child care are women's destiny. Ideologies of domesticity and femininity have played a significant part in women's place in the labour force and in the nature and conditions of the paid work which most undertake.

It is this recognition of the dual character of women's class position which is the most essential ingredient of the Marxist-feminist perspective on education. As Arnot (1981, p. 109) says, 'Ideologies of gender, of feminity and sexuality are brought into contact with ideologies of class differences and control.' In bringing together issues of class and gender, this perspective seeks to highlight the following matters. Patriarchy is seen to be experienced differently in different classes — that is, there is more than one social construction of its essential themes. This view is steeped in a belief that there are different cultures between class groups and that these intersect with domestic and labour force arrangements. It also draws from a belief that the gender arrangements of more powerful social groups tend to exercise a hegemony over these powerful groups, that this hegemony works through a range of social agencies, including schools, and that these may function to serve class interests.

Schools are regarded as sites within, and through which, the interrelated power structures of class and gender operate. Hence schools are seen to prepare students for their dual locations in the sociosexual division of labour, the relations of production, and in the relations of reproduction within the family. With regard to the last, they are complicit in 'forming and transmitting gender identities and sexual power relations' (MacDonald, 1979, p. 142). Collectively, what this work shows is that notions of masculinity and femininity have been central to education systems, and that they vary across time and between class groups. More specifically, what much of this work also shows is that education systems may, and do, make distinctions between the gender identities that they offer particular class groups, while at the same time selectively legitimating particular gendered class cultures.

This work is moving towards analyses which consider the interactions between structures and agents, and so explorations are being conducted of the intersections between the subjectivities which groups of students bring to school and the ideologies permeating the schools' operations. Gender definitions are not seen to be reproduced without conflict or change, and hegemony theory has proved useful in exploring these points, as the following lengthy but useful quotation from Arnot indicates. She points to

> the *active* nature of the learning process, the existence of dialectical relations, power struggles and points of conflict, the range of alternative practices which may exist inside, or exist outside and be brought into the school. Further it allows us to remember that the power of dominant interests is never total nor secure. Cultural hegemony is still a weapon which must be continually struggled for, won and maintained. Women in this analysis must offer consciously or unconsciously their 'consent' to their subordination before male power is secured. They are encouraged 'freely' to choose their inferior status and to accept their exploitation as natural. In this sense the production of gender differences becomes a critical point of gender struggle and reproduction, the site of gender control. (1984, p. 66)

The research on education which comes as close as any to exploring the actual rather than only theoretical complexities of the hegemonic process is that of the Home, School and Work project team (Connell, Ashenden, Kessler and Dowsett). Its work points to the complexity of the social structures which are gender and class; and to the range of institutions, interactions and cultural, sociological and psychological dimensions which they involve. As Kessler *et al.* (1982, p. 182) say and demonstrate, class and gender 'abrade, inflame, amplify, twist, negate, dampen and implicate one another. In short they interact vigorously ... with significant consequences for schooling.' The project team's publications exemplify Gramsci's notion of 'historic bloc'. They demonstrate the connections between the family, the school, popular culture, the labour market and, to a lesser extent, the state and show various ways in which each and all are involved in overlapping class and gender politics. They show clearly the changing nature of gender and class relationships and their tensions, contradictions and constant production. Within this framework, this body of work offers an account which integrates class and gender, one which recognizes a range of different femininities and masculinities, but which recognizes that certain patterns dominate at the level of practice and of myth. The school, they argue, 'arbitrates among different kinds . . . by providing a setting in which one kind or another becomes hegemonic' (Kessler *et al.*, 1985, p. 42). They see schools as having a particular gender regime, that is, 'the pattern of practices that constitutes various kinds of masculinity and femininity among staff and students, orders them in terms of prestige and power, and constructs a sexual division of labour within the institution' (1985, p. 42). As suggested in the preceding discussion, class cultures also have a 'gender regime' and this is complicit in the formation of class-specific gendered subjectivities and in the relationships between classes.

Thus much of the literature considering the relationship between private schools and social class is deficient as an attempt to understand the role of the schools in gendered class formation and relations. The matter is much more complicated than identifying the class location of parents and products. Connell *et al.* (1982) Kapferer (1986a, 1986b) and Teese (1981, 1986) all indicate that the schools are active in developing the dominant classes, not in any mechanical way but rather in ways which require the engagement of the parties involved. The schools assist their clients as a class, and their clients help the school, often possibly with self-interest in mind, but with the class group as beneficiary. My work elsewhere (Kenway, 1987b) indicates the many aspects of this process of mutual self-help. Here, however, I wish to focus on consumption as an aspect of gendered class culture and on the ways in which this articulates with the use to which private schools are put by their client class.

The Culture of Consumption

The notions of markets and consumption are not unfamiliar in the critical literature on private schooling in Australia. Indeed, a force underpinning parents' power, or sense of power, over the private school is what Connell *et al.* (1982) call the 'private school market' and Kapferer (1986a, 1986b) calls 'consumer patronage'. The former argue that private schools' clients have a certain amount of power over the school via the forces of the private school market and that the school will both direct its activities in accordance with the demands of the market and contribute to the forces operating within the market. As a consequence of the school's need to attract and retain its clients, school staff are expected to pay reasonable heed to, and even to anticipate, parents' wishes. They emphasize the power which parents exert over teachers' employment and the curricula by virtue of this financial exchange. Parents are also seen to exert power over the schools, given the schools' 'vulnerability' within the education market. Without client support the school's existence is not guaranteed. Client power is an important component of the Connell *et al.* argument, even though they also note the forces operating against it — including religion, family tradition, geography, teacher professionalism and, in particular, strong-minded principals. Recognizing differences in the clientele, Connell *et al.* are also prepared to differentiate between both the capacity and the preparedness of individual families to exercise direct power and the values and motives parents bring to the school. Nonetheless, most parents are seen to bring an attitude of 'calculative appraisal' (1982, p. 135).

A second feature of the market forces which Connell *et al.* observe is that which provides a mechanism by which schools can change 'in response to change in the ruling class' (p. 137), one which is effective, for all its diversity and tensions. The school is seen as an active part of its class, helping to organize, renew and reconstitute it in changing times. In order that they may 'modernize ruling class education', the schools must have a certain autonomy. The exercise of power is not unidirectional and not all located in parents' hands.

Evaluated here is another dimension to the notion of markets and consumers, one to do not so much with exercising power as with legitimating it. I am referring to a way of thinking arising from the logic of consumption, my contention being that neither Connell *et al.* nor Kapferer take the matter of markets and consumers far enough. Private schools are immersed in, and shot through with, an ideology of consumption, and certain of the discourses of the schools unwittingly endorse this while others, in attempting to challenge it, often become overwhelmed by its logic. Some background to the notion will indicate its strength within the cultural context of private schools and thus how it impinges upon them.

Market capacity, consumption patterns, life-style, social honour and the relationship between status and class have been tied more to Weberian than to Marxist class analysis. Marxists have traditionally concentrated on production and markets in labour, the commodification of labour power and the ethos peculiar to capitalism which equates money and worth, and subjects everything to the logic of profit. However, as theories of ideology and hegemony have developed to encompass many aspects of civil society, neo-Marxist analyses of class have increasingly come to acknowledge consumption as a mechanism in social structuring. While one tendency has been to discuss consumption as a form of ideological co-option by a dominant economic order, another approach has considered it, in part at least, as an act of creation or what dc Certeau (1984) calls 'consumer production' or 'secondary production hidden in the process of [its] utilization' (p. xiii).

The role of consumption in class cultures and its use as a means of social definition as the assertion of identity are increasingly acknowledged; as is its use in class relations as a mode of legitimating existing power relations and of asserting opposition to them. Austin (1981, p. 29) points out that, in effect, Weber focused on the role of ideology in the realm of consumption, showing the way in which 'patterns of consumption and their ideological representations may complement and affect production relations.' My intention here is to draw from some neo-Weberian studies, particularly Veblen's (1970) classic, in examining the relationship between consumption and the private schools of this study, noting further that class and consumption are intricately caught up in matters of gender. In the following few pages I draw out some of these intricacies as they impinge upon the clients of private schools in the suburban contexts in which they live their daily lives.

One matter seldom mentioned in the private school literature in Australia is the relationship between private schools, their clients and urban geography and culture. While not addressing it in any detail, Connell *et al.* (1982) note some of the implications of the suburban concentration of the wealthy and the 'comfortable', how the 'private housing market segregates people along class lines' (p. 71). Both state and private schools are caught up in this process of social segregation except that, as they note, those with financial resources have a degree of choice about where they live and thus have greater control over their lives than do those without such resources and that this has implications for the ways families are shaped and connected with larger social structures (Connell *el al.*, 1982, p. 71). Further to this line of thinking, I suggest that the locale is also an important site for the construction of subjectivity.

All suburbs are invaded by the products of 'captains of industry and consciousness' (Ewen, 1976). 'We live and breathe an atmosphere where mass images are everywhere in evidence: mass produced, mass distributed. In the streets, in our homes, among a crowd or alone, they speak to us, overwhelm our vision. Their presence, their messages are given; unavoidable' (Ewen, 1976, p. 8). Sharing this and other features, suburban areas also have their own distinctiveness which reflects and helps to direct the culture of the classes to which they 'belong'. The use to which space, property and even vegetation are put, and the forms of leisure and other forms of consumption which develop, are determined by a range of characteristics of the inhabitants and provide one means by which progeny experience class and gender and become classed and gendered subjects.

The suburbs which provide the contexts for the three schools of this study are theatres for display, operating essentially with the class group itself as an audience, participating in a script, with competitive posturing through consumption as one of its themes. The consumption of property, leisure and adornment are the distinctive features focused on here, each providing a vehicle for the display of pecuniary strength and for staking claims to social esteem and respectability. For, as Veblen (1970, p. 36) says, 'In order to gain and hold the esteem of men [sic] it is not sufficient to merely possess wealth or power. Wealth or power must be put in evidence, for esteem is awarded only on evidence.' Clearly, too, there are acceptable and unacceptable ways of displaying such strength and demanding esteem. Display must be infused by what are considered decorous canons of taste. Learning these as second nature, and intuitively adjusting to their changing content, is part of being inducted into the culture. A theatre for display, the suburb also invites emulation or 'invidious comparison' (Veblen, 1970, p. 16). As the codes signifying honorific achievement are set, they are inevitably broken, adjusted and transcended as the imperatives of display and competition engage in a fierce dialectic.

The three schools of this study are located in Perth's most esteemed suburbs. The area's demographic, ethnic and socio-economic characteristics are described in considerable detail in *Perth, A Social Atlas* (1983), a document produced by the Division of National Mapping and the Australian Bureau of Statistics from the 1981 census data. The *Atlas* indicates that the suburbs associated with this study contain pockets which are characterized by extreme wealth and privilege. Further, and very generally, it indicates that in contrast with most other suburbs of the city of Perth, this area has higher levels of income, bigger and more owner-occupied private dwellings, a greater number of people employed in professional, technical and administrative occupations and working in the central business district, fewer unemployed, fewer rented dwellings and fewer overseas-born residents. The participation of married women in the paid labour force is average to below to significantly below average depending on the area. The picture thus painted is of a region of the city which, although including a range of indices of class membership (within stratificationist terms), contains only a very restricted range.

If one looks more closely at the area as a social landscape, a signifying system, with regard particularly to the cultural symbols mentioned earlier (visible property, leisure and adornment), it contains its fair share of solid 'respectable' family homes, but their number would certainly be equalled by combining the stately mansions, the elegant units, the luxurious edifices to architectural imagination and the fashionably restored older dwellings. It is this latter set which establishes the pecuniary standard, inviting emulation. Amid all this there are no signs of squalor, decay, poverty or even clutter or mess — only the 'conspicuous waste' born of money, one of the many waste forms engendered by capitalism. This locality contains the street which real estate agents call 'Millionaires Row', some of the most expensive urban land in Australia. The vast state of Western Australia, with its capital city one of the most isolated in the world, is often regarded as the 'last frontier' by Australian business speculators. It contains more millionaires per capita than any other state, most of whom live in this region, in some cases appalling even the locals with ostentatious displays of wealth, and certainly overstepping the marks of 'good taste'. Conspicuous consumption, restrained and 'tasteful' display, and homely comfort are set among the carefully — formal or casually — landscaped gardens of the smaller blocks or the sweeping lawns of the larger, their greenery merging into the blues of the river to the south and the ocean to the north.

Such waters improve property values and suburban status, adding an aesthetic and important cultural dimension to suburban life and providing opportunity for the conspicuous display of leisure. Expensive water sports belong to suburbs such as these. As forms of leisure, they have a value beyond the pleasure they induce — their utility as a means of gaining the respect of others. Symbols of potency, they demonstrate, particularly for the males of the area, a capacity to pay and a physical prowess achieved through the luxury of time to learn in a culture disposed to it. The acquired skills of sailing, surf skiing, wind surfing, wave jumping and even surfing are in some ways class-based and in many ways gender-based. Suburban waters, river or beach, generate particularly male forms of 'action' oriented consumption. These include water sporting goods, the style of apparel which accompanies them for different age groups and the drinking rituals and settings which 'top it all off'. For many of the boys of Perth Boys' Grammar such consumption constitutes their out-of-school way of life. The water is the male sphere which females may ornament, observe or use, but not, like their male counterparts, 'control'. On no occasion is the ownership of the river more clear than when the rowing teams of all the prestigious boys' schools assemble for the annual Head of the River Regatta and when all manner of water craft invade the river, proclaiming loudly the connections between the schools and privilege, demonstrating gender-inflected modes of consumption.

For most weekdays these particular suburbs are the domain of women in unpaid or part-time labour, children and the elderly. The men and the 'working women' leave them daily, in part at least in order to sustain them. Ostensibly a green refuge from the production and commerce of the central business district, suburbs such as these have isolated women from the world of 'real work' and have led them to fill their lives in other ways beyond, of course, the 'non-work' of reproducing the family. For some the competitive, individualistic, monism of the suburb is counteracted by a sense of community generated through leisure activities such as golf, tennis and bridge and through their social networking associated with luncheons and chats over coffee. For others the suburb has become a site for vicarious living through husband and children. The notion of the 'private school family' implicitly recognizes the potential insularity of life in suburbia and offers the opportunity for community membership while maintaining the service role of the female sex. Further, suburbia remains connected to business, industry and 'production' via shopping centres. Females are the main targets for their goods, their receptivity to particular types depending very much on the way history has culminated in the present for women and girls of their class, their class-based experience of a general experience of being female.

Part of the history of the privileged women and girls of this study finds its distant roots in women's place in the leisured classes (Veblen, 1970). To the men of such classes women were, in many ways, regarded as trophies to be displayed among other property as evidence of success and reputability and to be deployed in such interests. Historically, these women absorbed this ethic to the extent that much of their leisure time was spent in the labour of acquiring and applying various forms of adornment, thus demonstrating their own worthiness as trophies sought and reflecting favourably upon the male's prowess and pecuniary capacity once acquired. Having been acquired, the women extended their well nurtured talent for adornment to the home, where the freedom from drudgery permitted by money and domestic service allowed for ongoing cultivation of the talent. Clearly, there has always been more to privileged women than this glimpse at their history acknowledges, and as current scrutiny shows (e.g. Branca, 1975; Russell, 1988), but even so, consumption, adornment and display are part of their story, then and now. Although occurring in a very different historical, social and cultural complex, the shopping centres in wealthy suburbs help to produce and indulge (but never assuage) this emphasis on adornment and display in the culture of privileged females.

Servicing the area of the three schools are the 'usual' supermarkets, fast food outlets and petrol stations, but these are interspersed by 'up market' shopping streets, dotted liberally with quaint cafés, trendy bars, art galleries, antique shops, expensive little boutiques, places for buying health food, gourmet food and articles for decorating the home. The shops are mainly small, thus individualizing the more prestigious end of the mass market. The culture of good living is demonstrated and sold in these streets, where the pecuniary standard for the area is set and regularly reset as fashions in dressing, dining, drinking and living change almost seasonally. These are the places where canons of taste and style for the class and the gender are established, centres for 'invidious comparison'. Seeing and being seen is no less important than seeing how one should be seen, learning a commodified, class-based version of masculinity and femininity, while at the same time chasing fantasies through objects which promise fulfilment for the price on the ticket. Consumption, leisure, pleasure and work merge in these streets as desires are produced and eternally unmet.

The overwhelming emphasis on goods for the adornment of the self and the home attests to the essential 'femaleness' of these street cultures. During the day women outnumber men by about ten to one. The cafés are their lunchtime province. While it would be an overstatement to identify the women of the district with the women of Veblen's leisure class, what we see here is very much a modern equivalent. As Ewen (1976) and Ewen and Ewen (1979) point out, the work of housewives has increasingly become associated with consumption management and 'the survival tactic of allurement became appended to it as the most conspicuous form of self definition'. For women 'sexuality was the duty of leisure, and consumption "provided the idiom for the unity" of women's work and women's leisure' (Ewen, 1976, pp. 182, 183). The home is a further demonstration of the woman's style; body and home are both sites for display.

The message these streets give is that, whatever else these women include in their spheres of effort, their function is still to beautify the household in a stylish and elegant manner and be its 'chief ornament' (Veblen, 1970, p. 180). The woman's ability to spend in these regions demonstrates not only her household's capacity to pay but performs for her male counterpart Veblen's 'vicarious consumption'. At the same time her family identifies and is identified with her 'personal', 'individual' good taste, which is little more than her selection from 'a general class taste and the particular ideals promoted by that class' (Coward, 1984, p. 65).

If life in the suburban home is unfulfilling, the streets promise pleasure and satisfaction. They are one of the many places in society where female desire is defined and 'courted with the promise of future perfection, by the lure of achieving ideals.... Achieve these ideals and you will feel better! Female dissatisfaction is constantly recast as desire, as desire for something more ... dissatisfaction displaced into desire for the ideal' (Coward, 1984, p. 13). With all their marks of modernity it is not easy to recognize that the pleasure/desire axis of the sophisticated suburban street is ultimately conservative, promising improvement in 'their lives without any major social changes' (Coward, 1984, p. 15); in fact, sustaining for women the patriarchal expectation that they will ornament and nurture their world.

In mid-afternoon the local youth spill out of their various private (and other) schools, many into the most immediate and most 'up market' shopping street. For a while the colour of the street crowd is dulled by the browns, blues, greens and greys of meticulously worn private school uniforms, incongruous, even archaic, in such a setting. The uniform is 'frozen fashion' as Ewing (1977) says, but it is also a banner, its minute insignia advertizing rank within the group, and for outsiders its more general features symbolizing exclusivity, solidarity and superiority. It provides private school students with a means of identifying themselves and others. It gives them social stature and a sense of secure membership of an esteemed social class. Given its connotations of attachment to a privileged culture, the school uniform is also an expression of parental ambition for children and a means of displaying their own rank or market capacity.

Often in mid-afternoon mothers shop with daughters, almost ritualistically inducting them into the notion of housework as consumption and the search for personal satisfaction and social worth through esteemed modes of consumption. Preparing the young for comfortable membership in dominant culture requires learning 'discrimination as to what articles of consumption are decorous and what are the decorous methods of consuming them' (Veblen, 1970, p. 50). As many point out, women are often custodians of the status symbols of the class, as well as frequently generating and servicing its social networks, 'maintaining and supervising class distinctions' (Game and Pringle, 1979, p. 5). Their daughters, presumably, must acquire the skills of boundary maintenance through consumption.

In the evenings and on late week or weekend nights a more even numerical balance is achieved between the sexes. Uniforms are replaced by another trademark of the area, casual chic. Consumption is more clearly amusement at these times. Seeing and being seen has as much to do with markets in sexuality or gender advertizing as with learning the appropriate codes for the consumption of goods for pleasure. Night is the time-province of the leisure and pleasure vendors. Dining, drinking and the mateship and mating rituals associated particularly with drinking sites are a common form that leisure takes. If the mating rituals are performed with greater intensity here than in other parts of the city, if the air is a little heavier in this regard, perhaps the single-sex schooling for large numbers of the local young has something to do with it. For the younger adolescents, particularly boys, street leisure takes the form of 'hanging about' at the video shops, hamburger bars and their adjacent parking areas. Several groups form and promenade waiting for 'something to happen'. Occasionally, the superiority of this privileged youth culture is 'confirmed' as members of another, with different symbols of value, invade it, sometimes demonstrating their 'baser' instincts in the form of verbal and physical violence.

It is not possible to go into the connections between sexuality and consumption so usefully highlighted by psychoanalytic theory, but what has been outlined above suggests the different significance which commodities have in the life of males and females and the way consumer capitalism taps into and constructs desire, the relentless search for pleasure and fulfilment, in gendered ways. The modes of consumption employed by males in the area are largely directed towards demonstrating potency and control in the ways esteemed for and by men and boys of their social group. The females' modes of consumption are largely directed towards confirming their superior feminine identity in the eyes of others. As Game and Pringle (1979, p. 11) write, of consumption in the suburbs,

> A woman's value as housewife and mother is reflected in her success as a consumer, filling the cupboards and fulfilling herself. Thus the idea of femininity is promised not only through commodities related to self-adornment (clothes, cosmetics, hairstyles) but also through those connected with the care of home and family. All these commodities take on an erotic significance connected with her sexual identity. A desire for 'the other' to fill a psychic emptiness took the form of a desire for objects: the ideals of femininity and masculinity being offered via commodities.

Consumption promises happiness.

This is a manipulated consumer oriented population in one sense, but it is also one which puts consumption to its own use. Within the class culture it offers gendered measures of success, confirms an identity and provides emblems signifying group membership. In class *relations*, consumption is part of the process of social distancing and closure, helping to define 'us' and 'them'. The 'organic intellectuals' of the dominant class culture, those in the worlds of art and design, furnishings and fabrics, image makers and their propagators, provide the cultural symbols and help to construct the aesthetic standards by which social distinction may be demonstrated and through which a cultural 'hegemony over definitions of design, taste, style and elegance' (Coward, 1984, p. 68) is restlessly exercised. The canons can only be emulated in the most 'odious' of ways. This point can be illustrated through the example of dress. As Ewen and Ewen (1979, p. 233) observe: 'Clothing has become — for more and more people — and arena of social dialogue in which desires are expressed, and symbolically met. Within the expansive parameters of fashion, questions of *class*; *sexuality* and *gender*; and conflicting vectors of *resistance* and *conformity* have played themselves out visibly and dramatically.'

Dress is a social language of great force, particularly among the females of the area, and the most acceptable dress encompasses a plethora of styles, ranging from the sophisticated sensuality of 'continental chic' to 'Gucci punk'; but what is common to them all is their distance from markets for the masses by virtue of expense. Veblen (1970, p. 130) indicates that valued objects 'must conform to the requirements of beauty and expensiveness both'. The two elements are blended and confused.

> The ceremonial inferiority or uncleanness in consumable goods due to 'commonness' or in other words to their slight cost of production, has been taken very seriously by many persons. . . . What is common is within the (pecuniary) reach of many people. Its consumption is therefore not honorific, since it does not serve the purpose of a favourable invidious comparison with other consumers. Hence the consumption, or even the sight of such goods, is inseparable from an odious suggestion of the lower levels of human life, and one comes away from their contemplation with a pervading sense of meanness that is extremely distasteful and depressing to a person of sensibility. (Veblen, 1970, p. 161).

The cheap emulation of expensive fashion indicates that the 'real thing' cannot be afforded. Once emulated and part of a mass look it is then tainted and must be abandoned. Departures from the code and thus from 'aesthetic truth' (Veblen, 1970, p. 13) are often no more acceptable unless, as Wilson (1985) points out, they are part of some interesting or cultish movement of resistance which is often co-opted by the market anyway, thus losing its cutting edge. Cheapness and difference are both regarded as indecorous, if not repugnant, and usually signify not just a sartorial defectiveness but an entire cultural deficiency.

Although variations exist, difference is not a feature of the area in which the three schools are located. It is not like the city described by Ewen and Ewen (1979, p. 241), which 'functioned to enlarge a world-view.... Cities did not hide the world, but gave it new dimensions, in the flow of migrations, in a mosaic of cultures, languages and skin tones that reverberated in the streets. Sexual possibilities were expanded by the very proximity of bodies. Different worlds were always in contact and collision, as work and life commingled, inexorably interwined.' This area is a retreat from difference. To see any significant signs that life, even suburban life, can be otherwise, one must travel some distance to suburbs mostly on the other side of the city. To the extent that most needs and wants can be satisfied locally, and as the young tend to be restricted in their movements, the privileges and comforts of the area are signified as normal. A broader vision is neither required nor made available.

The Logic of Consumption and Private Schooling

Just as the locality has its distinctive approach to the consumption of goods, so too it has distinctive preferences in education. As one mother said 'Private schools are the norm in this area.' Indeed, of the secondary schools there are two state schools and seven private schools: four girls', two boys' and one co-educational. Two of these are Catholic and five Protestant. One of the state schools is set in the midst of the private schools and is regarded by parents and students alike as 'the pits'. The other, Hale, located on the margin of the area but close to the University of Western Australia, is considered a 'state, private school'. Its students include many academics' children, and its results and retention rates are high. The oft-repeated notion of a 'private, state school' speaks volumes. State education of any 'quality' must be redefined as 'private'. The market claims a virtual monopoly on quality, at least at its most prestigious end.

The region described does not simply provide a context in which local private schools sit, their inhabitants immune to its effects, like some monastic order. 'In a consumer society, the language and meaning of objects are fused with those of the market place' (Ewen and Ewen, 1979, p. 233); here too the 'language and meaning' of education for private school clients have become 'fused with the market place'. While consumption may well be the way of life of us all, its effects differ according to our place in the labour process and our market capacity. The world of these three schools is one in which money not only buys goods but a range of intangibles, such as desired outcomes, including success or the appearance of it. This culture of consumption and display has important consequences for private schools. It helps to explain *why* they are used by many parents and *the way* they are often used by parents and students, commodifying their offerings and evaluating them according to market values; hence such terms as 'I expect to get my money's worth' and 'I'm paying that school to . . .' are not uncommon among parents.

Certain private schools have always been 'owned' by certain class groups; an integral part of the class culture, their use a social habit, their reputability unquestioned. Purchasing an expensive private school education is, and always has been, a social statement resonant with meaning; an insignia of honour. It signifies at 'least' a capacity to pay, and so some pecuniary strength, and at 'best' membership of the dominant orders, custodians of educational and cultural value. Hence, as a teacher at PBG observed: 'Round here, one of the first questions that would be asked of somebody is "Where did you go to school?" That's a measure of his parents — a measure of his life concept.'

Private schools have also provided their clients with an honorific means of cementing, promoting and celebrating their own class standing; a means for accumulating esteem and social stature — what Weber calls status honour. Once bought, they place their clients in valuable social networks and thus assist further their social ambitions. A school councillor at PBG demonstrated this point rather vividly in the following remark:

> Take PBG, because of its high academic record you are going to have a heap of boys here that in later life are going to run into one another again. Professional, successful business men, or successful doctors and lawyers and accountants, architects and so on. Certainly there is an advantage to be able to have something in common with these people. You are growing up with valuable peers, educationally, academically, from the same socio-economic group . . . . Fine, they are much more comfortable and they know who they are talking to, they are not at a disadvantage when for the first time they run into some bloke. They know his background and strengths and weaknesses, he is not a stranger and they are on a very much more equal footing, of course they are, because it breeds a certain confidence.

These social benefits accrue even to those who fail in the school culture of conspicuous success:

> I'm a person who has not been very academic. I left school at fifteen and I was working before I turned sixteen but I've got by

> in life, I believe, largely as a result of the people and the associations I made at Hentey's School and I unashamedly admit that I've used my social background and the school that I went to, many times, to achieve my aims in life. If it's done nothing else it has done that for me.

To make these points is to indicate what thc schools do, and have done, for parents. The issue is not usually couched in this way, and most studies which seek to elucidate the reasons for parental choice of private schools rate such matters as low priority (e.g. Smolicz and Moody, 1978; Partington, n.d.). There are various reasons why this is so. In the studies themselves the problems often emanate from the nature of survey research, its superficial assumption that everything is accessible to consciousness and that respondents have access to, and are prepared to share, 'the whole truth'. From the parents' point of view a number of reasons exist (see Kapferer, in progress, pp. 19–20). Among them is the possibility that, for some, social and educational habit is not necessarily conscious and, second, for those conscious of such matters their explication could be somewhat embarrassing. It is definitely 'non u' to be seen to be trying to elevate one's class position and one would presumably want to suppress the unpleasant fact; indeed one might well repress it from consciousness. The 'non u' uses to which private schools are put must be explained in other terms, for example, as a rational and respectable *educational* choice. This is, it seems, one reason why the parents of this study felt compelled to be so relentlessly negative about what they had not chosen — i.e. the state system. Further, to a reasonable number of the parents in this study the discussion of class or class and education proved most unpalatable and prompted hot, vigorous denials, often as we sat among all their symbols of wealth and power in, for example, a judge's, a solicitor's and an accountant's plush offices and in houses resplendent with expensive, often antique, furniture and/or river views. Among the school population the general tendency is to deny class differences within the schools, at the same time as deploying hegemonic 'all walks of life', 'struggle and sacrifice' themes.

Of course, schooling is usually thought of in terms of what it does for and to children. As Connell *et al.*'s work demonstrates, buying one's children expensive private education was, and still is, a means of buying their induction into a class culture. For those students already suitably classed, by and large it confirms the home. For those on the 'ascent', it helps to provide the requisite social, cultural and educational tools and tastes. Witness the words of a teacher at the Ladies School of Perth: 'Things that you'd expect children to learn at home, basic courtesy and good manners have to be taught in the boarding school. Using the correct knives and forks, and knowing how to set the table and knowing how to dress correctly to go to dinner in the evening ... Some parents don't send their children to boarding school well equipped, dress-wise and shoes-wise and with the basic sort of knowledge.'

Private schools continue to try to teach decorum, the manners supposedly associated with 'breeding' and their polite usage at formal and ceremonial occasions. One has only to attend school assemblies and speech nights to observe both the teaching process and the demonstration of such knowledge. On a school speech night I saw a stream of schoolgirls cross the stage and hurriedly and awkwardly curtsey to the Governor as they received their school prizes, the curtsey and the Governor embodying signs of courtly deference from another country, another age. Of course, there are other desirable social skills which are also inculcated — particularly, as in the following case, for boys: 'If you are talking about the bottom 30 or 40 percent of students you are talking about PBG as a finishing school in how to get on in the world in ways not related to tertiary studies — an ability to hustle in business for instance – how to make money, use your contacts etc'. This point is confirmed by remarks by PBG students.

B: 'A lot of people, even at school, want to know who you know, who's going into what. You need to know who your mates are.'

B: 'Even now people are organizing profit making societies — like shares, seeking things, able to get hold of things. It doesn't have to be underhanded and they're the people who are going to get far even if they do it underhandedly — every business man uses contacts.' (Year 12)

The PBG boys also jointly learn other social skills, as a teacher found to his surprise:

> I went to a student's home to deliver an assignment. School had finished at 3.30 and there at 4.00 were he and five or six of his mates having cocktails in the lounge room — they invited me into the party. They weren't into stuff like beer — but spirits and sitting around — civilized, almost the adolescent parody of a business man's drink at a private home.

The teachers talked of the self-assurance of many of the students, their well developed social skills, their apparent sophistication. As one teacher said, 'They've got all the social graces under the sun.' However, there were often qualifications such as:

> They know how to address you and manipulate you. The things they know are how to behave at an afternoon tea or a cocktail party, where to put the silver on the table, how to freeze a waiter with your eyes. Yes, and they do it to us because here, many of the kids again pick up the attitude of their parents that teachers are beneath consideration and they really do treat us as servants. (Teacher, St Jerome's)

Students also absorb the codes of the culture, which include its negative referents, such as people whose disreputable identity and baser instincts are exhibited in their 'choice' of school, labour and leisure and in their use of ignoble consumable goods.

The ethic of consumption which pervades parental use of private schools encapsulates the view that what is best for their children may be bought, its purchase a form of insurance for their children's futures. Marketable credentials, and academic motivation and application, the right peer group and social distance from 'bad influences', good teachers and religious commitment can all be bought. Indeed, as many teachers in all three schools insisted, some parents believe that the school can compensate for their children's lack of educational 'ability'.

> I think that . . . the parental perception is very strongly that, even if their kids are in reality as thick as a brick, this is an academic school and why isn't my child doing better, and you dare suggest that so and so couldn't. . . . Quite seriously, they expect the School to *do* things for the students, above and beyond any recognition of what the students are 'capable of doing'. (Teacher, LSP)

Even a daughter's sexual purity can be ensured for longer in a single-sex girls' school, or so some mothers of this study wishfully thought. The degree of protection and surveillance which the girls are subjected to in the boarding house and on public occasions testifies to the school's responsiveness to this thinking in the education commodity market. For some parents the school takes on a role as surrogate, assisting in their struggle to control turbulent youth. Even beyond the boarding houses the teachers are expected to achieve the results which parents often cannot: 'the *teachers* should make them work, get their jewellery off, make them get their hair cut. Teachers should make them go to bed early.

The teachers should be their parents' (Teacher LSP). The right purchase in the educational market will gratify all individual needs, wishes and desires.

Always a commodity put to social use, in current times the perceived use-value of private schools has increased. I have suggested that the ethic of consumption is competitive individualism. This ethic has also been a structural feature of schooling, one which has reached new heights in an era of high unemployment, stringent entry quotas to tertiary study and credential mania. Educational 'success' has become a scarce resource and increasingly regarded as a commodity, all the more within one's grasp through investment in private schooling. Private schooling, it is believed, provides the competitive edge. Merit is 'captured by those with private means' (Marginson, 1986). 'Merit' is not an end in itself though; it is an investment in tertiary study which is an investment in an esteemed future embodying control over one's own life and power over others. One father, a 'Leftist' academic, said to me at a parents' night: 'I know private schools produce the ruling class and I want my daughter to be one of them.' Such naked admissions of parental ambition are rare.

The parents of this study most frequently said such things as, 'We want to give him/her the best'; 'We want the best we can afford for our kids, its only natural'; 'We want to give him/her every chance'; 'All you can give your kids is the right start in life', and 'If you care about your kids you'll give them a good education.' Understandable and commendable as such sentiments are, they indicate no sense of the historical basis to notions of 'best', 'chance', 'right start' and so forth. Yet such notions are clearly tied up with the honorific canons of educational consumption attached to the dominant classes. Veblen (1970, p. 52) said of decorum: 'It is this highest class that also gives decorum its definitive formulation which serves as a canon of conduct for the classes beneath.' To rephrase, the point would equally apply to costly private schools: 'It is the expensive private schools that give education its definitive formulation which serves as an educational canon for schools beneath.' Such notions are also tied up with the culture's habit of equating cost and merit, educational standards being related to the educational costs borne. For instance, one father from St Jerome's classified a school's class in relation to fees:

> To put it crudely, I think there is upper class, middle class and lower class and I think St Jerome's is middle class. PBG for example is upper class, it has to be, you can't afford to send your children there unless you've got a lot of money and it is as simple as that. You either have the money to send them to that school or you don't, so therefore you go down the scale until you hit the scale you can afford.

Yet a school's place in the market is not determined solely by fees. His school has a particular place because it is Catholic *and* located in one of Perth's wealthy suburbs. Those Catholic members of the dominant classes who want a Catholic education for their children are well positioned by both geography and generous federal funding to enjoy an educational bargain — private, prestigious and *cheap* schooling for their offspring. Because of its low fees, St Jerome's is certainly differently placed, but because of its suburban location and history it does have a certain 'snob' value. Yet its parents define it as different, in class terms, from the Protestant schools in the neighbourhood. They see it as less 'up market', more 'middle-class'. Nonetheless, despite such gradations, the consumption of such private education is honorific, as it serves the purpose of a 'favourable' comparison with most other educational consumers. Like goods of slight cost, education of no cost, i.e. state schooling, connotes commonness and inferiority. By buying, one may 'avoid the mortification that comes from unfavourable comment' (Veblen, 1970, p. 169) directed at a parent who does not care enough to choose 'the best' for her child, or who has defied the magical logic of consumption and made no choice at all.

Kapferer (in progress, p. 36) suggests that private school marketing, like other educational marketing, plays 'upon the anxieties of parents [and] intimating selfishness, dereliction of duty, even dishonour among those who fail to make the "necessary" expenditure.' Guilt is the other side of the market, parental guilt at not spending, student guilt at wasting parental investment. For example, the girls at the LSP are systematically taught that through the purchase of a private school education they gain facilities, opportunities and advantages above and beyond those made available through a state school. As one teacher said: 'Because their folks have to pay for their education they feel they are different, they are apart from the girls who go to the ordinary Government school.' Another teacher developed this point: 'The parents often feel the higher the fees the better the education. It must be a good school because the fees are the highest in WA. The girls do tend to think they are a little above the Seabourn High School girls. They say things like "She's *only* at Seabourn High "or" She's *only* from Melway".'

The girls also constantly acknowledge that because they go to a private school they gain a debt to their parents which must be repaid in the appropriate manner with hard work, 'high ambitions' and a meritocratic career. The greater the debt, the greater the dues.

G: 'If you come to private schools, you are not just going to leave and get married.'

> *G*: 'I feel I've got a duty to be a doctor or something, because my parents have sent me to a private school all my life.'
>
> *G*: 'If I wasn't going to *do* anything just stay home, get married and have kids, I wouldn't have come to the LSP.'
>
> *G*: 'We have sort of had it put upon us — if you go to a private school you maybe shouldn't take jobs like . . . um.'
>
> *G*: 'A garage mechanic or something unskilled like that or just receptionist or secretary or something like that. They expect more of you.' (Year 10)

Half-hearted application and an inappropriate choice of a future are to 'reneg on' the debt, a gross waste. The term 'waste' is a popular one among the girls and is applied to almost any future which does not involve tertiary study. To make alternative low status choices in the labour market or to opt for the domestic sphere is largely regarded as a 'waste of education', a 'waste of ability', a waste of the school's efforts and a failure 'to get my money's worth'. 'A friend of ours, when she leaves the LSP, she'll just go home to the farm, and we think "Oh god, what a waste of five years at a private school. She could have gone to a public school for that!"' (Year 10) It is clear from what the girls say that this investment logic is constantly deployed by parents and the school as a means of committing them to their study and to the tertiary-bound path. The money paid by parents is also seen to place certain obligations upon the teachers. Giving the parents their money's worth is what the teachers are expected to do, too. Where dedication and ambition are lacking in the girls, they must be cultivated. Thus, with fees at its centre, a circuit of obligations and expectations is produced.

The ideology of consumption commodifies social life and educational practice. Knowledge, schooling, effort and achievement are an investment directed towards the rule of profit — be it wealth, power, status or accumulation. Witness the following remark by an English teacher at PBG.

> This is the general sort of ethos of the school. There's an implicit assumption that one should succeed, not just succeed but one should win. . . . Currently drama is being given a big boost and music already has been, but funnily enough, it's as if one has to win in music and win in drama. It's not enough to play an instrument or something, one has to play it better than everybody else and in drama, I'm sure we are going to have to make more money and be more successful than everybody else. It's not

> enough that the thing is done for it's own sake, which is what culture should be all about, I would have thought. No, I'm getting a feeling that we've got to win.

Of course, the conspicuous display of private school success, be it in the form of examination results leading to esteemed credentials, the assumption of public leadership, achievement in sport, culture or otherwise is, in Kapferer's (in progress, p. 33) words, 'proof of purchase', and we are reminded again that it is the private schools which 'come up with the goods'.

Although private schools have only recently begun appointing public relations/marketing/fund-raising officers in various guises (St Hilda's recently advertized for a Director of Development, see *The Weekend Australian*, 3–4 December 1988, p. 48), they have always been conscious of 'marketing', hence their obsessive concern for appearances and their insistence that all students, parents and ex-students become standard-bearers for the cause; advertizing their own investment. It is apparent to the boys at PBG that the school has a vested interest in their success, and the more conspicuous it is the better.

> The reason they push us into the academic subjects is that they want a lot of glory later. They want people to know that *he* went to Perth Boys' Grammar School. He's made it — he's a millionaire, or we trained him in sport and that sort of thing. Like I tried to be excluded from sport and they said 'No', and I said 'Why'? and they said 'Do you want it in a nutshell? We want to say that we trained you if you make it to the Australian squad. We want to say that PBG was there and we were the force beyond you'. They mean well but it's also free advertising for the school. (Year 12)

Those boys with sporting talent are obliged (to put it mildly) to make it available for school use. School teams, school status, must come first. Displaying their success to themselves and outsiders is normal practice, a narcissistic exhibition of superiority and a bid to capture esteem and desirable clients.

Like the display windows of high status consumer-land, expensive private schools nourish and feed on parental desires and fantasies. As Connell *et al*. (1982) show, these are often generated by parents' own dashed hopes, particularly mothers'. Fantasies about what private schools might achieve for offspring are also generated by our British traditions, in children's and adults' literature, including television and film, and to a lesser extent some Australian literature. As I have pointed out elsewhere (Kenway, 1981, pp. 3–5), such works, in conjunction with a general media adulation (Kenway, 1987b), tend to present a stereotypical, glamorized and somewhat mythical image of the schools, emphasizing their connections with power, achievement and privileged life-styles. For those living vicariously through children, private schools provide a 'second chance', a bleak bid for renewal. What comfort there is for a parent in the reflected glory of a son who is 'Head of School' or a daughter who is Dux, the best of the best! Private schools offer parents the 'inside lane' in the pursuit of parental pleasure and gratification through a child's schooling, more ready rewards for their proclaimed sacrifices. As was implied earlier, they also tap into the potential loneliness experienced in the atomized culture of suburban consumption where, for their price, one can buy membership of an extended school and church 'family', always there, providing, particularly for women, a social avenue of escape from the home, even if its cost is the expectation of more servicing of others in the form of unpaid school labour.

The ideology of consumption prompts a particular form of subjectivity which may be in direct opposition to certain of the schools' activities. This is a matter of considerable concern to many teachers, who note the ways in which students interpret their education through a market lens. Due to their parents' payment of fees, the students apparently feel a certain sense of power over the teachers. As one teacher at PBG said, teaching 'is a service industry. A lot of kids would see it that way. I've heard kids say — "Jesus we're paying these fees — we expect a pound of flesh".' Such overt arrogance and manipulation is not at all uncommon. 'It's been said many times to St Jerome's teachers, "We pay to come here".... Other comments like, students will say to teachers "I can get you sacked for not doing that properly". Comments, even in jokes sometimes, about — "If you don't do this, I can do such and such and then you'll get the sack because of it".'

Usually, however, these power relations are somewhat more subtley expressed and felt. A St Jerome's teacher described them this way:

> In private schools the teachers do a lot for the kids. A lot of them do just about everything and the kids expect to have it all done for them and if you don't have it done 'Why haven't you done it?' they'll say that to your face. And then the demands of, 'When will you mark our work? When will you give us this assignment. When will you give us these notes?' There's a sense of having to perform for them, do everything for them.... They're sitting

> there watching you do everything all the time as if they are pulling the strings and you have to jump.

Within the classroom the students conduct a form of surveillance over which work should or should not be part of the course.

> When I'm teaching Maths often in the past if I tried to do anything with them that's slightly off the course but may just broaden their education and open their eyes a bit, a response would often come from the kids. 'Will this be assessed?' 'Will I need it?' 'How will this help me?' As if everything I do has to be justified in terms of them getting where their parents are. (Teacher, St Jerome's)

From what the teachers say, many students are also fiercely competitive and most work for marks: '"Is it going to be marked?" is the first question, always and then "What level is this work?" And "If this work is ordinary credit level, what does that mean I can do after that and what jobs does that prepare me for?" It's hard to get something done just for the sake of learning and education' (Teacher, St Jerome's). Equally, many parents approach their children's learning with a similar investment mentality. They know which forms of knowledge have the greatest investment potential and put considerable pressume on the schools to ensure that their own children are not exposed to low status school knowledge.

> It's one of the difficulties that we face in a school like this. They come from higher socio-economic levels, the parents have high ambitions for the girls and it shows up very much in subject choices in Year Ten. We talk the girls into doing courses like Early Childhood Studies, General English and time and again the parents ring up and they say, 'No, we want the girls to do the regular Tertiary Entrance English course', or 'Early childhood studies doesn't count to get into anything, she must do Chemistry', and she is totally unfitted to do Chemistry. (Teacher, LSP)

As a teacher at PBG pointed out, the matter does not stop there: 'Parents don't come to me and say I'm worried about so and so's English per se, they're worried about how they'll cope with law if they are not very gifted at expressing themselves. It's always a worry in the future. What little Johnny is going to do and be in his life rather than how he is coping as a person at the moment, that is rather low priority.' Parents, like their children, are also often seen to define 'doing well in life' in relation to money and consumption. 'Having the wherewithal to travel, to have a Mercedes, own a swimming pool, launch to go to Rottnest Island holiday resort, very much in material terms.'

The logic of consumption also distorts those subordinate curricula in each school which potentially challenge current social arrangements; not just standing as a seductive challenge to them but providing a translation discourse through which the schools' meanings may be changed. For example, the schools' emphasis on appearances, on market interests, and the community's emphasis on display combine to undermine any school programs aimed at teaching students that personal worth goes beyond surfaces. As a girl at the LSP confidently proclaimed 'We are taught that what we appear to be is what we are.' This statement rings particularly true for the girls in relation to dress. They define themselves, girls from other private schools and from state schools according to appearance and fashion.

> *G*: 'Most LSP girls are all really good looking. That's what you notice. A lot of times you classify them as far as clothes go and so you think of them sort of as designer clothes and exclusive boutique clothes. Our school's more Espri, or Cherry Lane around that, not really sort of boutique exclusive, except for a few people.'
>
> *G*: 'St Bridgettes has got a really poor reputation, sort of boggish.'
>
> *G*: 'Yeah, they're not like a private school. They're sort of all fat and ugly.' [laughter]
>
> *G*: 'Right. I've never seen a good looking girl from there.'
>
> *G*: 'No, you don't see them very often at all. They're all really butch — and big.' (Year 12, St Jerome's)

Such matters are no less important in structuring social groupings within and outside the private school system:

> *G*: 'If you wear nice clothes you can be surely guaranteed that you won't be treated badly. If you can't wear the nicest clothes and have a nice hair style and live in a nice area, well then you've got worries with the girls' groups.'
>
> *G*: 'I have a group of friends at the LSP and what matters to them is purely what people have. Boats, where their moorings are, who they know. One friend in particular, she would never dream of speaking to anybody that wasn't dressed properly, or spoke badly or, — um — or drove a

funny car or things like that. It really matters to her and it's silly, but it matters to all of us.' (Year 12, St Jerome's)

Clothes and appearances combine with other consumer items as mechanisms of social differentiation and distinction. What follows is a discussion among a group of girls from the LSP about their preferred versions of masculinity. To prefer private school boys is natural, often because similarities of wealth produce similar patterns of leisure consumption.

G: 'We do all the same things as private school boys do. We go wind-surfing, we've got the money to do it.'

G: 'That's it money, money. If I went out with someone from Glengala, I'd probably get about as much pocket money in one week as he got in a year, I'd probably sort of be paying for him. I've been brought up to expect things like, you know, he can pay.'

G: 'If you've got a boyfriend and he's from private school then he'd take you out to dinner once in a while but others just take you to the drive-in.'

G: 'Video, they've all got videos. Instead of skateboarding and riding bikes they do other things. Spas, saunas and other things.'

G: 'I live in Rowallen and the guys from the school down there [interjections:Bogans] an ideal Friday night to them — go to the bowling alley — don't bowl — sit there and watch everyone — pick up a few chicks — go over to the oval and get drunk or stoned then go over to Point Peron in the car and stop and have a big drink-up.'

G: 'State school boys are really crude and tough, sort of bogan.'

G: 'We know some state school ones, they are tougher, they are crude, they are disgusting and they are older than their age.'

G: 'Yeah, and smoking and stuff like that, drugs.'

G: 'I know when we went to that sports thing and we were sitting next to those kids and they all had their John Forrest High bags and they were John Forrest and everyone immediately thought "Oh, yuk". No matter, we knew what they were like.'

G: 'They don't shop around, they like to shop somewhere like Target.' [giggles]

G: 'They don't all come up here and get the real expensive boutique clothes.' (Year 10, LSP)

Evident in this conversation is the way in which the consumption of schooling is also an important ingredient of social stature and closure. High status private schools service cultures of affluence and both set hegemonic canons of taste; both help to construct subjectivity for those inside and outside the culture. Those firmly located inside the culture of privilege can buy social, cultural and educational empowerment.

Conclusion: Education Policy and the Market Metaphor

This chapter has shown some of the connections between class culture, gender, consumption and private schooling. While alluding to more 'macro' social features, the empirical analysis has been largely at the level of 'micro' cultural and educational politics. It is important to recognize, however, that the logic of consumption, display and commodification which pervades private schools has much wider educational significance than that mentioned above. Elsewhere, I have highlighted the ways in which such thinking informs the public rhetoric of the private school lobby, the educational Right and the New Right (Kenway, 1990). With the assistance of the media, this loosely linked political amalgam has throughout the 1980s constantly and loudly propagated the notion that educational excellence and efficiency are best guaranteed by subjecting education to the logic and forces of the market. Within this line of thinking, private schools have a monopoly on educational excellence and success, and this is regarded as a consequence of the free play of market forces. The virtues of the market are juxtaposed to the evils and inadequacies of 'state intervention' in education. State schools are presented as 'in crisis' because, in part, they are administered by an inefficient, alienating and remote bureaucratic monolith. Private schools are free to succeed and to 'care' because of their 'independence' from the state, which should certainly assist with funding but should otherwise leave these schools free to excel. In this view, accepting public money does not imply that the schools should be accountable to the government or the public. State support is encouraged only insofar as it permits the educational market to operate; beyond that, private schools must be private in order to operate effectively. To require accountability is regarded as an affront to privacy, a bureaucratic intrusion upon the individual rights of those who are managing their schools more efficiently than state governments are managing their 'failing investment' — state schools.

While the privatization, consumer sovereignty ethic has certainly enhanced the cultural and educational capital and drawing power of private schools generally, and certain private schools in particular, it has also led to the subtle privatization of state schools. Increasingly, such schools are expected to emulate their private school competitors, to transfer power, or at least the illusion of power, to the school community, to market themselves, to raise money from parents and extract their unpaid labour. The more that state governments transfer educational authority to the 'educational consumers' at the local level, the more they relinquish any of their (admittedly often latent) capacity to direct education in socially just ways, in universal rather than sectional interests. The privatization of state schooling has caught Leftist educational thinkers with their pants down. Community involvement and control was always a strong, but deeply ambiguous and rather naive, plank in their educational agenda. Its naivety is demonstrated in a failure to recognize the ways in which dominant interests construct both educational markets and the thinking of educational consumers. It is the socially constructed educational market, premised on competitive individualism, the commodification of knowledge and the 'cult of selfishness', which helps to direct people to their educational desires, preferences and 'choices'. Throughout the 1980s education has come to be considered less and less a means of individual development, a personal and national social and cultural benefit, or a way of effecting just social change. Increasingly, it is perceived as an investment, for individuals in a job and for the nation an investment in economic growth.

The privatization of state schooling also implies the privatization of educational equity. What this means is that although governments may continue to espose notions of social justice, they nonetheless minimize their capacity to effect such social change. The responsibility for educational equity is transferred to the educational manager and consumer in the local school. In an economic and social climate where a social conscience is increasingly deemed something of a fad associated with the luxuries of the long boom and the late 1960s/early 1970s, the transfer of this responsibility must be regarded as deeply problematic. In the early 1990s, an era of economic and moral uncertainty, it is most unlikely that parents in an atomized education system will encourage their school to implement a strong social conscience. Markets and their consumers have no responsibilities beyond self-gratification. Indeed, although seductive, the market has a momentum which is both fierce and cruel. Despite its celebration of choice, it really only offers choice and control as delusions. The education market, like other markets, in fact diminishes real choice and increases economic and social inequality. It offers an educational utopia premised on the values of consumer culture. In true hegemonic fashion it promises satisfaction to all, but in effect gives the greatest opportunity for satisfaction to those with the greatest pecuniary strength. It implies that security and even status and power are best achieved by purchasing a private school education; and that these attributes are available to anyone who can afford the fees. This ignores the connections between esteemed modes of consumption, educational and otherwise, and their *distance* from mass markets. It also ignores the fact that markets almost invariably operate in the interests of the powerful and privileged and let the weak 'go to the wall'.

References

ABERCROMBIE, N. and URRY, J. (1983) *Capital, Labour and the Middle Class*, London, George Allen and Unwin.

ARNOT, M. (1981) 'Culture and political economy: Dual perspectives on women's education', *Educational Analysis*, 3, 1, pp. 97–116.

ARNOT, M. (1982) 'Male hegemony, social class and women's education', *Journal of Education*, 164, 1, pp. 64–89.

ARNOT, M. (1984) 'A feminist perspective on the relationship between family life and school life', *Journal of Education*, 166, 1, pp. 5–25.

Association of Independent Schools Surveys, 1974, 1975, 1978.

AUSTIN, D. (1981) 'Ideology in class society: The contribution of Max Weber', in HILLER, P. (Ed.), *Class and Inequality in Australia: Sociological Perspectives and Research*, Sydney, Harcourt Brace Jovanovich.

AUSTIN, D.J. (1984) *Australian Sociologies*, Sydney, Allen and Unwin.

BARRETT, M. (1980) *Women's Oppression Today: Problems in Marxist Feminist Analysis*, London, Verso Edition.

BRANCA, P. (1975) *Silent Sisterhood: Middle-class Women in the Victorian Home*, London, Croom Helm.

BROOM, L., JONES, F.L. and ZUBRZYCKI, J. (1968) 'Social stratification in Australia', in JACKSON, A.J. (Ed.), *Social Stratification*, Cambridge, Cambridge University Press, 212–233.

CARPENTER, P. (1985a) 'Type of school and academic achievement', *Australian and New Zealand Journal of Sociology*, 21, 2, pp. 219–37.

CARPENTER, P. (1985b) 'Single sex schooling: Girls' academic achievements', *Australian and New Zealand Journal of Sociology*, 21, 3, pp. 456–73.

CONNELL, R.W. (1977) *Ruling Class, Ruling Culture: Studies of Conflict, Power and Hegemony in Australian Life*, Cambridge, Cambridge University Press.

CONNELL, R.W. (1983) 'Logic and politics in theories of class', in *Which Way Is Up? Essays on Class, Sex and Culture*, Sydney, George, Allen and Unwin, 83–97.

CONNELL, R.W. and IRVING, T. (1980) *Class Structure in Australian History*, Sydney, Longman Cheshire.

CONNELL, R.W. and IRVING, T.H. (1981) 'A working paper towards a historical theory of class', in Hiller, P. (Ed.), *Class and Inequality in Australia: Sociological Perspectives and Research*, Sydney, Harcourt Brace Jovanovich.

Connell, R.W., *et al.*, (1982) *Making the Difference: Schools, Families and Social Division*, Sydney, George Allen and Unwin.

Coward, R. (1984) *Female Desire: Women's Sexuality Today*, London, Paladin Books.

de Certeau, M. (1984) *The Practice of Everyday Life*. Trans by S.F. Rendell. Berkeley, Calif., University of California Press.

Encel, S. (1970) *Equality and Authority: A Study of Class Status and Power in Australia*, Melbourne, Cheshire.

Ewen, S. (1976) *Captains of Consciousness: Advertizing, the Social Roots of the Consumer Culture*, New York, McGraw-Hill.

Ewen, S. and Ewen, E. (1979) *Channells of Desire: Mass Images and the Shaping of American Consciousness*, New York, McGraw-Hill.

Ewing, E. (1977) *History of Children's Costume*, London, B.T. Batsford.

Game, A. and Pringle, R. (1979) 'Sexuality and the suburban dream', *Australian and New Zealand Journal of Sociology*, 15, 2, pp. 4–15.

Gramsci, A. (1971) *Selections from the Prison Notebooks*, Ed. and trans by Quintin Hoare and Geoffrey Nowell Smith, New York, International Publishers.

Henriques, J., Hollway, W., Urwin, C., Venn, C. and Walkerdine, V. (1984) *Changing the Subject: Psychology, Social Regulation and Subjectivity*, London, Methuen.

Higley, J., Deacon, D. and Smart, D. (1979) *Elites in Australia*, London, Routledge and Kegan Paul.

Hogan, D. (1982) 'Education and class formation: The peculiarities of the Americans', in Apple, M.W. (Ed.), *Cultural and Economic Reproduction in Education: Essays on Class, Ideology and the State*, London, Routledge and Kegan Paul, 32–79.

Hunt, F.J. (1976) 'Fathers' occupation and the secondary school', in Browne, R.K. and Magin, D.J. (Eds), *Sociology of Education*, Melbourne, Macmillan, 282–92.

Kapferer, J. (1986a) 'Curricula and the reproduction of structural social irregularities', *Curriculum Inquiry*, 16, 1, pp. 5–31.

Kapferer, J. (1986b) 'Schools for the state: Public and private education in Australia', paper presented to AARE conference, Melbourne.

Kapferer, J. (in progress) *The Conspicuous Consumption of Schooling or Keeping Up with the Kidmans*, Adelaide, Flinders University.

Kenway, J. (1981) Position and Opposition: Conflicting Images of Independent Boys' Schools in Australia 1931-1980, unpublished honours thesis, Murdoch University, Perth.

Kenway, J. (1987a) 'Left right out: Australian education and the politics of signification', *Journal of Education and Policy*, 2, 3, pp. 189–203.

Kenway, J. (1987b) High Status Private Schooling and the Production of an Educational Hegemony, unpublished PhD thesis, Murdoch University, Perth.

Kenway, J. (1990) 'Education and the right's discursive politics: Private versus state schooling', in Ball, S. (Ed.), *Foucault and Education*, London, Routledge and Kegan Paul.

KESSLER, S., ASHENDEN, D., CONNELL, B. and DOWSETT, G. (1982) *Ockers and Disco-maniacs: A Discussion on Sex, Gender and Secondary Schooling*, Sydney, Inner City Education Centre.

KESSLER, S., *et al.* (1985) 'Gender relations in secondary schooling', *Sociology of Education*, 58, January, pp. 34–48.

MACDONALD, M. (1979) 'Cultural reproduction: The pedagogy of sexuality', *Screen Education*, Autumn/Winter, 32–33, 1, pp. 143–53.

MACDONALD, M. (1980) 'Socio-cultural reproduction and women's education', in DEEM, R. (Ed.), *Schooling and Women's Work*, London, Routledge and Kegan Paul, 13–25.

MACDONALD, M. (1981) 'Schooling and the reproduction of class and gender relations', in DALE, R., ESLAND, G., FERGUSON, R. and MACDONALD, M. (Eds), *Education and the State*, Lewes, Falmer Press, 159–79.

MARGINSON, S. (1986) 'Are students human capital? The free market theory of education', *ATF Research Notes*, No. 5, pp. 11–44.

Partington, G. (Ed.), (n.d.) *Parents Who Change Schools*, mimeo, Adelaide, Flinders University.

Perth, A Social Atlas (1983) Atlas of Population and Housing, 1981 census, Vol.6, Australian Government Publishing Service.

PRAETZ, H. (1983) 'The non-government schools', in BROWNE, R.K. and FOSTER, L.E.(Eds), *Sociology of Education*, Melbourne, Macmillan, 34–46.

RADFORD, W.C. and WILKES, R.E. (1975) *Schools Leavers in Australia, 1971-1972*, Melbourne, Australian Council for Educational Research.

RUSSELL, R. (1988) *Significant Pauses: The Language of Class and Femininity in Melbourne 1860–1880*, Roger Joyce Lecture, Melbourne University.

Schools in Australia: Report of the Interim Committee for the Australian Schools Commission (1973) Canberra, Australian Government Publishing Service.

SMOLICZ, J.J. and MOODY, J.M. (1978) 'Independent schools as cultural systems', *Melbourne Studies in Education*, pp. 1–66.

TEESE, R. (1981) 'The social function of private schools', in *Melbourne Working Papers*, University of Melbourne, 94–142.

TEESE, R. (1986) 'The traditional structure of the university market in Australia', *Australian University Review*, 1, pp. 17–21.

THEOBOLD, M. (1984) 'Mere accomplishments? Melbourne early ladies schools reconsidered', *History of Education Review*, 13, 2, pp. 15–28.

THEOBOLD, M. (1986) 'The awful fascination of the Presbyterian Ladies College: Reflections on the reform of female education in nineteenth-century Australia', paper presented to the AARE Conference, Melbourne.

THERBORN, G. (1980) *The Ideology of Power and the Power of Ideology*, London, Verso Editions.

THOMPSON, E. (1963) *The Making of the English Working Class*, Harmondsworth, Penguin.

THOMPSON, E.P. (1978) *The Poverty of Theory and Other Essays*, Britain, Merlin Press.

VEBLEN, T. (1970) *The Theory of the Leisure Class*, London, Unwin.

WILD, R. (1974) 'Social stratification or statistical exercise', in EDGAR, D. (Ed.), *Social Change in Australia: Readings in Sociology*, Melbourne, Cheshire, 227–235.

WILD, R. (1978) *Social Stratification in Australia*, Sydney, Allen and Unwin.

WILSON, E. (1985) *Adorned in Dreams: Fashion and Modernity*, London, Virago.
WILLIAMSON, J. (1986) *Consuming Passions: The Dynamics of Popular Culture*, London, Marcon Boyars.
WRIGHT, E.O. (1976) 'Class boundaries in advanced capitalist societies', *New Left Review*, 98, pp. 3–41.
WRIGHT, E.O. (1980) 'Varieties of market conceptions of the class structure', *Politics and Society*, 9, 3, pp. 323–370.

Chapter 5

The Idea of Ethnicity and the Politics of Multicultural Education

Fazal Rizvi

In recent years the idea of ethnicity has acquired an important place in contemporary social and political theory. Sociologists have increasingly utilized it to describe the nature of social relationships in modern pluralist countries. Among some of the more influential writers on the subject Glazer and Moynihan (1975) have argued that ethnicity is a conceptually autonomous notion which occupies a major place in contemporary sociological theory along with, perhaps even ahead of, such categories as class, nation and gender. They (1975, p. 18) have not denied that class and nation are central concepts that should be used to analyze contemporary society, but have insisted that 'it's also true that we must add ethnicity as a major new focus for the mobilization of interests, troublesome both to those who wish to emphasize the primacy of class, and those who wish to emphasize the primacy of nation.'

The idea of ethnicity has not only been accorded the status of theoretical primacy in sociology, it has also provided an important political focus in the development of the public policy of multiculturalism. A succession of government reports in Australia has emphasized the need to celebrate ethnic diversity. Within the policy arena there is now a great deal of talk about identifying the special needs of 'ethnic minorities' in, for example, education, social and community services and housing. For the last two decades political theorists have debated the nature, size and possible impact of 'the ethnic vote', and politicians have tried to ensure that they win it. After a brief, but bitter, political controversy in 1988 concerning its relevance to the formation of Australian national identity (see Collins, 1988), 'multiculturalism' has once again been restored to its status as one of those rare policies which enjoys the support of both major political parties in Australia.

Within the educational sphere there is now pressure to ensure that teachers and administrators are aware of the distinct language and culture of 'ethnic minorities', and of the implications of these for teaching in schools. In some urban areas there has been consideration of the implications for religious instruction and co-educational schooling now that children of diverse backgrounds attend Australian schools. Teachers and curriculum advisers have been asked to ensure that curriculum materials are not ethnocentric. To be consistent with the policy of multiculturalism, schools have been encouraged to provide courses in ethnic cultures and ethnic (community) languages. Not only the much criticized Galbally Report (1978), but also the more recent documents of government policy in Australia, such as the *Agenda for Multicultural Australia* (1989), have emphasized the importance of rethinking our educational policies so that *all* schools begin to develop in *all* children what Galbally has referred to as a 'multicultural attitude' (p. 107).

All expressions of the public policy of multiculturalism embody an understanding of the idea of ethnicity — the way it manifests itself in social relations, the way social life is organized around it, the significance it has for the political economy of the nation and the part it plays in the organization of politics. While there are different conceptions of ethnicity in sociological literature, incorporating differing assumptions concerning its role in the structuring of political life, it is suggested here that successive official policies of multiculturalism rest on a particular understanding of the idea of ethnicity. Though it is seldom made explicit, it is an idea that informs the various practices of multicultural education that have been developed over the past decade. However, the assumptions upon which this idea of ethnicity is based are flawed on a number of counts, and generate a view of multiculturalism that rests on an inadequate account of social relations, constituting an unsatisfactory basis for developing an egalitarian politics. Three of the most influential accounts of ethnicity found in the literature will be examined. While these accounts, of Van den Berghe (1981), Barth (1969) and Glazer and Moynihan (1975), are rooted in different theoretical perspectives, they are nevertheless based on a similar set of assumptions and emerge from a common problematic. It is these assumptions which remain implicit in most formulations of the policy of multiculturalism and practices of multicultural education.

It is commonplace to think of ethnicity as involving communal ways of thinking, feeling and acting that constitute the essence of culture. The three accounts of ethnicity discussed in this chapter all take cultural identity and affectivity to be the defining characteristic of ethnicity. Equally, however, the three accounts take culture at its face value, as something objectively given and abstracted from its historical and structural circumstances. In contrast to this widely held view, I shall argue that culture does not exist in a social vacuum, nor is it fixed or unchanging. Ethnic patterns, insofar as they involve cultural traditions, are related to historical and material contexts in which they are embedded. Accounts of Van den Berghe (1981), Barth (1969), and Glazer and Moynihan (1975) are flawed for a number of reasons, but most significantly because they define ethnic groups without reference to, or in opposition to, the class structure in the social formation of which the identified persons live.

This limitation has major implications for multiculturalism and multicultural education. For one thing, it implies that the promotion of multiculturalism, in its present and official guise, has been hegemonic and ideological because it has served to defuse and obscure the issues of class inequality and other patterns of social relations in Australia. Given this criticism, multicultural education, which in its popular form involves no more than the simplistic cataloguing of superficial ethnic differences, in the hope of developing a 'multicultural attitude' in children, is essentially misguided. A sounder approach to multicultural education would involve a study of the nature of the specific social relationships between ethnic groups within the broader historical and political context. Moreover, instead of reifying ethnicity as a static category and creating the illusion that there is something ineffable about ethnic phenomena, teachers should encourage students to understand cultural relations in terms of their material and structural sources.

The 'Revival' of Ethnicity

There can be little doubt that 'ethnicity' as an explanatory category, as well as a focus for policy development, has acquired a pervasive presence in Australia. This raises questions of why and how this widespread and apparently escalating role of ethnicity in social life has come about. It is important to note that the concept of an 'ethnic group' has its origin in cultural anthropology, and that it has in recent years undergone considerable transformation, especially since sociologists and political theorists have begun to use the concept to discuss issues located in urban industrial contexts. The concern of anthropologists to document differences between cultural traditions has now been replaced by the concern of sociologists who attempt to highlight ethnic differences in urban locations. But while anthropologists have documented differences between societies which may have never met each other, sociologists study ethnic groups which allegedly define themselves in terms of their economic and social relations with the other groups which comprise the society.

According to Smith (1981), the current interest in ethnicity can be viewed as a 'revival' which has emerged as a result of the recognition by liberal theorists that their cosmopolitan ideals, which involved the rationalistic expectation that cultural differences would disappear in modern society, were misguided. Smith argues that liberal theorists had generally taken the view that 'as mankind [sic] moved from a primitive, tribal stage of social organization towards large scale industrial societies, the various primordial ties of religion, language ethnicity and race which divided it would gradually but inexorably lose their hold and disappear' (Smith, 1981, p. 2). With mass migration and with the expansion of industrial capitalism, it was expected that a time would come when it would be necessary to organize production and trade on a global scale. The rational use of labour would mean that old cultural differences and political divisions would become increasingly irrelevant. The growth of mass tourism, the expansion in communication systems and the standardization of mass culture would inevitably, so thought the liberals, lead to a global cosmopolitan culture. According to Smith (1981), however, this pre-shadowed dissolution of ethnicity has not occurred. Indeed, he maintains, if anything, modern history has demonstrated that economic and industrial trends have tended to reinforce ethnic and cultural divisions.

The assimilationist and 'melting pot' integrationist policies which Australia followed for most of this century were broadly consistent with the liberal ideals identified by Smith. The policy of assimilation was deceptively simple and was couched in liberal democratic terms. It had stipulated that all Australians, regardless of their origin, were gradually to attain the same manner of living, come to share a common culture, live as members of a single Australian community enjoying the same rights and privileges, accepting the same responsibilities and observing the same customs (see Foster, 1988, Ch. 4). All Australians would be influenced by the same beliefs, hopes and loyalties. Post-World War II immigrants from Europe, whose numbers have now significantly changed the cultural landscape of Australia, were thus expected to assimilate into the social and economic structures that existed at that time. Towards the end of the 1960s, however, it was clear that assimilation was not as easily attainable as policy-makers had thought. Successive studies (e.g. Jupp, 1966; Martin, 1972) clearly showed that not only was it difficult for migrants to shed their cultural traditions but also that many did not wish to do so.

It was also recognized that, contrary to the government rhetoric which claimed that migrants had an equal opportunity to take an equal and informed part in the creation and maintenance of Australian society, almost invariably they occupied low paid, low status and insecure jobs at the lower end of the occupational structure, jobs which many native-born Australians were reluctant to accept (Birrell and Birrell, 1981, p. 144).

Lacking adequate educational support facilities, non-English-speaking immigrants found, moreover, that their disadvantages were reproduced for their children. Widespread racism and xenophobic attitudes of native-born Australians represented a further structural barrier to the migrants wishing to participate in Australian life.

By the mid-1960s the ideology of assimilation was clearly discredited. Far from promoting liberal and egalitarian ideals of a cosmopolitan society, assimilation represented enforced Anglo conformity. It meant a denial of any significance to migrant cultures and life-styles. This recognition led in the late 1960s to experiments with the policy of integration, imported to Australia from the United States where the Johnson presidency had earlier rejected assimilationist ideas in favour of a 'melting pot' ideology. The central objective of the 'melting pot' integrationist policy in Australia was to encourage the creation of a society in which different cultural groups, including Anglo-Australians, participated and contributed *full and equally* in the development of the nation's social, political and economic institutions. The rhetoric of integration suggested a view of intercultural relations in which all groups lived with each other in a climate of mutual accommodation. The most fundamental problem with this position was, however, that equal participation in a society in which political structures and institutions were essentially derived from Anglo-Saxon traditions could hardly have been possible. It was recognized that the dice, so to speak, with which the 'melting pot' game was played was already loaded in favour of the existing power structures. In the end integration, while representing a shift in policy away from the emphasis on Anglo conformity in cultural terms, remained assimilationist, for it required from migrants their complete political integration into a predominantly Anglo system.

Integration, in no less a subtle way than assimilation, emphasized the liberal ideal of a homogeneous Australian community. The need to develop a culturally and politically indivisible nation continued to be stressed. The assumption was that the Australian community had to have a single uniform culture. It is this assumption that has been challenged by those who see in the notion of ethnicity a central focus for a more satisfactory social and political analysis, an analysis which leads them to advocate multiculturalism. The policy of multiculturalism rejects the idea of cultural homogeneity as either possible or desirable. It is argued by the proponents of multiculturalism that ethnicity is a natural phenomenon of human society; therefore, policies promoting cultural homogeneity cannot succeed even in modern industrial societies which are characterized by their preference for large and uniform institutions. Indeed, the need for cultural identification in such societies is even greater than in traditional societies. Ethnicity is thus thought to be a permanent feature of human society, which a policy responding to cultural diversity would do well to recognize.

Ethnicity and Multicultural Education

The policy of multiculturalism in Australia has been articulated through a series of reports. While it has undergone some minor changes, it has emphasized three key principles: the right of ethnic groups to maintain their cultural identity; the promotion of equality of opportunity; and the need to ensure social cohesion. It is in line with these principles that practices of multicultural education have developed.

The idea of multicultural education is perhaps most clearly stated in the 1982 report of the Australian Council of Population and Ethnic Affairs, *Multiculturalism for All Australians* (the Zubrzycki Report). This report insists that 'the means to achieve multiculturalism are to be found in two areas: public policy and community attitude' (p. 13). In the area of public policy it argues that 'multiculturalism must be based on support for a common core of institutions, rights and obligation' and that the principle of a common national identity must be recognized. Social cohesion is thus regarded as a unifying political value around, and within the framework of, which diverse ethnic groups are encouraged to celebrate their cultural traditions. It is in the area of the development of desirable community attitudes that multicultural education is thought to be of crucial importance. Multicultural education is thought to be 'primarily affective, about attitudes, and only instrumentally cognitive'. The Zubrzycki Report (1982, p. 17) claims that multiculturalism is a 'way of looking at Australian society, and involves living together with an awareness of cultural diversity. We accept our differences and appreciate a variety of lifestyles rather than expect everyone to fit into a standardized pattern.'

Multicultural education, then, is largely a matter of developing appropriate attitudes of tolerance and intercultural understanding in all Australians. The Zubrzycki Report provides a range of arguments in support of this view of multicultural education. In instrumental terms it suggests that the 'recognition of, together with assistance for maintaining, different identities result in greater self-confidence and self-esteem for individuals and their families.' Ignorance, the report contends, 'breeds suspicion and intolerance', and 'multicultural education is one of the keys to achieving a society in which cultural differences are understood and appreciated' (p. 18). Zubrzycki's thinking rests on the assumption that maintaining and nurturing cultural and linguistic heritages within Australia would inevitably lead to greater communication between members of one cultural group and those of others. For Zubrzycki, the school system has an important role to play in ensuring that children develop a 'multicultural attitude'. He argues that 'The Australian school system, despite regional and sectional variations, plays a central role in a multicultural Australia. Through the curricula, it provides a common body of knowledge that forms part of what it means to have an Australian culture. It also provides an opportunity for shared experiences between children of different cultural backgrounds' (1982, p. 18). The report argues that intercultural understanding, tolerance of and respect for cultural patterns other than one's own are fundamental conditions of all truly multicultural classrooms.

The Zubrzycki Report's general analysis of multicultural education has been largely shared by federal and state Departments of Education in Australia. Through the Schools Commission, the federal government has ensured that multiculturalism remains high on the agendas of the state governments and schools when they come to make decisions about their educational policy. Though these have become smaller in size in recent years, up to the mid-1980s substantial funds were made available to support initiatives in multicultural education. These initiatives can be broadly classified into five interrelated categories.

First, Education Departments in all states have encouraged studies of ethnic cultures. Programs based on the comparative study of cultures have now become commonplace in schools. Through the study of ethnic cultures, argues Smolicz (1984), not only have migrant children come to value their ethnicity but they have begun to understand and respect cultural heritages other than their own. In this way ethnic studies as an area of curriculum is as relevant to the Anglo-Australian children as it is to the migrants. Smolicz (1984, p. 130) argues that since ethnicity is always 'dormant', ethnic studies can help activate a migrant child's normative identification with his heritage. Smolicz (1984, pp. 133–4) maintains that 'ethnic heritage, in its folklore, religious and artistic aspects and customs, also serves to strengthen identity.'

The second set of educational initiatives under the rubric of multicultural education has emphasized the need to have all school practices, curricular as well as administrative, reflect a multicultural attitude. This way of looking at multicultural education is summed up by an early report of the Schools Commission:

> the multicultural reality of Australia needs to be reflected in the school curricula — languages, social studies, history, literature,

> the arts and crafts — in staffing and in school organization. While these changes are particularly important to undergird the self-esteem of migrant children they also have application for all Australian children growing up in a society which could be greatly enriched through a wider sharing in the variety of cultural heritages now present in it. (Schools Commission, 1975, quoted in Bullivant, 1984, p. 60)

A multicultural curriculum is thus seen as embodying an overall attitude to be developed in all children, as well as a value which must be embedded in all educational practices. Lippman (1981, p. 24) argues that '... multiculturalism is a perspective which needs to infuse all parts of teacher education, in the selection of educational materials, in the examples chosen for illustration, and in the choice of resource personnel.'

A third initiative in multicultural education has meant that the support structure for teaching English as a second language to migrant children, and adults alike, has been significantly strengthened. The Zubrzycki Report (1982, p. 19) affirms its support for English as the pre-eminent language of public affairs in Australia, and argues that intercultural understanding cannot occur unless English is established as the principal means of communication between members of different cultural groups. Without appropriate skills in English, it is argued, migrants cannot fully participate in Australian cultural life and are therefore denied equality of occupational and social opportunity.

A fourth initiative in multicultural education involves the promotion of the teaching of community languages and bilingualism. The Zubrzycki Report (1982) argues that if 'language is the deepest manifestation of any culture and enables the expression of features unique to that culture, the preservation of cultural heritage entails the retention of minority languages' (p. 19). The rationale for bilingual education is backed up by various research findings (see Phillips and Houston, 1984, Chs 8 and 9) which demonstrate that the children who maintain their mother language are likely to be more successful in their schooling.

A fifth initiative in multicultural education is related to the developments of ethnic schools which, while they have always existed, have only recently received institutional support. 'Ethnic school' is a very general term, which refers to a range of programs, in addition to children's normal school schedule, which vary from a few hours on Saturday mornings to longer weekly periods. Kaldor (1981, p. 11) claims that 'the ethnic school movement has been gathering considerable momentum in recent years, as an increasing number of parents and ethnic communities have felt the need to initiate action to ensure that their children maintain their ancestral languages and develop literacy in their mother tongues, while also gaining some knowledge of their culture.' The debate on the role of ethnic schools is a complex one. There are those who see ethnic schools as an additional institutional burden on children. Kaldor, on the other hand, sees them as a useful back-up system for multicultural education in the state schools and a communication link with members of ethnic groups.

To sum up, multicultural education is seen as involving a complex of three educational objectives:

1 to promote intercultural understanding, 'tolerance' and respect for cultures other than one's own through improved communication between members of different ethnic groups;
2 to encourage maintenance of the culture and linguistic heritage of all ethnic groups in Australia; and
3 to devise administrative structures and programs which result in the provision of greater equality of educational and social opportunities to non-English-speaking children in Australia.

These educational goals and initiatives, while they represent separate strands and forces in education, are nevertheless seen as being integral parts of multicultural education.

Various attempts have been made in most schools in Australia to achieve these goals of multicultural education through initiatives such as offering courses in ethnic studies, infusing the entire curriculum with 'a multicultural perspective', providing greater institutional support for teaching English as a second language, community languages and, to a lesser extent, ethnic schools. However, the extent to which these initiatives have made any difference to school practices remains contentious. According to Foster (1983, p. 436), while at a rhetorical level multiculturalism has found some acceptance and support in schools, institutional support for multicultural programs and services remains at a fairly low level. Others, such as Jayasuriya (1987), believe that multicultural education has become entrenched in Australian schools, and that ethnicity is now recognized as indispensable to thinking about social relations in schools. Certainly, according to *The National Agenda for a Multicultural Australia*, ethnicity is a major determinant of social experience in Australia and schools have increasingly recognized this fact and sought to incorporate in into their thinking about curriculum and pedagogy.

But in the development of the policy of multiculturalism, how is the idea of ethnicity conceptualized? In what way does ethnicity define social experiences? And how does multiculturalism serve groups to maintain their ethnicity? While it is true that there are no uniform answers to these questions, there appear to be certain common assumptions implicit in official statements of multiculturalism and the practices of multicultural education to which they give rise. These assumptions are largely derived from a number of prominent theories of ethnicity.

Van den Berghe's Primordialism

Van den Berghe (1981) develops his analysis of the ethnic phenomenon by rejecting both the assimilationist ideology and what he refers to as the liberal tradition in race and ethnic relations. According to Van den Berghe (1981, pp. 2–3), the liberal tradition in ethnic and race relations is constituted by the following propositions:

1 All humans are members of a single species, and there are no biologically meaningful subspecies within it. 'Races' are social constructs corresponding to no biological reality.
2 Differences between human populations are smaller than within them, and such differences as exist (e.g. in I.Q. test performance) are largely if not entirely the product of the social environment.
3 Racism and ethnocentrocism are irrational, dysfunctional attitudes, if not downright aberrations, to which certain rigid, authoritarian types of personality are especially prone. Such attitudes must be combatted through a social therapy promoting equal status contact between groups.

Van den Berghe argues that the liberal tradition in social science rests on the mistaken assumption that all human behaviour can be explained entirely in terms of the cultural environment. Impressed by the attempts of E.O. Wilson (1975) and others to integrate the biological and social sciences into a single evolutionary paradigm, Van den Berghe suggests that in studying human behaviour we should look at 'the genetic evolution of man [sic], as one species of organism interacting with many others in a physical and biotic milieu *as well as* in the cultural environment of his [sic] own making . . .' (Van den Berghe, 1981, p. 3).

Using this sociobiological paradigm, Van den Berghe contends that assimilationist and melting pot ideologies are fundamentally misguided because they rest on the assumption that cultural diversity can be eradicated through the forces of urbanization, industrialization and modernization. Cultural diversity is, for Van den Berghe, a necessary condition of human evolution and adaptation. He maintains that as for all other animals, human genes are selected in an adaptive response to a multiplicity of ecological conditions. Our natural selection grows out of our specifically human capabilities, the configuration of which we call culture. Van den Berghe insists that culture is part and parcel of nature and cannot be dissociated from it. He (1981, p. 11) goes on to argue that:

> Like other animal societies, human societies are held together by the self-interest of their individual members. This self-interest is best measured in terms of reproductive success, for it is through differential reproduction that biological evolution of all life forms takes place. Individuals, human or nonhuman, interact competitively or co-operatively to maximize their individual fitness. They do so in three basic ways: through kin selection, reciprocity and coercion. The human variations on these three basic mechanisms are much more complex than those observable in other species, but they are not categorically different.

On the basis of this view of human behaviour, ethnicity, according to Van den Berghe, has something to do with kinship, a deeply rooted biological affiliation, which is often referred to in the social science literature as primordialist. According to Van den Berghe, it is this kinship and biological affiliation that bring people together to have common cultural attributes like language, religion, rituals and other customs, and that these are constitutive of ethnicity.

Humans, like other social animals, claims Van den Berghe (1981, p. 35), are biologically predisposed to be nepotistic because, by favouring kin, they maximize their 'inclusive fitness'. This notion gives rise to the ideas of physical boundaries of territory and social boundaries, violations of which explain mistrust, avoidance and, not infrequently, open conflict over scarce resources. Van den Berghe argues that even in industrialized mass societies of today, the urge to maintain collectivities and social boundaries on the basis of biological descent remains strong. He contends that 'a wide variety of ethnic markers are used to define collectivities of descent, but their choice is not capricious' (Van den Berghe, 1981, p. 35). Van den Berghe thus insists that in recent years ethnicity has not been so much 'revived' as has always persisted, for its existence is an objective matter, governed by biological laws. While ethnicity may be something variable, situationally defined or subjectively expressed, it nevertheless has a natural foundation in the biological make-up of human beings. Nepotism and ethnocentrism, however expressed, are therefore 'biologically evolved mechanisms serving the pursuit of individual self-interest' (Van den Berghe, 1981, p. xii).

There are a number of criticisms that can be made of Van den Berghe's account of ethnicity; four will be mentioned here. The first criticism relates to the inadequacies of the theoretical framework which Van den Berge assumes. The epistemological status of sociobiology is, at best, dubious. Sociobiology claims to be science, but its claims are essentially unfalsifiable. If we accept Popper's (1972) view that science is demarcated from non-science on the grounds that scientific propositions are falsifiable and non-scientific propositions are not, then sociobiology turns out to be an explanatory scheme which cannot be empirically refuted. As Burnley, Encel and McCall (1985, p. 26) point out, '... we cannot disprove that lurking deep in the human bioprogram is the imperative of inclusive fitness. Equally, though, Van den Berghe cannot show that it is, except circumstantially because it might work out that way and some people say they believe it....' For every example that may be provided to support the contentions of biologically grounded ethnic behaviour, there are equally good counter-examples.

The claim of Van den Berghe that ethnicity is an innate human characteristic which manifests itself differently in different cultural contexts would also appear to be vacuous of any explanatory significance. For unless we know exactly how gene sharing and the like occurs in conflict over our scarce resources (Van den Berghe, 1981, p. 38), we cannot explain specific instances of ethnic competition in terms of sociobiology. Van den Berghe provides an elaborate taxonomy of the stages of ethnic relations (pp. 40ff). Such a scheme suggests a theory of social stratification which is not examined in any detail by Van den Berghe. But, as Burnley, Encel and McCall (1985, p. 25) argue, Van den Berghe's argument can be applied equally to other classificatory schemes in respect of social differentiation, such as caste. The biological processes which Van den Berghe describes 'are similar because they serve human populations to distinguish one from the other, on a micro or macro level' (Burnley, Encel and McCall, 1985, p. 25). Van den Berghe has not identified the distinctive features which might be constitutive of ethnicity.

Having stated boldly that nepotism, ethnocentrocism, self-interest and kin identification are innate human characteristics, Van den Berghe is careful to assert that his is a scientific theory, rather than one which is concerned with making value judgments on the characteristics he finds universal in all human behaviour. He claims (Van den Berghe, 1981, p. xii) that his description amounts to a 'statement that the behaviour of most people most of the time is consistent with that paradigm, whether one likes it or not.' Van den Berghe's account evidently rests on the assumption that it is possible to distinguish facts from values. This is a highly questionable assumption. Most post-empiricist philosophers of social science (see Bernstein, 1976) now admit that not only are descriptions of social phenomena necessarily informed by categories of evaluation and appraisal, but also that sociological descriptions have ideological implications. Concepts such as ethnicity cannot be regarded as purely 'scientific' constructs; for every sociological concept and theory has an ideological force by reason of its influence upon the actions of human beings in their everyday life. As Bottomore (1966, p. 20) points out, '... it may have this influence either because it is impregnated with a social doctrine, or because, while it excludes any immediate doctrinal influence, it nevertheless draws attention to and emphasizes certain features of social life and neglects others, and thus persuades men to conceive of their condition and their possible future in one set of terms rather than another.' By describing human behaviour as biologically nepotistic and ethnocentric, Van den Berghe also seems to rule out the possibility of political action through which nepotism and ethnocentricity might be overcome.

On his sociobiological account Van den Berghe assumes inequality to be a permanent feature of the human condition. It is this assumption that leads him to argue that social and cultural hierarchies are inevitable (Van den Berghe, 1981, p. 38). The ideological implications of this claim are immense, as de Lepervanche (1984b) has explained. In Van den Berghe's view ethnic inequalities and social stratification appear as natural, 'biologically given' phenomena over which humans have no power. But if ethnocentricity and ethnic nepotism are, at their foundation, biological, then there seems little point in spending millions of dollars of public money in an attempt to reduce, through educational programs, levels of prejudice that currently exist in a plural society!

Van den Berghe's biological determinism can, however, be challenged. While what human beings can and cannot do may be governed, at a very general level, by our biological make-up, this does not mean that how social groups relate to each other is also determined by biological laws. Social behaviour is produced and reproduced by human beings and may, therefore, be radically transformed. Moreover, our social relations should be viewed not so much as biologically defined but as conceptualized and maintained by us within historical and structural conditions in which we find ourselves. The fact is that inequality is a social relation between individuals or groups of people and like all other social relations can be transformed. The possibility of altruism is as strong among human beings as are the possibilities of nepotism and self-interest (see Midgley, 1980).

Barth's Interpretive Account of Ethnicity

One of the most influential critiques of the primordial conception of ethnicity, as represented by the work of Van den Berghe, can be found in Barth's introductory essay to his *Ethnic Groups and Boundaries* (1969). Barth emphatically rejects the views that ethnic groups have a primordial quality, that is, the characteristic of being biologically self-perpetuating, and that they share fundamental cultural values, realized in overt unity in various cultural forms. His main objection to the primordial view is that it begs all the critical questions concerning the place of ethnicity in human society and culture; for, 'while purporting to give an ideal type model of a recurring empirical form, it implies a preconceived view of what are the significant factors in the genesis, structure and functions of such groups' (Barth, 1969, p. 11). Barth argues that the primordial view also allows us to assume that ethnic boundary maintenance is unproblematic and that it occurs in relative cultural and social isolation, 'mainly in response to local ecologic factors, through a history of adaptation by invention and selective borrowing' (Barth, 1969, p. 11).

In Barth's view, what is missing from the primordial view of ethnicity is any account of how individuals come together to see each other as sharing a common culture, and others as having a distinctively different culture. Barth accepts the view that the classification of persons and local groups as members of an ethnic group depends on their exhibiting the traits of a particular culture, but denies the assumption that this is something that can only be 'judged objectively by the ethnographic observer, regardless of the categories and the prejudices of the actor' (Barth, 1969, p. 12). For Barth, what is of crucial importance is the subjective interpretive dimension of ethnic classification.

Barth sees ethnic groups as a form of self-identified social organization, which has a membership which not only identifies itself but is also identified by others as constituting a cultural category distinguishable from other categories of the same order. According to Barth, his definition enables ethnicity to be seen as involving a dynamic relationship, for actors use ethnic identities to categorize themselves and others for purposes of social interaction. Barth maintains that:

> It is important to recognize that although ethnic categories take cultural differences into account, we can assume no simple one-to-one relationship between ethnic units and cultural similarities and differences. The features that are taken into account are not the sum of 'objective' differences, *but only those which the actors themselves regard as significant*. Not only do ecologic variations

> mark and exaggerate differences; some cultural features are used by the actors as signals and emblems of differences, others are ignored, and in some relationships radical differences are played down and denied. (Barth, 1969, p. 14; emphasis added)

In contrast to Van den Berghe's analysis, Barth is concerned with the social processes by which groups identify themselves and maintain their difference from other groups. Barth explains these processes by reference to his concept of boundary maintenance. He argues that it is the 'ethnic boundary that defines the group, not the cultural stuff that it encloses. The boundaries to which we must give attention are of course social boundaries, though they may have territorial counterparts. If a group maintains its identity when members interact with others, this entails criteria for determining membership and ways of signalling membership and exclusion' (Barth, 1969, p. 15). Boundaries between ethnic groups are thus self-ascribed and represent the collective act of a group of people to recognize and maintain in their interaction with other groups their distinctiveness in terms of various cultural criteria, such as emotional, symbolic and linguistic. This definition presupposes not only an awareness but also a degree of contact and interaction between ethnic groups. Ethnicity is understood as a reactive concept. If we accept Barth's analysis of ethnicity, then research into ethnic relations must begin with people's perception of a sense of difference in relation to others who are perceived to be 'not us'. The analytical focus thus shifts from an attempt to identify some allegedly 'objective' cultural traits to an investigation of the social boundaries that are drawn on the basis of the recognition and maintenance of cultural differences.

Barth's analysis of ethnicity is certainly an advance on Van den Berghe's sociobiological account. Barth's view of ethnicity represents a rejection of Van den Berghe's static primordial classification of cultural traditions and traits. The theorists writing in the tradition of Barth's work correctly stress that ethnicity is reactive; an allegedly objective basis of differentiation between groups is rightly rejected in favour of a view which emphasizes a 'subjective component' in the criteria used in the process of categorization. As Wallman (1986) points out, the ascription of ethnicity is the recognition of 'significant difference'; and the normative basis for what counts as significant, or the difference, is neither set absolutely nor defined by reference to some supposedly objective set of properties. In an earlier work Wallman (1979, p. 6) contends that ethnicity is 'culture in-adaptation-to, in-response-to, up-against "others" within a context shared by both sides of the ethnic boundary, and it is shaped by the aims, constraints and opportunities of that context as they pertain to each side.' Wallman argues, moreover, that no a priori assumptions can be made about what cultural and phenotypical criteria will be used in the process of ascribing ethnicity. For example, two persons who possess similar phenotypical and cultural features and are engaged in social interaction may not necessarily attribute any social significance to this similarity. They would not, therefore, share any ethnic identity.

While the interpretivist approach of Barth and his followers might seem promising, it too is flawed. To begin with, Barth's, and particularly Wallman's, definitions of ethnicity are far too general to be analytically useful. The use of 'ethnicity' to refer generally to the perception of group difference means that the term is being made to refer to any criteria by which one might distinguish one group from another. Barth's definition would allow us to describe any group which defines itself as being different in some way from some other group, and as sharing some identity, as constituting an ethnic group. On this view, liberal voters, country women, Rotarians and the like can all describe themselves as belonging to some ethnic group. If, however, we insist that an ethnic group is a culturally distinct minority with some specific attributes, then we have isolated a criterion which is not self-ascribed. This would be contradictory to Barth's insistence that ethnicity be subjectively defined.

Barth and Wallman are correct in emphasizing the importance of the subjective dimension in the recognition of ethnicity, but the scope of their analysis is limited by its predominant focus on interpretive perspectives of individual actors. They provide no theoretical scheme which might account for the *construction* of the subjective meanings that individuals might have of their ethnicity (Mearns, 1989). It is true that human behaviour must initially be understood in terms of the meaning and significance that that behaviour has for the individual. But this understanding is necessarily limited, for to stop at this juncture is to fail to ask further questions about the origins, causes and results of people accepting certain interpretations of their behaviour and social life as being valid. It is also to neglect problems of social conflict and social change that arise when we attempt to understand the significance of our social classifications. Interpretivist accounts such as the one provided by Barth and Wallman are generally incapable of explaining the macro-social, political and cultural structures within which self-ascription of ethnicity makes sense. Discussing the tradition of interpretive social science, Carr and Kemmis (1983, pp. 94–5) correctly observe:

> Because it emphasizes the 'subjective meanings' of social action and the way in which social reality is constructed out of a plurality of 'definitions of the situations', the interpretive approach

> cannot help but neglect questions about the relationships between individuals' interpretations and action and external factors and circumstances. But while it may be true that social reality is constructed and maintained through the interactions of individuals, it is also the case that the range of possible interpretations of reality that are open to individuals is limited and constrained by the structural elements of a particular social order. Social reality is not simply something that is structured and sustained by the interpretations and perceptions of individuals — it is also a major factor in determining the kind of interpretations of reality that are appropriate for a particular group of individuals to possess.

Carr and Kemmis (1983, p. 96) argue that the interpretivist approach is also mistaken because in emphasizing the fundamental importance of grasping the subjective meanings that individuals have of their own ways of viewing the social world, it 'offers no way of identifying and examining the ideological character that these meanings and actions possess, and the purposes they serve in social life.' The interpretivist view provides us with no criteria for distinguishing those ways of looking at social phenomena which are sytematically distorted and those which are not: genuine insights and illusions, rationalization and deceptions are placed on the same plane.

The place ethnicity has, and how it is related to, and located within, economic and political circumstances of a plural society like Australia are highly complex questions. The issue of how ethnicity is linked to questions of material inequalities and questions of class structure is no less problematic. But the crucial point here is that an analysis of ethnicity and of the processes of social categorization which is based solely on the interpretive understanding of actors themselves is unlikely to be theoretically useful. Nor would these self-understandings, unrelated as they often are to broader structural questions, provide sufficient basis for critical judgments or evaluation of the theoretical work that the notion is required to do in the development of official policies of multiculturalism.

A good example of the limitations of the interpretivist approach to an analysis of ethnicity can be found in what Zubrzycki has to say about ethnicity in Australia. He maintains that Australians belong to an ethnic group in similar manner to their membership of football clubs. Just as it is possible for a person to be an Australian as well as a supporter of a football team, similarly a person may be both an Australian and, say, a Greek. This analogy is fundamentally misleading; yet it is an inevitable consequence of the interpretivist view of ethnicity. Ethnicity is related to the structures of the state in a way that membership of a football club is not. It has economic and political significance in a way that a private preference for a football club does not. Ethnicity cannot be 'privatized'.

Another example of the limitations of the interpretivist approach to ethnicity can be found in the work of Issacs (1976), who studied a number of Sydney schools with large numbers of Greek immigrants. Her book, *Greek Children in Sydney*, is an interesting catalogue of Anglo-Australian attitudes towards Greek migrants and attempts of Greek-Australians to understand their ethnicity. An impression that is conveyed by Issacs' account is that, as an ethnic group, Greek-Australians are generally uncertain about their ethnicity and that they lack any continuous, conscious sense of identity as a common collectivity. This should not be surprising, for there are such profound differences among Greek-Australians along class, occupational, religious and regional lines (and also how they view their life in Australia) that to speak of a homogeneous Greek ethnicity would seem to be totally inappropriate. Furthermore, Issacs' attempt at developing primary categories of explanation by reference to individuals' own interpretations means that she ignores the underlying historical and structural processes within which such interpretations are located. Arguably, these processes set the parameters which are instrumental in defining class boundaries as well as ethnic divisions, often created to serve particular state functions. Since a recognition of these parameters, as they manifest themselves in Australia, is not necessarily evident in individuals' own understanding of their social behaviour, Issacs' analysis of Greek ethnicity is essentially flawed.

Glazer and Moynihan's Account of Ethnicity

Both Van den Berghe and Barth either ignore class issues or present their accounts of ethnicity in opposition to, or parallel to, class analysis. For Barth and the interpretivists generally the primary object of analysis is self-ascribed cultural differentiation of ethnic groups. Ethnic beliefs and behaviour are assessed in terms of their cultural distinctiveness, but the issue of how such beliefs and behaviour may be linked to class relations, and located in economic and political structures, is not explored. Indeed, as de Lepervanche (1980, p. 28) points out, 'the vast bulk of the material on ethnicity is exceptionally empirical in emphasis and implicitly or explicitly critical of class analysis.' Even when Barth mentions systems of stratification and power, he refers to these phenomena as being conceptually linked to values and culture, rather than to unequal social and economic relationships. The functionalist assumptions in his account become evident when he claims that 'stratified poly-ethnic systems exist where groups are characterized by differential control of assets that are valued by all groups in the system' (Barth, 1969, p. 27). In Barth's analysis, moreover, it is implicitly assumed that inequalities are natural and necessary means of ethnic differentiation, a mechanism which is seen as the organizing principle of modern social life.

In contrast to Barth's analysis, Van den Berghe's account represents not so much an obscuration of class issues as an assertion that class and ethnic analyses of social relations are logically independent of each other. Van den Berghe (1981, p. 244) warns that 'any attempt to reduce ethnicity to class is a serious distortion of reality' and claims that any '*a priori* theoretical position that one is more important than the other is untenable.' According to Van den Berghe, while social classes are grouped according to common material interests, ethnic groups are organized by real or positive common descent — ultimately, on the basis of common genetic interests. Van den Berghe thus assumes that biologically grounded cultural interests are logically distinguishable from those interests which are social and political. This is a fundamental assumption which permeates almost all recent analyses of ethnicity. It is an assumption upon which the current official theory of multiculturalism in Australia, a theory which celebrates cultural diversity and yet requires political integration of migrants into existing structures, is based. It is argued below that this distinction between the cultural and the political is untenable. But first it is appropriate to examine briefly a highly influential argument of Glazer and Moynihan (1975), who see in ethnicity the emergence of a social category which supersedes class.

Glazer and Moynihan argue that just as class was an idea which helped people conceptualize their social and political identity in the nineteenth century, in the twentieth century it is ethnicity which is the organizing principle around which people define their identity. As a political idea, Glazer and Moynihan (1975, p. 20) claim, 'ethnicity in our time has spread around the world with the curious consequence of sameness and difference that is encountered with other such phenomena.' No longer, they contend, is class normally the basis of group mobilization; rather, it is ethnicity which has come to have strategic efficacy as a basis for asserting claims and negotiating with governments. In the past it was through an identification with a particular class that groups expressed not only their interest but also their conflicts. But, argue Glazer and Moynihan, one element of the present situation is that 'interest is pursued effectively by ethnic groups today as well as interest-defined groups; indeed, perhaps it can be pursued even more effectively. As against class-based forms of social identification and conflict — which of course continue to exist — we have been surprised by the persistence and salience of ethnic-based forms of social identification and conflict' (Glazer and Moynihan, 1975, p. 7). An ethnic group is recognized in terms of its having a distinct set of interests and needs which require collective organization in order that they be pursued and defended. Ethnicity comes to have a political dimension. But as a social, and explanatory, category, it is quite distinct from class. Glazer and Moynihan claim that class analysis is not capable of explaining the kind of conflict that now exists between migrant groups and the dominant majority group in modern industrial societies. Not all interests are determined by economic position, and increasingly in the modern world interests that guide people into social action derive their significance from specific ethnic attachment.

Glazer and Moynihan (1975, p. 19) suggest that an important reason for the pervasive salience of ethnicity and its effectiveness in advancing the interests of particular groups is that 'it involves more than interests'. Quoting Bell, they (1975, p. 19) argue the 'ethnicity has become more salient (than class) because it can combine an interest with an affective tie.' On the other hand, in the case of class, 'what had once been an ideology had now become almost largely an interest.' This is a highly dubious argument, as Eipper (1983) has demonstrated. Eipper (1983, p. 433) has correctly pointed out that class is no less capable than ethnicity of combining an interest with an affective tie: 'again and again historiography shows us that class consciousness and class solidarity acquires its political potency from the way economic interest is expressed in and through cultural ties.' Indeed, it could reasonably be argued, as Bonacich (1980) does, that it is the underlying class conflict that has given rise to the assertion of ethnicity as a possible avenue for class transformation. Glazer and Moynihan (1975, p. 25) themselves admit that ethnic self-assertion and conflict are 'simply the form that class conflict has been taking on certain occasions in recent decades, and without the notion of class exploitation nothing else would follow.' But they do not recognize the full implications of this observation: for if a revival of ethnicity is an expression of class struggle, then ethnicity cannot be a theoretically fundamental property.

Eipper (1983) is correct in pointing out that the conceptual difficulties Glazer and Moynihan lead themselves into are largely due to their adherence to a very narrow economistic conception of class. They see class as a stratificational hierarchy, as an economic category which coheres with a set of interests. But is we see class as a broader notion, in the way Marx (1906) and even Weber (1948) meant it to be seen, as involving the whole spectrum of ideological, social and economic relationships, then ethnicity as a category would have to be accounted for in terms of these relationships, rather than the other way around.

For Glazer and Moynihan, inequality between ethnic groups in plural societies is inevitable. They assert its universality by maintaining that just as human beings are not equal, ethnic groups are also unequal. Plural societies are, moreover, constantly in a state of negotiating, both formally and informally, consensus between contending interests and between conflicting or antagonistic values and beliefs. Inequality prevails because, through these negotiations, different sets of values, beliefs and interests come to acquire higher or lower status. Glazer and Moynihan (1975, p. 14) argue that, 'in a situation of mixed ethnic groups where one group is dominant, which is to say that its norms are seen as normal not just for it but for others also, there follows an almost automatic consignment of other groups to inferior status.' Racial discrimination is thus 'the relationship between two groups of people, *wherein one group has defined the rules by which the other group must act.*'

The main problem with this account of interethnic relations and competition is that it is presented in a totally ahistorical manner. That is, no attempt is made to describe the historical and structural conditions which promote interethnic competition in the first place; nor is any account provided of the hegemonic mechanisms by which those who constitute the dominant group continue to arrive at 'consensus' that is invariably advantageous to them. Glazer and Moynihan are also mistaken in assuming that ethnic groups have uniform values and interests. As was argued earlier, the essential interests of people are often determined on the basis of their location in class structure, rather than their cultural identification. Insofar as migrants, who are more commonly referred to as 'ethnics' than is the dominant group, are motivated in their migration by a desire for economic and social advancement, they are acutely cognizant of their class position.

Glazer and Moynihan, because they abstract ethnic differentiation, and the notion of group identity which derives from this difference, from production relations, fail to identify class dimensions within the culturally distinct ethnic groups. While it may be true, for example, that a Greek clothing factory owner may share with his employees his language, diet and faith in Greek Orthodoxy, the differences between them are still profound. This sharing of a common ethnicity tells us nothing about the conditions under which the production of clothes proceeds and, therefore, about the factors concerning the purchase and sale of the labour power of the fellow 'ethnics'. We know nothing about the material and structural basis upon which the owner of the factory is able to maintain his ownership, and therefore his class position. It terms of this description of economic relations among the people belonging to the same ethnic group, we cannot assume that they will have identical interests in the manner that Glazer and Moynihan suggest.

Shared Assumptions

While Van den Berghe, Barth and Glazer and Moynihan locate their analysis of the ethnic phenomenon in very different sociological traditions, and while they have radically different theoretical interests, there analyses are based on a set of common assumptions. The notion of ethnicity that serves to legitimate the ideological appeal of multiculturalism in Australia shares these common assumptions.

Van de Berghe's account of ethnicity is based on his assumption that ethnicity is biologically primordial and that it constitutes a foundational category for the purposes of explanation of human behaviour. This assumption is partly shared by Barth who, while rejecting Van den Berghe's emphasis on ethnicity as an objective category, nevertheless claims that people do come to classify themselves into various ethnic categories on the basis of their distinctively different cultures. How cultural differences originate and come to acquire significance in a particular society is an issue that neither Van den Berghe nor Barth explores. In contrast, Glazer and Moynihan see ethnicity as a sociopolitically mobilizing concept, through which common social and political interests are expressed. The term 'ethnic groups' is used by Moynihan and Glazer to refer 'to any group of distinct cultural tradition and origin' (Glazer and Moynihan, 1975, p. 4). Why certain cultural differences acquire significance at a particular time in particular ways is an issue left unexplored by Glazer and Moynihan.

All three accounts assume cultural traditions to be static unchanging phenomena, divorced from the broader social context in which they acquire meaning. In each case, because ethnicity is accepted as the primary explanatory concept, the dynamics of cultural change are either pushed aside as being irrelevant or else ignored. In short, culture is reified. Reification occurs whenever culture is treated as though it is a thing unto itself, independent of other spheres of life. The reification of ethnic values has made a mystique of ethnicity, creating the impression that there is something foundational (natural) about ethnic phenomena that does not lend itself to rational explanation. This is particularly the case when ethnic groups are assumed to be endowed with a given set of cultural values which are taken to be unrelated to the material and political context in which they arise and acquire significance.

The accounts of Van den Berghe, Barth and Glazer and Moynihan assume that the cultural form and content of ethnicity are entirely separable from the social and political origins. There is no exploration of how social forces influence assertion of ethnicity and how there might be a dialectical relationship between ethnic factors on the one hand, and a broad array of historical, economic political and social factors on the other. The failure to tackle these questions leads to not only the reification but also the mystification of ethnicity. As in other Western countries, in Australia this has meant that the celebration of ethnicity has come to serve an ideological function.

Jakubowicz (1984, p. 15) points out that in much of the literature on the subject in Australia 'a theoretical primacy is accorded to "ethnicity", however ill-defined the term may be, and however idealized and ahistorical is the referent.' Ethnicity has taken on 'a first cause' role in such a way as not to require an explanation of its form and origin in terms of relationships with such concepts as class. Jakubowicz shows how this abstract way of looking at ethnicity has not only permeated the work of such influential sociologists of ethnic relations as Zubrzycki and Martin, but also most of the official statements of the policy of multiculturalism. Multiculturalism has thus been represented as the celebration of ethnic diversity. But the ethnicity that is encouraged is apolitical ethnicity, divorced from the larger, sociopolitical matrix in which it is embedded.

This view of ethnicity is encouraged not only in Australia but also in the United States, where, as Glazer and Moynihan admit, US governments have found ethnicity efficacious and have employed 'ethnic categories for distributing its rewards' (Glazer and Moynihan, 1975, p. 10). But why have governments done this? In responding to this question, Eipper (1983, p. 435) argues that:

> Glazer and Moynihan do in theory what governments do in practice; they deny that ethnicity can be decomposed into linguistic, national, religious, tribal, racial etc. divisions, at the same time using ethnicity to decompose class: it becomes a devise for buying-off groups, a devise for mitigating the polarising effects of class. It does so because vertical links and dependencies are created by making the criteria of eligibility and the channels for receiving state-patronage ones based — if not legally, then certainly substantially — upon cultural statuses.

In developing the policy of multiculturalism, Australian governments have been no less keen than United States governments to promote this understanding of ethnicity, and in so doing to mask and obscure the nature of the relationship between ethnicity and class. Multiculturalism has served as an ideology which, by portraying ethnicity as a reified static category divorced from political concerns, is instrumental in defusing and masking the more fundamental political issues of class inequality and other patterns of social and economic disadvantage in Australia.

It has to be admitted, however, that the policy of multiculturalism represents a considerable advance on the earlier assimilationist and integrationist policies in a number of important respects. First, multiculturalism has encouraged an awareness of the nature and extent of cultural heterogeneity in Australian community, and among migrants. All migrants are not the same, and they all have significant heritages which can contribute to the development of a richer Australian identity. Second, multiculturalism has highlighted people of non-English-speaking background as active subjects of experience and not simply as objects of an abstract economic policy, to be manipulated in the interest of the demands of capital. With the assimilationist policies, migrants had come to be viewed unidimensionally as objects of other people's beliefs and behaviour. By stressing identity and the facts of cultural differences, the multicultural perspective presents migrant groups in a context in which they are now seen as having the capacity for self-activity. Third, the recognition of cultural diversity in Australia has meant that the political economy of labour migration has become a significant topic for research. By viewing migration as a political process, at least some room has been created for examining the important issues of the reasons for migration and its effects on Australian economy as well as on the lives of individual migrants. Fourth, largely as a result of the promotion of multiculturalism as a public policy, the nature and extent of migrant disadvantage are being explored by academics working in a range of social sciences. Multicultural discourse has enabled the existence of widespread prejudice and racism, at both individual and institutional levels in Australian society, to be highlighted.

While these developments constitute an advance on earlier policy perspectives, they represent an inadequate basis for egalitarian politics, because they are rooted in an analytical framework which is generally uncritical of the economic structure and the social system that gives rise to the problems minority groups face in the first place. The following section demonstrates how the theoretical assumptions upon which multiculturalism is based are limited at one level, and misguided at another.

Multiculturalism's False Problematic

Multiculturalism stresses the importance of celebrating ethnicity and cultural identity. The celebration of ethnicity involves highlighting the significance and meaningfulness of preservation of 'ethnic' languages, 'ethnic' religion, kin ties, 'ethnic' customs and folk life-styles and their role in the formation of individual and group identities. A range of Australian writers, including Issacs (1976) and Smolicz (1984), portray the maintenance of ethnic identities as a moral right, essential for human dignity and intrinsically valuable. But their understanding of the notion of ethnicity has much in common with the accounts of Van den Berghe, Barth and Glazer and Moynihan which were criticized above. They assume ethnicity to be a primary object of social analysis and present their discussion of the nature of ethnic relations in a way abstracted for class and other patterns of social relations. This limitation constitutes a false problematic within which the theory of multiculturalism is located.

Throughout his theoretical writings Marx (1906) makes a fundamental distinction between phenomenal form and essential relations. Miles (1982, p. 31) explains Marx's use of this distinction in the following manner.

> By phenomenal form, Marx was referring to the way in which the phenomena of the external, social world are respresented in human experience while the notion of essential relations was used to refer to the conditions of existence of the phenomenal forms. Phenomenal forms are, therefore, obvious and apparent to the human agent, such that they may even be regarded as natural and inevitable: they constitute the surface appearance of the way in which the world is organized. Indeed, this surface appearance may actually obscure the real, underlying relations, i.e. the essential relations which explain why the phenomenal form is the way that it appears.

Marx's distinction between phenomenal form and essential relations can be used to demonstrate how recent writings on ethnicity are located in a false problematic. It can be shown that recent research into ethnicity by the proponents of multiculturalism has been concerned to highlight only the phenomenal features of cultural life, thus obscuring the essential class relations which are crucial for understanding migrant experience.

It has to be recognized that people do conceive of themselves and others as belonging to certain ethnic groups and do describe certain sorts of situations and relations as being 'ethnic relations'. But this does not mean that the categories of everyday life can be automatically taken up and employed analytically. Social analysis, as was shown earlier, should not be restricted to the interpretive analysis of the actors themselves. For the categories of description used in everyday discourse, because they are uncritical and are confined to the direct experience and appearance of the social world, are likely to provide a false and misleading explanation.

The social experience of migrants in Australia is not confined to their cultural behaviour. Migrant groups occupy a particular position within the class structure of Australian society, and play an important role in the production of economic relations, a role about which they are often not able to theorize. Their inability to theorize about essential relations should not, however, be taken to imply that these relations are not important, or irrelevant to a sociological analysis of ethnic relations. As de Lepervanche (1984a, p. 32) points out, studies of multiculturalism 'too easily focus on descriptions of observable regularities in behaviour and of people's expressed beliefs. They capture a series of normative facts, and provide us with much empirical data but little analysis of the way in whch these normative orientations of the social factors are governed by underlying structural relationship, such as class.'

So, if ethnic phenomena are analyzed only by using the interpretive understanding of the actors themselves, we are in danger of reifying the phenomenal forms, that is, analyzing them as if they are real, active subjects. The important task should be to make the phenomenal categories of 'ethnicity' and 'cultural identity' the object of critique, and ask how they have come to be constructed and reproduced in the way they have. How have certain cultural differences come to be regarded by migrants themselves as more significant than others? How have ethnic traditions evolved in their specifically Australian contexts? These are questions which are seldom asked by the proponents of multiculturalism, who assume ethnicity to be a static category, resistant to change, even when it has become historically relocated through the process of immigration.

Multiculturalism involves an emphasis upon 'ethnic groups' as self-defined groups whose beliefs, customs and behaviours have to be assessed in terms of their culturally determined distinctiveness. But such an emphasis, as Miles (1982, p. 67) argues,

> ... tends to abstract the facts of cultural differentiation in the course of making them the primary object of inquiry. At one level this can lead to a simple cataloguing of cultural difference (a dictionary of the 'exotic'), while at another it presents an analysis of the interaction between culturally distinct groups either with-

> out reference to or even in direct opposition to class relations. Thus, culture comes to be portrayed as a universal, collectivist characteristic and is used to explain the totality of the belief and behaviour of the individuals who constitute the 'ethnic group'. A simple cataloguing of cultural difference may satisfy a sense of curiosity, but it cannot by itself solve any analytical problems. And it is when attempts are made to grapple with such problems that the primary emphasis upon cultural difference comes to exhibit its most general limitation.

The consequences of such abstraction of ethnic differentiation from their politicohistorical locations, from production relations, are significant. For one thing, there is a failure to identify class divisions which exist within culturally distinct ethnic groups. White the 'ethnic' shop owner may have some cultural characteristics in common with the workers of the same ethnic group as he, the differences between them in respect of economic relations are also extremely important. The economic relationship between the 'ethnic' boss and the 'ethnic' worker is not an arbitrary one, dependent solely on their cultural characteristic; rather, it is historically determined by the condition present in the whole sector of commodity production. Exclusive emphasis on cultural differences obscures this fact of commonality across ethnic divisions. We must explore not only the facts of cultural differences, but also how these facts might be used to obstruct the development of a class unity among workers across diverse ethnic groups. Cultural attributes are only one of the important determinants of social relations. To focus analysis exclusively upon the establishment and maintenance of ethnic boundaries (language, dress, diet, etc.). irrespective of production relations, is not only misguided but also ideological (see Miles, 1982, pp. 67–8).

Moreover, it is mistaken to assume that cultural differences are of primary importance to all members of an ethnic group equally. Economic circumstances always have the potential of bursting the 'ethnic' bond between the employer and the employees if the conditions of production necessitate the imposition of those conditions upon the employee which for material and political reasons they find unacceptable. In this respect there is little difference between class relations within Anglo-Australian groups and those within migrant groups. Moreover, in response to the demands of the production process, the possibility of the development of collective motivation and aspirations across all cultural boundaries, of both employers and employees, must be acknowledged. In this process the possibility of the migrant employer assuming the position of a petit bourgeois whose interests are similar to those of Anglo-Australian employers has to be recognized. Yet much of the recent research on ethnicity largely fails to provide an account of the ethnic petit bourgeoisie, and of the material conditions that permit the formation of such a class position within an ethnic group. A fundamental conceptual error made by most proponents of multiculturalism is that they assume a degree of uniformity and homogeneity among members of ethnic groups which seldom exits.

The crucial issue at the heart of any debate about multiculturalism is not about the catalogue of cultural differences but about the class position which many migrants come to occupy in Australian capitalism. It is also about the material forces which determine the migration process. What is so striking about the various migrant groups in Australia is not their cultural differences, but rather the similarity of the material and economic circumstances that they experienced before their migration and the experience they had of the migration process itself.

Thus the apolitical approach to ethnic relations, which multiculturalism assumes, is fundamentally misguided. An adequate grasp of migrant experience in Australia is not possible unless we pay attention to the political nature of ethnic relations and the dynamics of change and class conflict, and the place of migration in the overall production of social relations in Australia. To study comparative cultural differences in abstraction from these issues is to identify only a phenomenal process which, as Miles (1982, p. 17) points out, '... has real political and ideological effects on, inter alia, the development of class struggle and the formation of class consciousness. But, equally, one must recognize that the persons who constitute a group which is formed and identified on this basis also have a position in essential relations. That is, they have a position in production (and, thereby, class) relations.'

The issue of racism and intercultural understanding, as a particular example of ethnic relations, is linked to these considerations. An apolitical and ahistorical account of ethnic relations, such as the one the proponents of multiculturalism assume, views racism as a manifestation of the phenomenological experience of individuals. According to this interpretivist view, racist attitudes are irrational pathological phenomena that are a function of either an individual's inadequate personality or his lack of understanding of other cultures' mores and customs. The proponents of multiculturalism recognize the long history of the existence of racist attitudes in Australia. However, they fail to provide a satisfactory historical explanation of why such penetration has been so systematic and complete. Their view is that it is ignorance which causes racism, and that once ethnic groups learn to live with each other in a climate of mutual accommodation, prejudiced attitudes would simply disappear or at least be greatly reduced. The Galbally Report (1978) thus emphasizes the need to develop in children 'a multicultural attitude' through educative programs which involve teaching about diverse cultural traditions. Galbally hopes that by learning about other cultures children will be able to 'communicate' better with members of other cultural groups, and that this communication will inevitably be enlightened.

While there is great merit in intercultural communication, learning about cultures alone cannot significantly reduce instances of racism in Australia. If the arguments in this section are correct, then an analysis of racism in terms of individual psychological factors is fundamentally mistaken. Racism in society is ultimately a manifestation of an ongoing collective process of group interaction, whereby the status and behaviour of minorities are defined and redefined in relation to the dominant group. However, these definitions are not arbitrary, for the collective processes of group interaction are linked to modes of production and the structures of the state. Castles *et al.* (1988, Ch. 5) point out that in capitalist societies racism against migrants is linked to the creation and maintenance of class divisions within the working class. They contend that prejudiced attitudes as such do not cause the discrimination that immigrants experience. Discrimination against migrants has its source in conflict over economic and social interests. Prejudiced attitudes emerge as a justification for discrimination but, once institutionalized, may in time become intensified, as a consequence of a complex interaction of economic, political and ideological relations. Castles *et al.* (1988, p. 95) maintain that during times of economic downturn, an 'increase in racism must be linked to the problems of maintaining ideological legitimacy for the nation-state at a time when it is demonstrably not satisfying large sections of the populations.' They conclude that antiracist programs cannot succeed unless we also attend to the economic and social conditions which help produce and reproduce racism in the first place.

Omi and Winant (1986) have helped us to understand how the 'individual pathology' view of racism is misguided. They (1986, p. 76) have argued that racism can be built into the very structures of the state, '*institutions*, the policies they carry out, the *conditions and rules* which support and justify them, and the *social relations* in which they are inbedded.' If the analyses of Castles *et al.* and Omi and Winant are correct about the nature of prejudice and racism, and I believe they are, then the hopes of the proponents of multicultural education would appear to be misplaced. For it would be mistaken to assume that by simply learning about other cultures we can promote intercultural understanding and lead to reduction in levels of prejudice directed against minorities. As de Lepervanche (1984a, p. 194) observes, 'education *per se* will not lead to the removal of prejudice and discrimination or to the institution of equal opportunity.' If racism is linked to socio-economic conditions, then we cannot expect to change prejudiced attitudes simply by encouraging cultural tolerance in classrooms. Racism cannot be effectively tackled unless we also attend to the economic and social conditions which help produce it. Multiculturalism, however widespread the acceptance of its rhetoric, is incapable of doing this because it is presented in a form which renders any critical examination of the existing structures unnecessary.

Multiculturalism as an Ideology

Proponents of multiculturalism have rarely confronted the issue of how Aboriginal people fit into their pluralist scheme. Aboriginal groups have always maintained that they have certain prior rights to Australia's material resources (Barlow, 1984), but how these claims can be accommodated within a policy which affirms equality of status to all cultural groups is a question which has not been adequately dealt with by advocates of multiculturalism.

This issue highlights a major problem with multiculturalism. Multiculturalism is a doctrine which lacks a historical perspective. The Aboriginal claim to land rights is a historical claim and derives its validity from the premise that the dispossessed should be adequately compensated, and not treated in the same manner as, other cultural groups in Austalia. As a liberal-individualist theory, multiculturalism, on the other hand, assumes the status quo, with its attendant patterns of social and economic inequalities, to be perfectly natural, and prescribes equality of access within existing economic circumstances.

It is no wonder that those who stand to benefit from maintaining and reinforcing boundaries are those who are already strongly enough positioned to ensure that their ethnic status would be advantageous. It is of great comfort to the so-called 'ethnic' leaders to know that they would be at the centre rather than the periphery of Australian political life. Accordingly, multiculturalism proves most attractive to those who are already largely assimilated into the dominant culture. Indeed, in Australia over the past decade the ethnic groups who have espoused multiculturalism most vigorously have been those who stood to protect their class interests. As Jakubowicz (1884, p. 20) points out, it was the 'ethnic' petit bourgeoisie which most readily volunteered itself to assist the Fraser Government in promoting multiculturalism.

For the disadvantaged minorities, multiculturalism would bring few social and economic benefits. Steinberg (1981, p. 256) argues:

> a pluralism based on systematic inequalities is inherently unstable because ethnic groups at or near the bottom of the social ladder have little reason to endorse the ethnic status quo. On the contrary, groups aspiring to class mobility are typically forced to adopt strategies that are designed to advanced their class interests, but at the same time whittle away at the pluralist structure. Two such strategies may be observed, one within the disadvantaged group, the other in its relationship with more advantaged groups.

As long as ethnicity is associated with patterns of disadvantage, then powerful incentives exist for migrants to assimilate into the mainstream culture since, in economic terms at least, this will improve their chances for a better life. Indeed, the Australian experience demonstrates that most disadvantaged migrants have been willing to shed their public ethnicity in order to obtain greater economic security (see Birrell and Birrell, 1981). Given that structural features of Australian society are to remain the same under some spurious rhetoric of social cohesion, it would seem that equality of opportunity would be available only to those who are prepared to assimilate into those structures. In view of the existing patterns of the distribution of power, equal opportunity in practice means equal opportunity only for those persons whose ideas and values conform with those of the dominant Anglo-Australian culture — those who possess real power. In education, since the provision of equal opportunity is already defined in terms of goals which favour Anglo-Australian students, only the assimilated can succeed. For migrant pupils, this means that only those who absorb these Anglo-Australian values are likely to succeed academically and socially and have a measure of equality of educational opportunity.

Its proponents argue that multiculturalism is a theory of society in which ideals of democracy and pluralism come together in policy. But the effective implementation of this policy is only possible in a society where there is a basic parity among its constituent ethnic groups. Given that this is not the case in Australia, where some ethnic groups have historically come to occupy inferior class positions, pluralism cannot 'be innocent of class bias and consistent with democratic principles' (Steinberg, 1981, p. 261). Democracy and pluralism are, therefore, not as compatible as the proponents of multiculturalism claim, essentially because pluralist structures tend to reinforce existing class inequalities.

The idea, central to multiculturalism, that ethnic groups maintain their cultural identity is fundamentally ideological. As Collins (1978) points out, the encouragement of a culturally divided workforce to celebrate its differences has political implications. The celebration of ethnic differences serves only to divide the working class: in competition over jobs and social benefits, ethnic groups become increasingly suspicious of each other. Here we find the roots of prejudice and racism developing. In a political context, ethnic boundaries are strengthened at the expense of working-class solidarity. Emphasis on the celebration of ethnic differences also has the consequence of diverting attention away from structural class inequalities that currently exist in Australian society. As de Lepervanche (1984a, p. 208) observes: 'if we concentrate on drawing cultural boundaries too clearly there is the danger, in a class society of unequals, of isolating those who are occupationally segmented and culturally or racially distinct from others in a similar social position.'

Conclusion

In this chapter it has been argued that the 'revival' of ethnicity is regressive, and that multicultural education is fundamentally ideological, for in celebrating ethnic heterogeneity, it systematically obscures and legitimates the essential class inequalities which produce the disadvantages migrants in Australia face. Multiculturalism assumes, moreover, that culture is the most fundamental factor in addressing the problems of non-England-speaking migrants. It thus ignores other sociohistorical factors, such as class, which are more fundamental in explaining economic and social disadvantage. We already know that schooling systems are inherently conservative and that they often reflect the economic structure of the wider society, in which class stratification continues to play a major role in the maintenance of socio-economic structure. Social analysis which neglects these issues is bound to be inadequate. More importantly, it is an analysis which is ideological in the sense that it diverts us from confronting the history of political and economic exploitation which has had, perhaps, a more important role than ethnicity in the structural organization of Australian society.

Multiculturalism represents the use of a culturally determined set of ideas and practices to justify certain practices and protect specific interests. As a form of ideology, it represents an attempt to celebrate ethnic differences and practices in order to institutionalize those differences, and thus reproduce current patterns of social inequalities. In doing this, multiculturalism also tends to obfuscate the common experiences, histories and social and political conditions of migrant groups and hence obscure the degree of commonality of experience that exists between migrant and Anglo-Australian working class in Australia. Arguably, these commonalities, in terms of political and economic relationships, are more profound than the ethnic differences, based on cultural heritages or purportedly biologically determined entities.

Superficially, multiculturalism appears to represent a radical change from earlier assimilationist perspectives, but the analysis presented here reveals this change to be ideological, rather than structural. That is, as Jakubowicz (1984, p. 10) points out, it rests on a notion of ethnicity which 'mediated Australian class relations by reifying the history of people into a static category of theoretical labeling.'

It follows that the celebration of ethnicity should not be seen as a major element in the development of educational policy, designed to meet the needs and interests of youth. By all means, students, migrants and Anglo-Australians alike should be encouraged to examine the structure of their society, but this analysis should not be a simple cataloguing of ethnic differences. It should be an exploration of the relation between structures of dominance and their transformation and an examination of the way people can respond to oppression and promote effective social change. Arguably, the emphasis on the ahistorical and apolitical study of ethnic histories, customs, religions, music, languages and so on in current multicultural education programs has led to the celebration of differences. Yet it is only by highlighting historically constituted similarities of social experience that migrants, as well as other disadvantaged groups, by sharing their related interests, might hope to produce the kind of solidarity required to challenge the structural and symbolic forces that promote inequalities in our society.

Reference

BARLOW, A. (1984) 'The relationship between Aboriginal education and multicultural education', in PHILLIPS, D.J. and HOUSTON, J. (Eds), *Australian Multicultural Society: Identity, Communication and Decision-Making*, Melbourne, Drummond.

BARTH, F. (Ed.) (1969) *Ethnic Groups and Boundaries: The Social Organization of Cultural Difference*, London, George Allen and Unwin.

BERNSTEIN, R.J. (1976) *The Restructuring of Social and Political Theory*, London, Methuen.

BIRRELL, R. and BIRRELL, T. (1981) *An Issue of People: Pupulation and Australian Society*, Melbourne, Longman Cheshire.

BONACICH, E. (1980) 'Class approaches to ethnicity and race', *The Insurgent Sociologist*, 10, 2.

BOTTOMORE, T. (1966) *Elites and Society*, Harmondsworth, Penguin.

BULLIVANT, B. (1984) *Pluralism: Cultural Maintenance of Evolution*, Clevedon, Multilingual Matters.

BURNLEY, I., ENCEL, S. and MCCALL, G. (Eds) (1985) *Immigration and Ethnicity in the 1980's*, Melbourne, Longman Cheshire.

CARR, W. and KEMMIS, S. (1983) *Becoming Critical: Knowing through Action Research*, Geelong, Deakin University Press.

CASTLES, S., KALANTZIS, M., COPE, B. and MORRISSEY, M. (1988) *Mistaken Identity*, Sydney, Pluto Press.

COLLINS, J. (1978) 'Fragmentation of the working class', in WHEELWRIGHT, E.L. and BUCKLEY, K. (Eds), *Essays in the Political Economy of Australian Capitalism*, Vol. 3, Sydney, ANZ Book Company.

COLLINS, J. (1988) *Migrant Hands in Distant Land*, Sydney, Pluto Press.

DE LEPERVANCHE, M. (1980) 'From race to ethnicity', *The ANZ Journal of Sociology*, 16, 1, pp. 24–37.

DE LEPERVANCHE, M. (1984a), 'Migrants and ethnic groups', in ENCEL, S. and BRYSON, L. (Eds), *Australian Society*, 4th ed. Melbourne, Longman Cheshire.

DE LEPERVANCHE, M. (1984b), 'The naturalness of inequality', in BOTTOMLEY, G. and DE LEPERVANCHE, M. (Eds), *Ethnicity, Class and Gender in Australia*, Sydney, George Allen and Unwin.

EIPPER, C. (1983) 'The magician's hat: A critique of the concept of ethnicity', *The ANZ Journal of Sociology*, 19, 3, pp. 427–46.

FOSTER, L.E. (1983) 'The politics of educational knowledge', in BROWNE, R.K. and FOSTER, L.E. (Eds), *Sociology of Education*, 3rd ed. Melbourne, Macmillan.

FOSTER, L.E. (1988) *Diversity and Multicultural Education*, Sydney, Allen and Unwin.

GALBALLY F. (1978), *Report of the Review of Post-Arrival Program and Services for Migrants, Migrant Services and Programs*, Vol. 1, Canberra, Australian Government Publishing Service.

GLAZER, N. and MOYNIHAN, D. (Eds) (1975) *Ethnicity: Theory and Experience*, Cambridge, Mass., Harvard University Press.

ISACCS, E. (1976) *Greek Children in Sydney*, Canberra, Australian National University Press.

JAKUBOWICZ, A. (1984) 'State and ethnicity: Multiculturalism as ideology', in JUPP, J. (Ed.), *Ethnic Politics in Australia*, Sydney, George Allen and Unwin.

JAYASURIYA, L. (1987) *Education in and for a Multicultural Society: Issues and Strategies for Policy-making*, Canberra, NACCME.

JUPP, J. (1966) *Arrivals and Departures*, Melbourne, Cheshire-Lansdowne.

KALDOR S. (1981) *Perspectives on Multicultural Education*, Canberra, Australian Government Publishing Service.

LIPPMAN, L. (1981) 'The multicultural society and its implications for education', in SHERWOOD, J. (Ed.), *Multicultural Education: Time and Innovation*, Perth, Creative Research Press.

MARTIN, J. (1972) *Community and Identity: Refugee Groups in Adelaide*, Canberra, Australian National University Press.

MARX, K. (1906) *Capital*, Vol. 1, Chicago, Ill., Charles H. Keir.

MEARNS, D. (1989) *Understanding Ethnicity*, Geelong, Deakin University Press.

MIDGLEY, M. (1980) *Beast and Man: The Roots of Human Nature*, London, Methuen.

MILES, R. (1982) *Racism and Migrant Labour*, London, Routledge and Kegan Paul.

OFFICE OF MULTICULTURAL AFFAIRS (1989) *An Agenda for Multicultural Australia*, Canberra, Australian Government Publishing Service.

OMI, M. and WINANT, H. (1986) *Racial Formation in the United States*, Boston, Mass., Routledge and Kegan Paul.

PHILIPS, A.J. and HOUSTON, J. (Ed.) (1984) *Australia's Multicultural Society: Identity, Communication and Decision-Making*, Melbourne, Drummond.

POPPER K.R. (1972) *The Logic of Scientific Discovery*, 6th rev. ed. London, Hutchinson.

SMITH, A.D. (1981) *The Ethnic Revival*, Cambridge, Cambridge University Press.

SMOLICZ, J.J. (1984) 'Ethnic identity in Australia: Cohesive of divisive?' in PHILLIPS, D.J. and HOUSTON, J. (Eds), *Australian Multicultural Society: Identity, Communication and Decision-Making*, Melbourne, Drummond.

STEINBERG, S. (1981) *The Ethnic Myth*, New York, Atheneum.

VAN DEN BERGHE, P. (1981) *The Ethnic Phenomenon*, New York, Elsevier.

WALLMAN, S. (Ed.) (1979) *Ethnicity at Work*, London, Macmillan.

WALLMAN, S. (1986) 'Ethnicity and the boundary process in context', in REX, J. and MASON, D. (Eds), *Theories of Race and Ethnicity*, Cambridge, Cambridge University Press.

WEBER, M. (1948) *From Max Weber: Essays in Sociology*, GERTH, H.H. and WRIGHT MILLS, C. (Eds) London, Routledge and Kegan Paul.

WILSON, E.O. (1975) *Sociobiology: The New Synthesis*, Cambridge, Mass., Harvard University Press.

ZUBRZYCKI, J. (1982) *Multiculturalism for All Australians*, Canberra, Australian Government Publishing Service.

Chapter 6

High Technology, Work and Education

Peter Watkins

By the end of the 1980s the fascination with, and high hopes for, high technology which had held sway during that decade were being reassessed. Leading figures in the field of high technology such as Reinecke, writing in *Australian Society* (May 1989), and Forester, writing in *The Australian* (30 May 1989), have prompted a new look at the high tech vision of the world. This romance with high technology through the 1980s was frequently reflected in the headlines of the major Australian city newspapers. For example, the feature page of *The Herald* had emblazoned across it: '$75m. raised for high-technology' (5 June 1985), and *The Age* proclaimed 'Times are a changing with the help of technology' (15 January 1985). During this decade *The Australian* and *The Age* both had a regular weekly section headed 'Computers', which usually marvelled at the changes and wonders being conjured up in the realm of high technology. In this popular context technological change was viewed as progress, while progress was defined in terms of technological change.

Riche, Hecker and Burgan (1983) point out that there is no uniform or widely accepted definition of high technology. However, after examining various definitions, they argue that most definitions of high technology incorporate one or a combination of three factors: first, the use of scientific and technical workers; second, a high expenditure on research and development; and third, the nature of the product (Riche, Hecker and Burgan, 1983, p. 51). Macdonald (1983), however, sees high technology as being associated with venture and risk capital. He claims that technology is high because of the 'relatively high risk involved, the possibility of high return, its high pace of change and its high information intensity' (Macdonald, 1983, p. 331). More recently, Forester (1987) pointed to three main factors contributing to the high technology revolution: first, developments in microelectronics, which have resulted in steadily declining costs in computing; second, the digitization of information, which has permitted the use of a common language; and third, the deregulation and privatization of telecommunications, which has offered the lure of quick returns on invested capital. Morrison (1983) indicates those industrial sectors where these definitions might come together, including:

1 *electronic technologies* for the creation, storage, retrieval, transmission, manipulation and control of information, including information for the automated control of mechanical systems.
2 *biological and biochemical technologies* related to medicine, industrial processing and material fabrication, agriculture, food processing, and energy conversion.
3 *materials technologies* to achieve resource input efficiencies and/or achieve the strength, weight, durability and size characteristics needed for traditional and non-traditional applications. (Morrison, 1983, p. 239)

Low technology jobs, in contrast, are traditional, basic industrial jobs. But it should be remembered that high and low technology are contested terms. What is now considered low technology most likely was thought of as high technology in the past. Now low technology jobs often do not require a higher education, and they are becoming more frequently casual and part-time. While these jobs are often obscured by the glamour of high tech, the central argument of this chapter is that future job opportunities for the majority of young people will lie essentially with low tech rather than high tech forms of work. Central to this argument is the proposition that even in high technology industries a large proportion of the jobs are low technology jobs. If this is the case, then what should be the appropriate educational response? But first we need to look at the various arguments concerning technological change. One of these relates to technological determinism; another claims that technological change evolves through dialectical relationships. A major consideration in any discussion of technology is the concept of technological determinism. Here we will examine the works of Ellul and Winner, and contrast these with the works of Marx and Weber, who present a dialectical approach to technological change.

Deterministic and Dialectic Approaches to Technological Change

In this section of the chapter two ways of looking at technological change are presented. The first sees technology as an all-embracing entity, autonomous and determining the direction both it and society will take. The second view sees human beings and technology in a dialectic relationship with human agency, both being conditioned by and conditioning any technological innovations. In this dialectic, technology can be seen to mediate the interaction between labour and capital.

The Deterministic Approach

A certain view of technology sees technological development as evolving continuously in a fashion which is autonomous from human intervention and free from any value or ethical considerations but which contributes to the overall ordering of society. Technology is seen as having a life of its own and moving irresistibly in a determinate direction. This technological deterministic position is held, for example, by the French sociologist Jacques Ellul (see also Winner, 1977). Ellul has been concerned in both *The Technological Society* (1964) and his more recent book, *The Technological System* (1980), to highlight what he sees as the technological domination of our present society. In this view technology determines the production and distribution of raw materials, determines the social structures of society and limits whatever choices we have. Thus technology is the determining factor in all social, political and economic decisions. As Ellul puts it in his earlier *The Technological Society* (1964):

> In this decisive evolution, the human being does not play a part. Technical elements combine among themselves, and they do so more and more spontaneously. In the future, man will apparently be confined to the role of the recording device; he will note the effects of techniques upon one another, and register the results.... Anything and everything which technique is able to produce is produced and accepted by the consumer. The belief that the human producer is still master of production is a dangerous illusion. (Ellul, 1964, p. 93)

Technology is perceived to sweep inexorably forward, generating change and a set pattern of historical development within its own autonomous entity. This idea of autonomous technology is developed in greater depth in Ellul's later book; here he explains that by autonomous technology he means that 'technology ultimately depends only on itself, it maps its own route, it is a prime and not a secondary factor, it must be regarded as an "organism" tending towards closure and self-determination: it is an end in itself' (1980, p. 125). But Ellul also points out that this autonomy ascribed to technological change also corresponds to the notion of functionality. As a consequence it can be argued that:

> each technological element is first adapted to the technological system and it is in respect to this system that the element has its true functionality, far more so than in respect to a human need or a social order. . . . Performing this function, technology endures no judgement from the outside nor any restraint. It presents itself as an intrinsic necessity. (1980, p. 126)

Technology presented in this scenario is independent of human action and choice. However, Ellul distinguishes between technology being neutral of human values and absolutely neutral. While it is divorced from humans, technology is not absolutely neutral. Rather, technology contains its own law and meaning. In this sense it is autonomous, objective and value-free; separated from the whims and predilections of human beings. Thus Ellul puts forward the argument that technology 'is not an instrument that man can use as he likes. It has its own weight, which goes in technology's direction' (1980, p. 154). In this sense technology is reified with a force and sweep of its own. It is inevitably accepted, dictating the ways and means that it is used. Even though particular technologies may have disastrous effects on the human race, their deployment is inherently unavoidable, for, as Ellul puts it:

> We know the definitive risk that humanity is made to run by the bacteriological, chemical, and nuclear weapons, as well as by the general pollution of air and water, the domestic and agricultural use of countless chemical products. . . . But none of this matters; we must, above all, use what technology puts in our hands. (Ellul, 1980, p. 235)

Thus Ellul stresses that technological forces are the decisive factor in determining the direction of change in the social and economic environment. The evolution of technology in a particular form is the independent variable which decides on which path social change, the dependent variable, will take. The main agent of social change within society is an independent, autonomous technology which is separated from general social forces and considerations.

Winner, in his book, *Autonomous Technology* (1977), essentially agrees with Ellul's position on technological development. This position addresses the concern that technology has an independent, inexorable vitality which eventually leads to the technological control of society. Society is dominated by a technological imperative requiring certain decisions to perpetuate the technological order itself rather than any human concerns which may direct the technology towards human needs and interests. This domination reflects a reverse adaptation whereby 'technical systems become severed from the ends originally set for them and, in effect, reprogram themselves and their environments to suit the special conditions of their own operation' (1977, p. 227). In arguing the inevitability of the direction of technological change, Winner draws not only on Ellul but also on the anthropological determinist A.L. Kroeber. Kroeber discounted any idea of the significance of people and human choice in the technological process. Kroeber held the 'conviction that inventions may be inevitable, within certain limits; that given a certain constellation and development of a culture, certain inventions must be made' (Winner, 1977, p. 66). In this way, by fostering technology, human beings have eventually lost control of their lives, and choice becomes illusory because 'technology is now a kind of conduit such that no matter which aims or purposes one decides to put in, a particular kind of product inevitably comes out' (Winner, 1977, p. 278).

The picture presented by Winner is that of a linear path of technological development. There is virtually no relationship between human beings and technology, nor is there any consideration of values not subordinate to a technical rationality. Values relating to concerns for greater freedom, equity and justice are pushed aside. The neglect of any moral or ethical questions highlights the instrumentally functionalist progress of technology proceeding in a mechanical fashion. The presentation of technological change in such a predetermined, linear process precludes any consideration of human agency or practice which might render technology under control.

The technological determinist approach outlined above can take two directions in regard to its effect on human life, that of the optimist and that of the pessimist. The optimistic approach sees the march of technology as bringing about unprecedented human benefit. With the advent of new technology, according to the optimists, far more jobs will be created than will be lost. Not only will there be more jobs, but these jobs will be set at a higher intellectual level. The repetitive, routine jobs which had imparted so much drudgery on human beings during earlier periods of industrialization will be eliminated. If there is not the same number of jobs available as before, technology will bring about a new era of almost continual leisure. People will be able to pursue their hobbies and the arts without having to worry about work. Thus in Australia the Myers Report (Committee of Inquiry into Technological Change in Australia, 1980) suggested that the emerging technological revolution is not only inevitable but also desirable and should be encouraged and assisted. It argued that through the application of new technology Australia would be able to develop new products and processes from which would flow a new source of job opportunities (see also Watkins, 1984).

In contrast, the pessimistic view of technological change sees the advance of technology as inevitably leading to massive unemployment. But the pessimists argue that even in those jobs which do remain, there is still present an unremitting tendency for the jobs to be continually deskilled and degraded. In this scenario not only is physical, manual work deskilled and destroyed but so too is mental, intellectual work. So Braverman's view of the labour process in *Labor and Monopoly Capital* (1974) has been criticized as being basically deterministic, even though he attempts to dispel this criticism by stressing that relations between technology and society are beyond the reach of any simple-minded 'determinism' (1974, p. 19). Giddens (1982) and Mackenzie (1977) have highlighted a serious deficiency in Braverman's work. Mackenzie (1977, p. 249) notes that Braverman's work is 'devoid of dialectical under- or overtones'. In support Giddens argues that there is a failure in *Labor and Monopoly Capital* to embrace a discussion which exposes the reactions and resistances of workers to technology, the technical division of labour and the ideology of scientific management (Giddens, 1982).

The Dialectic Approach

The advocates of both the optimistic and the pessimistic view of technological change see the inexorable, unimpeded growth of technology. However, they deny that any implementation of technological change takes place at the direction of certain people and that any particular change takes place within a certain historical and social context. In this regard technology has to be seen as part of a social process deriving from particular historical milieux. For this reason Marx rejected any conception of technology and machinery which was historically and socially decontextualized. The analysis of machinery into basic components 'such as the lever, the inclined plane, the screw, the wedge etc.' offered an 'explanation (which) is worth nothing, because the historical element is missing from it' (*Capital*, 1906, pp. 405–6). Rosenberg points out that for Marx, 'new productive forces emerge, not exogenously or as some mysterious *deus ex machina*, but rather as a dialectical outcome of a larger historical process in which *both* the earlier forces and the relations of production play essential roles' (Rosenberg, 1983, p. 38). Similarly, MacKenzie (1984) emphasizes that technological change was, for Marx, a two-sided dialectical struggle. For 'capital uses machinery not only strategically ... but also for precise tactical purposes. Where workers' ... militancy poses a threat to valorization, capital can counter by promoting the invention and employment of machinery to undermine workers' power' (1984, p. 488). This dialectical relationship between technology and the social and historical structure which both enhance and constrain the direction and rate of technological change is also well caught by Giddens (1981, 1982). However, the dialectic might be best summed up by Marx writing in *Grundrisse* (1973): he argues that 'it must be kept in mind that the new forces of production and relations of production do not develop out of *nothing*, nor drop from the sky, nor from the womb of the self-positing Idea; but from within and in antithesis to the existing development of production and the inherited relations of property' (1973, p. 278). These recently translated writings, plus the scholarship of people like Rosenberg and Giddens, clearly indicate that Marx was not the technological determinist that he has occasionally been presented as (see Burns, 1969, Ch. 3). Rather, his dialectical method emphasized 'the mutual interactions and feedbacks between economy and technology' (Rosenberg, 1983, p. 36).

The thrust of technological change is related to 'the contractual encounter between capital and wage-labour' (Giddens, 1982, p. 42). Thus technology itself mediates the relationship between capital and labour. Consequently, the historical and social outcome of technological change reflects the dialectical interaction between the forces and the relations of production. With this interaction in mind, O'Connor (1984) also argues for a dialectic perspective of technological change where it is recognized that broader social perspectives both condition and are conditioned by any changes in technology. Nevertheless, he argues that

> the existing social relations of production may exert a decisive influence on the particular direction of technological change. Given alternative technological possibilities which are comparable in terms of their impact on economic efficiency, one or another may be preferred by those in a position to make decisions regarding the choice of technique depending on the dominant social relations of production in a particular society. (O'Connor, 1984, p. 5)

Weber also was critical of a deterministic view which saw technological developments resulting from the quest for more efficient productivity and necessarily leading to the benefit and good of society. In similar fashion to Marx, Weber stressed that technological innovations should be seen in their historical and social context. Thus he argued that

> it was and is certain *historically* given and historically alterable *social* conditions ie, constellations of *interests* of specific kinds, which made first possible (or even impossible) the utilization of *technical* discoveries in general, and that consequently the way in which the future of technological development takes shape is also dependent upon the development of these constellations of interests and no way upon purely technical 'possibilities' alone. (Weber, 1984; original 1909, p. 51)

Thus technology develops from the interaction of various interest groups who are located in a particular historical and social milieu. Weber considered that technology was a dependent variable. Technological innovations such as those in textile factories are worthless without large consumer markets and the ability to produce large amounts of wool and cotton. Indeed, technological inventions themselves are a consequence of a perceived 'need' which is located in a particular social relation. Moreover, the implementation of technology can be seen to enhance capital's profit at the cost of labour. Technology in this way is used to tip the balance of social relations in the workplace in favour of capital. Consequently, 'the tendency toward rationalizing technology and economic relations with a view to reducing prices in relation to costs, generated in the 17th Century a feverish pursuit of invention' (Weber, 1961; original 1923, p. 311). Costs could be reduced through either enhanced prediction and control of production or reduction of wage's. Neo-Weberians such as Collins discuss technological changes in terms of 'weapons' which are used by both capital and labour in a struggle for dominance. Technology should, therefore, be examined in the light of the interests and resources of those who implement it and the action/reaction of those on whom it impinges (see Collins, 1975).

If a dialectical view of technological change is accepted, then it should be clear that technological change is not autonomous and value-free but is, rather, the result of a chain of options which both condition and are conditioned by the bonds which constitute our social fabric. In this way technology reflects the social structure from which it originates. Technology is neither ideologically neutral nor has it been introduced in a neutral or random fashion.

A dialectical perspective also means that we should not view technology as having a form and rationality of its own. It is a misconception to create a vision of technology which is separate and divorced from its social context. It has been argued earlier that technology did not suddenly arrive out of nothing. The way in which technology is designed, developed and utilized is a reflection of the intellectual and creative energy of human beings. Technological development can take many directions and forms. In fact, technology can only be properly understood by placing it in its human context and questioning the present and potential forms of technological innovation. For technological innovation itself is not an inviolate determinant. Indeed, quite the opposite is the case, for, as Perrow (1983, p. 521) explains when discussing the structure of social relations in organization, 'rather than technology determining organizational structure, it would appear that machines and equipment are designed so that they reinforce existing structures and reproduce these structures in new settings.'

If this is the case, then it is unlikely that technology has been introduced in a neutral or random fashion. It embodies neither of these qualities, because by reproducing the unequal structure of society and institutions it also reproduces the dominant ideological position which justifies and gives support to the unequal distribution of power and rewards. Consequently, technology can always be seen as beneficial to some and detrimental to others. Who benefits and who is disadvantaged reflect in turn the conscious decisions of those in power, which give rise to the particular time and extent of technological innovation. This critical stance reflects the position which the followers of Ludd accepted. Although their approach toward technology has been distorted and vilified, some balance has been restored by the recent work of Winner (1977), Berg (1979), Webster and Robins (1986), Reid (1986) and, of course, the English historian E.P. Thompson.

Luddism

Closely associated with the vision of an ongoing march of technological development is the dismissal of those who oppose new technological innovations as Luddites and neo-Luddites. The term 'Luddite' refers to the followers of Ned Ludd who opposed the way technology was introduced into Yorkshire in the early nineteenth century; but the term still carries great force. For instance, the Australian Postal and Telecommunications Union was accused of 'postal union luddism' when it set out its opposition to new technology which would throw out of work many of its membership (*The Sun-Herald*, 9 June 1985). Similarly, even writers who are generally wary of a deterministic approach talk disparagingly of adopting a 'Luddite mentality' (Mere, 1984, p. 47) or a 'neo-Luddite abhorrence' (Ellyard, 1984, p. 84) toward the introduction of new technology. For many writers, any opposition to technology is mindless, and mindless opposition is a convenient label which has been identified with the activities of the Luddites. In this vein the writers of the Williams (Committee of Inquiry . . ., 1979) and the Myers Reports (1980) were quick to dismiss any so-called Luddite concerns in arguing for the continuing application of technology with its envisioned, taken-for-granted benefits to society and workers in general. But Ford (1984) has pointed out that such optimism associated with the introduction of new technology has not been vindicated by studies conducted in Australia at the plant level. He points out that such studies have

> found little evidence that technology had improved the quality of working life. In fact, those studies highlighted the appalling work conditions in many old and new industries. Similarly, the priority for the introduction of new technologies into offices in recent years has had little to do with improving the quality of working life. In fact the reverse is true. Tenosynovitis has reached almost plague proportions in some offices because of the failure to develop appropriate new working arrangements with the introduction of new technology. (Ford, 1984, p. 157)

In the light of such research findings it is not surprising that unions such as the Australian Postal and Telecommunications Union should be wary of the ideological structures built into the new technology and the likely outcomes on the unionists' lives which would follow its introduction. Similarly, as Berg (1979, p. 43) indicates, the followers of Ned Ludd were not against technology per se, but against the breaking of apprenticeship rules and wage agreements, and employer hostility to their unions. The Luddites were not against technology, but they were against the way particular technologies were developed and used in an attempt to break any power and control the worker may have had over the labour process.

The Luddites, as historians such as E.P. Thompson (1968) have shown, were not irrational zealots, blindly lashing out at the inevitability of technological change. Rather, Thompson has viewed the response of the Luddites as an attempt to put forward a working-class alternative to the political economy of the newly emerging business class. Thus 'the men who attacked Cartwright's mill at Rawfolds were announcing this alternative political economy, albeit in a confused midnight encounter' (Thompson, 1968, pp. 603–4).

The actions of the followers of Ludd sought, through their alternative, to put forward morality in place of laissez faire, and social priorities in place of control and profit. In this way they foreshadowed the efforts of those such as Mike Cooley at Lucas Aerospace, which will be discussed later, to employ technology in more socially useful ways. Webster and Robins sum up the activities of the Luddites in the following way:

> Luddism was a force that, if it looked back to better times in demanding 'full fashioned work at the old fashion'd price established by Custom and Law,' also looked towards the future of Labor organizations and aspirations. It does not deserve the sneering, indeed unthinking, dismissal it so frequently receives today. By most accounts this is not what it received from contemporaries; in spite of a large presence of troops, government spies, and rewards for informers, the detection rate for Luddite activists was remarkably small. The only satisfactory explanation is that Luddism enjoyed widespread popular if tacit, support. (Webster and Robins, 1986, pp. 3–4)

An examination of the historical evidence does not support the glib, distorted view of the Luddites which easily flows off the tongues of those debunking any opposition to a certain direction of technological change. The result is that many potential critics of the way technology is used are wary of confronting its implementation. In this way critique is deflected and contained within an ideology of inherent technological advance and progress. Consequently, 'in confronting the introduction of new technologies — already constituted as expressions of capital and *its* needs — it is necessary for us to adopt the ethical stance of critique, the stance that looks to a social reality other than that determined by capital' (Robins and Webster, 1983, p. 206; see also Webster and Robins, 1986; Thompson, 1976). This was the critical stance of the original Luddites. When critically examining any new innovation in the textile trade, they applied two basic, critical criteria. First, does the new device enhance the quality of the product being manufactured? Second, does the machine improve the quality of work? If the answer to one or both of the questions was 'no', they took action to try and block the implementation of the new technology (see Winner, 1977). In this way technology reflects an historical, social process through which practices are continually being constrained and enhanced through the ongoing transformation of social structures. In this dialectic human agents are acting on the outside world and transforming it, while simultaneously the nature of the human agents is also being transformed, enhanced or constrained, through this interaction. Thus 'this historical enterprise always contains a range of possibilities as well as necessities, possibilities seized upon by particular people, for particular purposes, according to particular conceptions of social destiny' (Noble, 1979, p. xxii).

Such historical possibilities and powerful forces can be best illustrated by examining an actual location of high tech industry. The foremost centre of recent high technology development is Silicon Valley in California, USA. It is important not only for its dominance of the industry but also because many people hope to copy its growth. By doing this successfully, the present ill winds of economic misfortune might be negated and a new era of prosperity generated. Therefore, because of its obvious importance, Silicon Valley will be examined in more detail in the next section.

The Silicon Valley Model

Silicon Valley is the name conjured up to describe the hundreds of low-slung, noiseless, smokeless, gleaming factories that sit between Freeway 101 and El Camino Real, the two main routes through this area of California. The factories found in the area are those like Zilog and Intel (recently bought into by IBM [Forester, 1987]) which are semiconductor companies concerned with putting information onto the small silicon chip and, like Apple and Hewlett-Packard, use the chips to manufacture the computer hardware. Also there are the satellite software companies designing the software which provides the computer with its program of action.

Silicon Valley epitomizes the traditional concept of classical capitalist development combining high elements of risk and uncertainty with venture capital, mediated by large slabs of luck. But, particularly after World War II, when there were lucrative federal government research funds and military contracts provided to win the Cold War, the region gained its major impetus (Saxenian, 1989). Much of the momentum in the high tech industry hinged on the work of William Shockley who, with the backing of millions of government dollars, invented the transistor in the late 1940s. Moving near Stanford University whose presence had fostered a number of electronics companies, Shockley worked for one of these at Palo Alto in the Santa Clara Valley. Here also a design team led by Hoff invented the microprocessor, a semiconductor chip containing thousands of integrated circuits as well as a memory (see Reinecke, 1983). The coincidences of Shockley going home to a location near Stanford which had creative graduates like Hoff looking for jobs and the initial input of huge amounts of government money as a result of the Cold War quickly transformed the Santa Clara County area. As Howard describes it:

> Thirty years ago, Santa Clara County was known mainly for its fruit orchards and the silicon chip did not exist. Today the county is blanketed with some 500 electronics firms ranging in size from 16,000 workers to 10 or less, and Silicon Valley has become the center of a $100 billion world electronic industry producing everything from calculators to cruise missiles, space invader computer games to industrial robots. (Howard, 1981, p. 22)

In the present era of economic downturn, of unemployment and plant closure, of deindustrialization, Silicon Valley stands out as the symbol and the future path that it is thought industry must tread if new jobs are going to be generated and new wealth accumulated. Consequently, the popular press in Australia and overseas proclaims that industries must look towards new high technology in order to generate new wealth and jobs. Moreover, it concludes that there are signs of a new consensus that Australia must embrace technology if its existing industries are to survive and if new industries are to flourish (*Future Age*, No. 3, 1984). Such sentiments are aptly demonstrated in the Victorian government statement of 1986 that: 'A major shift is underway in the composition of economic activity from resource intensive industries to knowledge intensive industries. Thus, economic growth is increasingly drawing on reserves of intellectual and technical skills rather than on resources of coal, iron ore and metals' (in Reinecke, 1989, p. 7).

The development of a high technology industry seems to many national and local governments to depend on the creation of new Silicon Valleys. In this vein the Australian government has encouraged the Australian Industry Development Corporation (AIDC) to become actively involved in the development of high technology industries. One aspect of this involvement has been the investment of $70 million in the AIDC's industrial research investment scheme. Paralleling this federal activity has been the involvement of a number of state governments through the establishment of technology parks in Adelaide and Perth and a centre for technology and design in Melbourne (*Future Age*, No. 3, 1984). Such developments are an attempt to emulate the Silicon Valley model, where high technology parks have arisen specializing in semiconductors, computers, telecommunications, robotics and biotechnology near major universities such as Stanford.

The rush to set up these technology parks is not only confined to Australia but also is a major concern of local and state governments in England and America. For example, Chicago and San Antonio have put forward plans to set up programs to foster the growth of high technology. Both cities aim to promote industries concerned with electronics, biotechnology and robotics. This promotion will be facilitated by the creation of investment funds and by redirecting education towards the needs of the new industry. This promotion will also involve locating the parks near universities not only for research interaction but also to attract federal research funds. Grubb (1984) illustrates that educational reform is seen as attracting much of the new high technology industry. In this way

> ... the robotics program at Oakland Community College (Michigan) has been justified as contributing to 'Michigan's salvation' by replacing jobs lost in the auto industry and the president of a community college in an area of high unemployment has declared that 'the development of high technology programs represent(s) our very best hope, not only of attracting new industry to one area, but for helping existing industry compete and prosper.' (Grubb, 1984, p. 432)

These communities hope that by creating a favourable economic and educational climate they will be able to compete from a position of advantage in attracting high technology corporations. By creating a supply of suitable workers it is hoped that a demand for their services will eventuate.

Several Australian states have taken a similar stance in seeking to train workers to meet the specific needs of industry. In Victoria in 1987 the Victorian government launched the Victorian Education Foundation (VEF) in an effort to more closely 'link education with busineses'. Education is seen as a catalyst both in stimulating the economy and in responding to the economy's needs. The business world is encouraged to pinpoint its requirements so that the VEF can contribute financial support in order that the 'strategic and competitive advantage of Victoria' is maintained. The priority areas designated in this instrumental, human capital agenda include mathematics, science, technology, business and management subjects. To fund these areas, employers are encouraged to divert 0.1 per cent of the 6 per cent state payroll tax into the Fund — as well as other financial contributions offered as a tax deduction! Similarly, New South Wales has in 1989 introduced legislation to establish an

Education and Training Foundation which gives businesses the choice of diverting 2 per cent of their state payroll tax to the Foundation. The money gathered in this way will be channelled into the creation and operation of educational programs which will both respond to industry's needs and encourage new industries to set up operations in the state.

However, scholars such as Macdonald (1983) have grave doubts on whether the success story of Silicon Valley can be transferred to a comparable site in Australia. He argues that it is a mistaken assumption to conclude that almost anywhere that can offer a pleasant climate, universities and large amounts of high risk capital can become another Silicon Valley. As a consequence, he argues, 'high technology policy is easily confused with employment, education and, particularly regional development incentives' (Macdonald, 1983, p. 335). Moreover, it is not so much an élite of high tech engineers that is the dynamic force in Silicon Valley but low tech service professionals. As he puts it, 'the major participants in the innovative process are such people as accountants, managers and salesmen — not high-status scientists and engineers' (Macdonald, 1983, p. 335). For the main concern in any capitalist enterprise is marketing and selling the commodity. The historical context of Shockley deciding to settle in Palo Alto and the consequent offsprings such as Fairchild Semiconductor, combined with the high mobility of the people in the industry, make it almost impossible to emulate Silicon Valley. Macdonald concludes that by putting into place the commonly accepted criteria on which it is thought that the Silicon Valley model is based 'there is only the prospect of chaos, waste and ultimate disappointment' (Macdonald, 1983, p. 344). Such disappointment has been amply illustratd by Reinecke in his survey of the attempts to promote high technology industries in Australia. He concludes that 'while the rhetoric remains, Australia is perhaps even further than it was a decade ago from creating an indigenous high technology industry that will provide a new and lasting wellspring of wealth' (Reinecke, 1989, p. 7).

But it is important to stress that all of the success of Silicon Valley has not been spread evenly. While there has been much wealth generated with the instant millionaires such as Wozniak and Jobs of Apple, not all high technology industries operate completely with high technology occupations (see Watkins, 1985). Much of the work is repetitive assembly-line work. In Silicon Valley this work is performed largely by women and minorities, made up increasingly of Filipino and Vietnamese immigrants. But even these workers are likely to command a wage which is considered too high by the corporate managers. Consequently, many of the companies have branches in Asia situated near airports where Jumbo Jets can shuttle the chips easily across the Pacific Ocean. These new assembly-line workers are in Malaysia, the Philippines, Indonesia and Hong Kong. In this respect Asian assemblers' hourly wages vary from about the $8.37 of the US norm to Indonesia with $0.35 and $1.58 in Hong Kong (Scott and Angel, 1988, p. 1054). They are typically women who are paid a minimal daily rate on the eye-straining work of wiring the chips to the minute circuit boards.

This ability of high technology to facilitate the transfer of jobs and production may mean that not just parts of the manufacturing process but almost the entire company may be moved to an overseas location. Levin and Rumberger (1983a), for instance, reported that Atari was considering shifting most of its production facilities to sites in Taiwan and Hong Kong. The immediate result was to be that 1700 workers in their Silicon Valley facilities would be sacked. In a transfer of this scale the impact of redundancy not only hits the production workers but also middle management.

Such activity indicated that all was not completely well in Silicon Valley in the mid- to late 1980s. It became obvious that the optimistic growth which others hoped to emulate had difficulty in being sustained. In fact during this period the semiconductor industry was described as being in mid-life crisis (*Electronics Week*, 17 May 1985). From August 1984 until June 1985, 18,000 jobs were lost in Silicon Valley. Both Apple Computers and Wang Computers sacked 1600 employees and more than 5000 jobs were lost overall in June 1985 alone (*Business Week*, 24 June 1985, *Australian*, 29–30 June 1985). Austerity programs were introduced into most companies. For example, Advanced Micro Services made its employees work longer hours for no extra pay. In addition, there were plans to put the majority of their 8000 workforce onto a four-day week with a 15 per cent cut in pay after closing the plant for a two-week period (*Australian*, 29–30 June 1985). The crisis was triggered by the almost total collapse of interest in the home computer and video game markets. The boom in consumer high technology during this period appeared to have burst. Consequently, personal computers and video games were dubbed by the popular press the 'hula hoops of the '80s' (*Australian*, 29–30 June 1985). Forester (1987) indicates that during the first half of 1985 the US semiconductor and computer industries had shed 27 per cent of their total number of employees. This trend was not confined to the USA; forecasts in the UK also predicted a decline of about 20 per cent in employment in these industries (Forester, 1987, p. 245) even though there would be a steady rise in output. Some loss of interest seemed to occur because people set about re-evaluating whether computers do provide information more efficiently, more easily and more productively. For example, is it easier to have cooking recipes displayed on a video screen or on cards which can be moved and placed next to the cooking utensils? The extent of the crisis which beset Silicon Valley should make those who blindly set out to follow Silicon Valley's pattern place their approach to high technology on more solid foundations.

Howard (1981) points out that many of the high technology industries actually work on the same basis as the mass production, assembly-line techniques of the car industry. Basically, there are three stages to the assembly-line process: first, workers look after process machinery, producing the quartz (silicon) and testing the integrated circuits; next, the circuits have fine wires attached under high-powered microscopes; last, different circuits are 'stuffed' into printed circuit boards.

To provide some idea of the work done by these high tech assembly-line workers, Howard presents a vignette of one of them.

> Susan Hoffman has worked in printed circuit board assembly at firms across the Valley. She has stuffed boards in 'clean rooms' where the environment is closely controlled for dust and workers wear rubber gloves, caps and smocks known as 'rabbit suits'. She has also stuffed them in a garage where during the summer the temperature hovered around 100 degrees. Either way, she says, stuffing 80 to 100 PC boards all day is 'dehumanizing work'. First, the worker places the circuits in the board, then passes it through a wave solder machine to fix the connections, then cleans it in an open tank of freon, a common industrial solvent. At the smaller companies, says Hoffman, the soldering is done by hand, the fumes from the burning metal are strong, but you can usually get a small fan if you ask for it. (Howard, 1981, p. 23)

The fact that many of the jobs in the high technology companies of Silicon Valley are repetitive, routine assembly-line jobs has caused distinct labour market segmentation to become evident. Saxenian's study of Silicon Valley (1985, 1989) confirms this segmented labour force by illustrating that the high technology industry there 'employs an unusually large proportion of professional and managerial employees alongside an equally large, but minimally skilled, production workforce' (1985, p. 83). This segmentation has had profound effects on social structure, class distribution and urban development. High income professional workers live in Palo Alto, while low income production workers live in San Jose.

The theory of labour market segmentation claims that there exist in the labour market distinct primary and secondary segments. The primary sector in Silicon Valley comprises the élite technicians, managers and sales personnel. In the secondary sector are the women and minorities for whom high technology industry 'means low-wage, dead-end jobs, unskilled, tedious work and exposure to some of the most dangerous occupational health hazards in all American industry' (Howard, 1981, p. 22). The existence of these two labour markets in high technology and the realization that high technology does not necessarily mean high technology occupations are matters which should be of great concern to educationalists. This concern should especially manifest itself when one reflects on the calls to link education, instrumentally, to a high technology future.

The Gender Implications of Technological Change

In the previous section an examination of the Silicon Valley example of high technology highlighted the presence of a segmented labour market. There were two distinct segments: a primary sector occupied by the high tech creators, accountants, and managers; and a secondary labour market occupied mainly by women and minorities who do repetitive, assembly-line, often part-time casual work. The Kirby Report (1985) perceived a similar general situation in Australia. It found that 'the incidence of part-time employment was particularly high among women.... [Also] some 17 per cent of female employment was in casual jobs, a far higher proportion than for any other group' (Kirby Report, 1985, p. 43). The findings in the Kirby Report also supported the evidence from the Silicon Valley example that the labour market is frequently divided on the grounds of gender. As the Kirby Report puts it:

> Underlying these patterns of inequitable access to employment is a high degree of labour market segregation on the basis of gender. Female employment is concentrated in relatively few major occupations and industry categories. For instance, in August 1984 over 33 per cent of women in the workforce were employed in clerical occupations. Many of them in low skilled jobs, compared with 8 per cent of males. In August 1984 over half of the female employment was concentrated in the community service, wholesale and retail trade industries, with low skilled, low paid jobs. Gender segregation in the labour market is an important reason why, despite the existence of the 'equal pay' principle, female earnings remain low relative to those of males. (Kirby Report, 1985, pp. 43–4)

As Apple (1985) suggests when looking at similar figures in the USA, these statistics indicate that the work women have traditionally done is related to both a vertical segregation, where women are disadvantaged compared with men, and a horizontal segmentation, where women are concentrated into specific types of work.

Kramar (1984), when studying the employment of women in the New South Wales Public Service, has bluntly stated that divisions within the service are based on sex. 'The sexual division of labour is hierarchical with men dominating senior authority positions, while women are concentrated in temporary subordinate and routine jobs' (Kramar, 1984, p. 200). The research by O'Donnell (1984) in Australia also supports the thesis that women have been disadvantaged through the sexual division of labour. Not only is the average female wage only about 67 per cent of the average wage for a male worker, but the position of women in the labour market is likely to be much more insecure than men while still occupying the lowest rung of the occupational hierarchy (O'Donnell, 1984, p. 147). With the introduction of high technology the division of labour based on gender has not been alleviated; rather, it has been exacerbated. Baldock, for instance, has found that 'the result of the introduction of new technology ... is more likely than not an artificial reclassification of labour, and a further strengthening of the gender division of labour' (Baldock, 1984, p. 276). Following the concern of these scholars, this section will examine the impact of high technology on those areas of work in which women are predominantly found. In particular the impact of high technology on office work and general 'white collar' areas of employment will be considered.

One of the major areas where computers and new information technologies are having the greatest impact is the working conditions of women. For instance, 'bank work has become increasingly routinised and repetitive', while the deskilling process 'in white collar work such as banking ... refers to a loss of knowledge of banking processes as a result of fragmentation' (Game and Pringle, 1983, p. 56; see also Garson, 1981). Increasing automation can be used not only to reduce secretarial skills in occupations which are predominantly female but also to centralize the work. For example, wordprocessing tends to be located in central workstations, involving routine, repetitive, keyboard-based data entry tasks which are fragmented and remote from the decision-making sources of the organization (see Downing, 1983).

The main thrust in the implementation of high technology in the office is to reduce the production costs per worker by automating the flow of work. The office worker is seen as not very productive compared to the blue collar worker in the factory. Windschuttle (1983) has pointed out that in the USA about 84 per cent of the office costs are labour costs, and in the last decade American office productivity has risen only 4 per cent compared to industrial productivity's 90 per cent. Capital expenditure per worker in American industry is $25,000; in offices only $2000. 'The most realistic predictions do not suggest that offices will match the efficiency of the factory, but there is still plenty of ground to be gained' (Windschuttle, 1983, pp. 81–2). In an attempt to match the factory, office work is being broken down into smaller fragments, while individual knowledge is being extracted and deposited on computer programs. In this vein Robert Noyce, Vice-Chairman of Intel, has commented that:

> We still have an enormous amount of paper in our society. If you look around the office, there is hardly a piece of paper that couldn't be eliminated with adequate file systems and retrieval systems — all of which will take more and more intelligence from the computer on the desk.... We are just at the beginning of mechanising all this intellectual activity going on — which represents by far the greatest portion of the work force.

Charles Sporck of National Semiconductor added: 'This technology can replace much of the manual labour now in use, and increasingly more of the skilled labour' (*The National Times*, February 1981).

The transfer of much workplace intellectual activity to management through the computer process makes office employees easier to control and easier to replace. Cooley (1980a) has argued that the introduction of high technology into traditional white collar areas of work will mean a decline in the quality of work to the office worker just as it has already done to the factory floor. He suggests that 'there are now good grounds for believing that we are beginning to repeat in the field of white-collar, intellectual and conceptual work, most of the mistakes we have already made at enormous cost at earlier historical stages when skilled manual work was subjected to technological change' (1980a, p. 524). Cooley concludes that high technology might be regarded as a 'Trojan Horse' to dehumanize and fragment work into minute repetitive tasks, each accurately timed (see also Watkins, 1986a).

But as Feldberg and Glenn (1983) show, because of the segmentation of the labour market and its relationship to family gender hierarchies (Feldberg and Glenn, 1979), the impact of technology in the office may differ for men and women. Examining the impact of new technology on occupational structure, they reached a number of conclusions. They found that the new office technology was labour-saving, reducing the number of people required in some jobs. Second, although there was a slight increase in the labour force, the number of traditional clerical jobs was reduced. Third, the introduction of the new technology was also used to reorganize the work. Occupations became narrower, more specialized and standardized, thus becoming independent of a worker's experience and knowledge. Fourth, the introduction of this high technology has increased the need for some more highly paid new positions. However, these are most likely to be a male preserve, with women most unlikely to move into these jobs. Thus Feldberg and Glenn found that 'with increasing automation, male/female stratification in the office became even more pronounced' (1983, p. 69). However, it would, perhaps, be wrong to see this as the result of an overt conspiracy on the part of men to degrade women. Rather, it can be seen as reflecting the commonly held, taken-for-granted assumptions which underpin perceptions of femininity and masculinity. It could be argued that many of these new positions are believed to require aggressiveness, ruthlessness and the ability to make tough decisions. However, such traits are ideologically linked to masculinity rather than femininity, leading to 'natural' segregation in the workforce (see Baker, 1964; Watkins, 1986b).

Such conclusions on the effects of high technology on women in the workforce are supported by a number of authors (Downing, 1980, 1983; Buchanan and Boddy, 1982; Arnold, Birke and Faulkner, 1981; Morgall, 1983). Morgall points out that wordprocessors in offices can be used both as a means of greater managerial control and further to widen the gap between what is seen as 'men's' and 'women's' work through the downgrading of skilled women workers. Similarly, Buchanan and Boddy (1982) found that the skill levels of the women working in offices were reduced by the introduction of wordprocessors. Work was created which was essentially specialized, repetitious, routine and boring with a reduction of the knowledge and understanding of the end product. But Morgall and Buchanan and Boddy argue that these situations were the result of managerial decisions. The wordprocessors could have been used in alternative ways. The technology could have been used to increase the intellectual involvement and skill requirements of the women operating the wordprocessors. However, management's preoccupation with better control techniques took precedence over any other considerations (see Buchanan and Boddy, 1982, p. 10). As Arnold, Birke and Faulkner (1981) conclude, with the emphasis on control, 'the patriarchal hierarchy, in which women are subordinate to men, is only likely to be reinforced and intensified by the advent of word processing technology' (Arnold, Birke and Faulkner, 1981, p. 336). To correct this reinforcement of the patriarchal hierarchy, Baldock proposes that technology should be reformulated on a more caring, concrete and personalized basis. There would be a recognition that women do not lose their skills through new high technology. Rather, the skills of women are undervalued and are excluded through the application of the new technology (Baldock, 1984).

While Feldberg and Glenn (1983) and Arnold, Birke and Faulkner (1981), for example, point out that the contradictory nature of the technological innovations, as well as the depressed economic scenario, have made any resistance to the way technology has been used muted and defensive, management is not necessarily seen as omnipotent. Downing (1983), in her research into female work in banking, has highlighted some ways in which women contest these new techniques of managerial control.

Downing (1983) reports that the introduction of new high technology by a major US bank into its San Francisco branch was expected by the women workers to increase their intellectual involvement and their autonomy. However, these expectations were not realized. Rather, work was reorganized on an assembly-line basis with increased monitoring and control. As one wordprocessor operator indicated to Downing:

> Everyone was excited to learn this new thing that was going to help alleviate boredom and make life easier and then they found out that they didn't do that at all — in fact they made it more boring. People felt that they were plugged into machines, that they were appendages to machines rather than people performing functions with other people. (Downing, 1983, p. 47)

The way the new technology has been employed and the consequent organization of work led the women to develop ways of using the technology to give vent to their dissatisfaction. So that they could break the repetition, they discovered and utilized the code for bringing the system down for maintenance. To counter the strict time deadlines, the women used strong magnets to erase the computer tapes 'by accident'. When the preoccupation with strict control became too much, the 110 wordprocessor operators would all rise at the same time to go to the toilet. Finally, Downing found that when things became extremely bad, the women 'would "forget" to key in their personal reference code which was necessary for their productivity count, and would proceed to key in obscenities which would come out in print' (Downing, 1983, p. 50). Because the work had been routinized and standardized, it was impossible to discover where to lay the blame. The consequence was that management was forced to re-evaluate the accepted IBM approach to the wordprocessor centre and to 'rethink' their philosophy on high technology and the organization of the wordprocessor operators.

In this section we have looked at the development of high technology and its application in the workplace. In particular, we have looked at the impact of new technology on white collar office work, which has traditionally been largely the domain of women workers. In the next section the likely consequences and implications of these trends on education will be examined.

High/Low Tech Jobs and Education

This section looks, first, at the influence high technology will have on future job opportunities and, second, at the educational response to these projected patterns.

High Tech/Low Tech Jobs

The increasing dominance of high technology in the lives of ordinary people has provided the hope of a new avenue along which the education of children might proceed. The production and servicing of these new advanced technologies are assumed to require a much more highly credentialled and qualified workforce. Pogrow (1983), for instance, puts the case that schools must produce more individuals skilled in high technology to meet the demands of the job market. This would include producing both students with high levels in maths and science skills to advance the frontiers of high technology and a plentiful supply of teachers to impart these skills. Education, Pogrow argues, must increase the number of individuals, scientists and engineers to satisfy the needs of the future high tech job market. In Australia a similar functionalist relationship between high technology and education is often presented. 'More than ever before education must seek to develop and enhance the talents of each individual and yet at the same time encourage that individual to contribute to a cohesive society based on understanding and respect' (Stranks, 1983, p. 143). Stranks sees the problem as one of essentially organizing the natural resources of human capital on a more efficient basis to cope with the demands of high technology. Citing the Williams Report, the Myers Report and the Keeves Report, Stranks claims that there is overall agreement that education 'much respond in ways that will enable us to manage and adapt technological change to our advantage' (1983, p. 143). A solution is offered by the example of Singapore, with that country's drive to foster increasingly higher levels of competence in mathematics. However, the call to link education instrumentally to the development of high technology is not limited to university professors like Stranks. Minister for Education, Employment and Training, John Dawkins has also called for higher levels of educational attainment to cope with the anticipated changes in the workforce. He has commented that the Commonwealth government believes that, as the hoped-for economic recovery takes place, the jobs which will be created for young people will require higher levels of education and training than in the past (Dawkins, 1987). Similarly, Johnson, the former secretary of the Department of Education and Youth Affairs, has commented on the Task Force on Education and Technology in the following way: 'The Task Force will develop options for policy and program initiatives to assist and encourage the educational system in stimulating, anticipating, shaping and responding to technological change and an increased level of technological innovation in Australia' (Johnson, 1984, p. 96).

However, not all educationalists are so confident in tying education to the high technology bandwagon. Sweet (1987) and Burke (1987) in Australia and Grubb (1984), Rumberger (1984a, 1984b, 1987) and Levin (Levin and Rumberger, 1983a, 1983b; Rumberger and Levin, 1985) have emphasized that high skill, high technology occupations will not be as important in the future as low tech, service jobs. In this vein Sweet argues that in Australia the skilled, attractive jobs have declined sharply for young people. His research indicates that technological innovation has had no impact on employment for young people. Rather, technological change can be linked both directly and indirectly to a decline in the opportunities for youth entering skilled occupations. But Sweet warns that:

> A recognition that technological change will not necessarily increase the demand for skills, that in some areas there has been a substantial deskilling because of the way technology has been introduced and that many past trends reflect supply and government expenditure rather than a technological imperative, carries risks for educational policy makers. (1987, p. 114)

The most obvious risk is that those who see education as being closely tied and instrumental to the demands of the workplace will call for cuts in education spending. However, education must be relocated from this narrow human capital agenda and placed on a more critical reflexive and transformative basis.

The trend towards low tech forms of jobs in Australia has also been noted by Ruthven of IBIS Corporate Services and John Brown, the former Minister for Sport and Tourism. Brown has pointed out that the leisure industry is creating about 30,000 jobs a year and with 400,000 people is Australia's biggest industry (*The Australian*, 28 July 1984, p. 19). Ruthven indicates that the leisure industry will probably create 730,000 of the 2.5 million new jobs Australia will need by the turn of the century. Most of these jobs will be of a casual or part-time temporary nature, requiring little training or skill. In the United Kingdom these low tech occupations have been called 'Mickey Mouse' jobs. However, Ruthven argues that any job is better than no job, and this type of work will be the only source of income for many people in Australia in the future (*The Australian*, 28 July 1984, p. 19).

In the United States of America a similar trend in work is evident. Rumberger (1984a, 1984b, 1987) and Levin (Rumberger and Levin, 1985; Levin and Rumberger, 1983a, 1983b) in recent papers have pointed out that, while high technology industries will be growing rapidly because of their low base, the actual numbers of jobs created by high tech will be quite low. Their projections indicate that only 7 per cent of the new employment opportunities created will be associated with high tech. In more general terms Etzioni and Jargowsky (1984) are also critical of the taken-for-granted orthodoxy that assumes that jobs in the United States economy are rapidly moving into the high tech areas such as microelectronics, telecommunications and bioengineering. While the high tech area is undoubtedly expanding, the great bulk of jobs will still be in basic, low tech industries. They found that basic jobs will continue to contribute a significant amount to the economy and will be an important sector in an integrated economy made up of both low tech and high tech industries. Similarly, Jamieson and Tasker (1988), during an intensive examination of the relationship of schooling with new technology, argue that, while there are spectacular instances of the applications of high technology, the actual workplace has undergone little transformation. They contend that 'changes in technology do not automatically bring about radical changes in the world of work. What changes new technology brings about, are always mediated by the political process, whether this is at the level of the individual firm or of society' (1988, p. 14).

The basis of the common orthodoxy rests with a number of misconceptions concerning high technology. Rumberger and Levin (1985) argue that misconception has arisen with regard to high technology and employment in three areas. First, as we have seen from our study of Silicon Valley, high technology industries have been confused with high technology occupations. In fact, less than a quarter of the jobs in high technology industries are high technology jobs (Rumberger and Levin, 1985). The majority of jobs are low tech, employing easily replaceable female and migrant labour. The second area of misconception relates to the comparative rates of growth for high tech and low tech industries. Any accelerated growth in the development of high tech industries does not mean a large absolute number of workers. This is due to the fact that compared with traditional areas of employment such as the manufacture of cars, these new occupations employ many fewer workers. Third, Rumberger and Levin (1985) show that, whereas previous technologies have reduced that physical demands of manual work, the present high technology is being used to take over mental, white collar areas of work. Thus it seems highly unlikely that the introduction of high technology will result inevitably in an increasing number of jobs in new areas of work. For example, the most recent user-friendly computers have made many computer programmers' jobs already redundant (Watkins, 1985). Indeed, an examination of the latest in, for example, personal computers which, through the use of 'windows', 'icons' and 'menus' have virtually eliminated any necessity to know a program language, makes any belief in the need for higher skill levels extremely difficult to hold. This impetus to reduce to a minimum any period of skill training by increasing the 'friendliness' of technology is a major aim of the high tech industry (see Guteri, 1984).

Similar to what we have seen as the likely trends in Australia, an examination of figures of the US Bureau of Statistics by Levin and Rumberger revealed that, while there would indeed be an increase in high tech occupations, by far the greatest increase would be in the low tech clerical and service occupations. They elaborated that:

> this picture is further reinforced by examination of individual high technology job categories. While jobs for computer systems analysts will increase by over 100 per cent between 1978 and 1990, only 200,000 new jobs will be created. In contrast there will be over 600,000 jobs for janitors and sextons. In fact, more new jobs for janitors will be created than new jobs in all the five occupations with the highest relative growth rates. Consider another example: about 150,000 new jobs for computer programmers are expected to emerge during this 12 year period, a level of growth vastly outpaced by the 800,000 new jobs expected for fast food workers and kitchen helpers. (Levin and Rumberger, 1983b, p. 5)

From the studies described in Australia and the United States it is evident that high technology is not going to solve the problem of youth unemployment or lead to large numbers of high technology jobs. Indeed, it is in the service industry where the fastest absolute growth will occur. The jobs most evident will be those such as custodians of buildings, nurses aides, salespeople, cashiers, waiters or waitresses. None of these fastest growing jobs is related to high technology. In the light of this evidence Rumberger and Levin (1985, p. 414) conclude that: '*not only will high tech provide few job opportunities in the future economy, but most new jobs will require no post-secondary schooling and will pay wages significantly lower than the average.*'

The Educational Response

The educational response should not be concerned with a blanket hostility towards technology but should introduce into the educative process a critical approach whereby we can reflect and explore the social and cultural ramifications of technology's introduction. Educationalists should prompt the consideration of basic questions regarding how and why certain technologies are being used in a particular way. In this way teachers can assist students to understand the values and structures which underlie the technological changes going on around them. The ongoing improvement of society and increased human autonomy are thus integral to a critical educative approach. Fay has highlighted the difference between an 'educative' and 'instrumental' approach:

> Both the instrumentalist and educative models promise freedom; but in the former it is the freedom that results from knowing how to achieve what one wants, whereas in the latter it is the freedom to be self-determining in the sense of being able to decide for oneself, on the basis of a lucid, critical self-awareness, the manner in which one wishes to live. In the educative model, the practical result of social theory is not the means for greater manipulative power, but rather the self-understanding that allows one's rational thinking to be the cause of one's actions: ie, social theory is a means towards increased autonomy. (Fay, 1977, p. 207)

Through an educative, critical approach in education about technology and work, a better understanding of the development of high technology and the society on which it impinges might be engendered. By engaging in such a practice education might be seen not merely as responding to the needs of the economy but to the needs of people. 'Thus education for the workplace needs to attack a finer division of labour, and it needs to give people the capacity to understand, and resist, the forces that are shaping the skills required of them at work' (Sweet, 1987, p. 115). Such an educative process would perhaps involve closely examining the rationale and strategy developed by Lucas Aerospace workers. Here the concern relies

> not merely on the fact that a group of workers for the first time are demanding the right to work on socially useful products, but they are proposing a whole series of new methods of production where a worker's hand and brain can really contribute to the design and development of products, and where they can work in a non-alienated manner in a labour process which enhances human beings rather than diminishes them. (Cooley, 1980b, p. 79)

For schools, comparable practice would not entail merely teaching such things as computer literacy devoid of any social and historical context. For, as Noble (1984) has argued, to do this merely reinforces the ideological notion of a predetermined technological future. Rather, the teaching of such literacy should be coupled to a critique of the economic, political, social and cultural foundations of society. Reinecke (1983) presents the case that the concept of computer literacy and of young people working with computers has a deceptive allure due to the fact that the degree of skill involved has been grossly overestimated. He suggests that this allure has masked the realization that access to, and working with, computers has the more basic underpinning of wealth and class. The result is that 'very often the people promoting computer literacy also accept a picture of a stratified society in which there will be a sharp division between the people Adam Osborne calls the capable and the incapable' (Reinecke, 1983, p. 187).

But through educative critique the imperative of technological determinism, which conceals powerful interests while segmenting society into an élite and their dependents, might be subject to scrutiny. For, as I have argued elsewhere,

> it would appear that, unless there is a massive transformation of the economy and society, there will evolve a highly educated elite who will develop and direct the form of technological change, while the majority of society will be occupied in fairly low-skilled service industries. In this way high technology is reinforcing the class nature of society while tending to accentuate the redistribu-

tion of power and the creation of increased imbalances between society's economic classes. (Watkins, 1985, pp. 32–3)

Any such transformation must have the school as one of the focal points in promoting educative, critical practices. However, it would appear that at present very few schools have tackled in depth the social effects of computers. Yet the need for schools 'forming attitudes and policies which ameliorate the unemployment created by computer technology and its effects on skills is one of the most pressing social needs' (Reinecke, 1983, p. 172). This need might be fulfilled by the Blackburn Report (1985) recommendation that the study of work in society be compulsorily undertaken as two units during the last two years of post-compulsory education. The Report suggests that the nature and organization of work should be examined in the social and historical context. It suggests a dialectic whereby the historical paths and the daily paths of human agency intersect and interact. Or, as the Report proposes, 'it essentially represents a form of socio-economic history brought forward into the present, interacting with the history of technology and involving contact with work places and the life experiences of various older men and women' (Blackburn Report, 1985, p. 29).

An educative critical view of technology would focus on the way technology can inhibit or constrain inequalities in the distribution of resources and power. Moreover, it would emphasize that technology, when viewed in a certain light, presents a particular ideology of the world (see Watkins, 1985). In contrast, a functional determinist view merely tends to facilitate a process whereby the essential facets of the status quo are reproduced. In educating students on the creation and implementation of technology, there is a need to bring about an understanding of the way technology interacts with social structures to produce and reproduce a particular construction of reality. Such a critical educative practice should also provide a capacity to illustrate where and how change might be generated from within the totality of society. For, as Connell *et al.* argue, 'the business of school is not propaganda; it is equipping people with the knowledge and skills and concepts relevant to remaking a dangerous and disordered world. In the most basic sense, the process of education and the process of liberation are the same' (Connell *et al.*, 1982, p. 208).

To relate this educative experience to practice in schools, Wood (1985) has suggested a number of ways in which meaningful participation in the choice and direction of technological change may be fostered. First, the development of critical basic skills should be a major facet of the school curriculum. Second, schools should strive to give students an understanding of their own historical and cultural context. Through this educative experience students can take up a position whether to support, oppose or change the status quo. Third, schools should expose the alternatives not only in ways of democratic living but also in ways of technological employment. Fourth, so that the fullest degree of participation in choices and decisions may be possible, change needs to come to the traditional authoritarian structure of schools. Lastly, schools should seek to foster values which facilitate equality, participation and a sense of human emancipation. Through such an educative process people will come to discover that education is not instrumental to a prescribed, predetermined technological necessity but rather technology is subject to human critique, human choice and human agency.

Conclusion

This chapter has attempted to demonstrate that an uncritical acceptance of the technological imperative popularly associated with high technology is likely to lead to contradictory outcomes. The functional determinism of two scholars, Ellul and Winner, on technological change was outlined. They claim that technology has got out of control by developing a life and rationale of its own. This argument leads to the aggregation and reification of the concept of technology. But perhaps most importantly, the argument of Winner in particular tends to equate all purposive human action with technological change, thus making technology by definition all-encompassing. The logical extension of this argument is that on every front people are dominated by technology. However, the emphasis on technology versus human beings ignores the potential of human beings to devise technological innovations with the capacity to liberate members of society. Technology can have inherent within it a range of values which can influence whether certain outcomes are seen as desirable or otherwise. This element of political reflexivity is a noticeable omission from the deterministic position. By neglecting to reflect on the political, social, economic and historical, especially the pre-modern period, the deterministic approach fosters a sense of helplessness. However, by reflecting on these concerns, a dialectic is revealed which helps dispel any feeling that human beings are now ineffectual in the way technology develops.

The model which most exemplifies the latest word of technological change is that of Silicon Valley. It was illustrated that there have been feverish efforts to copy the development of Silicon Valley in Australia and elsewhere. However, it was pointed out that there are many contradictory elements inherent in Silicon Valley itself. While it may be the mecca of current high technology, the work is frequently arranged on traditional assembly-line methods within, as Saxenian (1985, 1989) has illustrated, a strongly polarized social structure. The result of this organization of work is that most of the jobs are boring, repetitious and routinized. The main effect is to develop a segmented labour market where it seems that women especially, and migrants, do the poorly paid repetitive work, while men predominantly occupy the well paid, powerful positions in these corporations. This effect is not confined to Silicon Valley. Recent research indicates that one of the effects of high technology has been to accentuate the patriarchal hierarchy in organizations.

But many educators and educational administrators have argued that children must be more specifically educated, especially in the higher maths and sciences, to take their place creating and working the new technology (Pogrow, 1983). However, recent research in Australia and the USA indicates that it will not be in high tech occupations in which the majority of people will work in the future but in low tech positions, especially in the service sector of the economy. For instance, the work of Rumberger and Levin (1985) indicates that, while there will be undoubted growth in high technology occupations, these jobs make up, and will continue to make up, only a small percentage of the total labour market. Accordingly, the educational response should not reside in schools responding in a functional fashion to the needs of industry but rather in critically examining the practices and repercussions emanating from human choice in the creation and implementation of technology.

In conclusion, it has been argued that education should adopt a critical approach towards new technology. The legitimacy of the new technology, as well as its political foundations and power base, should be open to scrutiny. Through educative critique the apparent logic of determinism would be contrasted with the contradictions uncovered within the existing social order. In this way the functionalist unitary image of society engaging in coherent, rationalized actions would be set against, and discarded for, the dialectic of actual, daily practice interacting with the bonds of history and society.

References

APPLE, M.W. (1985) 'Teaching and "women's work": A comparative historical and ideological analysis', *Teachers College Record*, 86, 3, pp. 455–73.

ARNOLD, E., BIRKE, L. and FAULKNER, W. (1981) 'Women and microelectronics: The case of wordprocessors', *Women's Studies International Quarterly*, 4, 1, pp. 321–40.

BAKER, E.F. (1964) *Technology and Woman's Work*, New York, Columbia University Press.

BALDOCK, C. (1984) 'The skills of women in deskilled society', *Search*, 15, 9/10, pp. 275–78.
BERG, I. (1979) *Industrial Sociology*, Englewood Cliffs, N.J., Prentice-Hall.
BLACKBURN REPORT, *see Ministerial Review of Post Compulsory Schooling* (1985).
BRAVERMAN, H. (1974) *Labor and Monopoly Capital: The Degradation of Work in the Twentieth Century*, New York, Monthly Review Press.
BUCHANAN, D. and BODDY, D. (1982) 'Advanced technology and the quality of working life: The effects of wordprocessing on video typists', *Journal of Occupational Psychology*, 55, pp. 1–11.
BURKE, G. (1987) 'The structure and finance of education', in BURKE, G. and RUMBERGER, R. (Eds), *The Future Impact of Technology on Work and Education*, Lewes, Falmer Press.
BURNS, T. (Ed.) (1969) *Industrial Man*, Harmondsworth, Penguin.
COLLINS, R. (1975) *Conflict Sociology*, New York, Academic.
COMMITTEE OF INQUIRY INTO EDUCATION AND TRAINING (1979) (Williams Report) *Education, Training and Employment*, 3 vols, Canberra, Australian Government Publishing Service.
COMMITTEE OF INQUIRY INTO LABOUR MARKET PROGRAMS (1985) (Kirby Report) *Report of the Committee of Inquiry into Labour Market Programs*, Canberra, Australian Government Publishing Service.
COMMITTEE OF INQUIRY INTO TECHNOLOGICAL CHANGE IN AUSTRALIA (1980) (Myers Report) *Technological Change in Australia*, 4 vols, Canberra Australian Government Publishing Service.
CONNELL, R.W., ASHENDEN, D., KESSLER, S. and DOWSETT, G. (1982) *Making the Difference*, Sydney, Allen and Unwin.
CONNORS, L. (1984) 'The future of schooling in the age of technology', in Randell, S. (Ed.), *The Human Face of Technological Change*, Melbourne, The Australian College of Education.
COOLEY, M. (1980a) 'Computerization — Taylor's latest disguise', *Economic and Industrial Democracy*, 1, pp. 523–59.
COOLEY, M. (1980b) *Architect or Bee: The Human/Technological Relationship*, Sydney, Trans/National Co-operative.
DAWKINS, J.S. (1987) *Higher Education: A Policy Discussion Paper*, Canberra, Australian Government Publishing Service.
DOWNING, H. (1980) 'Word processors and the oppression of women', in FORESTER, T. (Ed.), *The Microelectronics Revolution*, Oxford, Basil Blackwell.
DOWNING, H. (1983) 'On being automated', *Aslib Proceedings*, 35, 1, pp. 38–51.
ELLUL, J. (1964) *The Technological Society*, New York, Alfred Knopf.
ELLUL, J. (1980) *The Technological System*, New York, Continuum.
ELLYARD, P. (1984) 'Towards a more innovative Australia', in RANDELL, S. (Ed.), *The Human Face of Technological Change*, Melbourne, The Australian College of Education.
EMERY, F. (1978) 'The fifth wave — embarking on the next forty years', in *Limits to Change*, Canberra, Centre for Continuing Education, Australian National University.
ETZIONI, A. and JARGOWSKY, P. (1984) 'High tech, basic industry, and the future of the American economy', *Human Resource Management*, 23, 3, pp. 229–40.
FAY, B. (1977) 'How people change themselves', in BALL, T. (Ed.), *Political Theory and Praxis*, Minneapolis, Minn., University of Minnesota Press.

FELDBERG, R. and GLENN, E. (1979) 'Male and female: Job vs gender models in the sociology of work', *Social Problems*, 26, pp. 524–38.

FELDBERG, R. and GLENN, E. (1983) 'Technology and work degradation: Effects of office automation on women clerical workers', in ROTHSCHILD, J. (Ed.), *Machina Ex Dea*, New York, Pergamon Press.

FORD, G.W. (1984) 'Review: Technological change and employment', *Prometheus*, 2, 1, pp. 156–9.

FORESTER, T. (1987) *High-tech Society*, Oxford, Basil Blackwell.

GAME, A. and PRINGLE, R. (1983) *Gender at Work*, Sydney, Allen and Unwin.

GARSON, B. (1981) 'The electronic sweatshop: Scanning the office of the future', *Mother Jones*, 6 July, pp. 32–41.

GIDDENS, A. (1981) *A Contemporary Critique of Historical Materialism*, London, Macmillan.

GIDDENS, A. (1982) 'Power, the dialectic of control and class structuration', in GIDDENS, A. and MACKENZIE, G. (Eds), *Social Class and the Division of Labour: Essays in Honour of Ilya Neustadt*, Cambridge, Cambridge University Press.

GRUBB, W.N. (1984) 'The bandwagon once more: Vocational preparation for high-tech occupations', *Harvard Educational Review*, 54, 4, pp. 429–54.

GUTERI, F. (1984) 'Technology '84: Personal computers', *IEEE SPECTRUM*, January, pp. 41–6.

HOWARD, R. (1981) 'Second class in Silicon Valley', *Working Papers*, 8, 5, pp. 21–31.

JAMIESON, I. and TASKER, M. (1988) 'Schooling and new technology: Rhetoric and reality', in HARRIS, D. (Ed.), *World Yearbook 1988: Education for the New Technologies*, London, Kogan Page.

JOHNSON, R. (1984) 'The Commonwealth Government's objectives for education and technology', in RANDELL, S. (Ed.), *The Human Face of Technological Change*, Melbourne, The Australian College of Education.

JONES, B. (1982) *Sleepers, Wake!*, Melbourne, Oxford University Press.

KIRBY REPORT, *see* Committee of Inquiry into Labour Market Programs (1985).

KRAMAR, R. (1984) 'The employment of women in the New South Wales public service, 1947 to 1978', *Journal of Industrial Relations*, 26, 2, pp. 200–25.

LEVIN, H.M. and RUMBERGER, R.W. (1983a) 'The low-skill future of high tech', *Technology Review*, 56, 6, pp. 18–21.

LEVIN, H.M. and RUMBERGER, R.W. (1983b) 'The educational implications of high technology', Project Report No. 83–A4, Institute for Research on Educational Finance and Governance, School of Education, Stanford University, California.

MACDONALD, S. (1983) 'High technology policy and the Silicon Valley model: An Australian perspective', *Prometheus*, 1, 2, pp. 330–49.

MACKENZIE, G. (1977) 'The political economy of the American working class', *British Journal of Sociology*, 28, 2, pp. 244–52.

MACKENZIE, D. (1984) 'Marx and the machine', *Technology and Culture*, 25, 3, pp. 473–502.

MARX, K. (1906) *Capital*, Vol. 1, Chicago, Ill., C.H. Kerr and Company.

MARX, K. (1973) *Grundrisse*, Harmondsworth, Penguin.

MERE, R. (1984) 'Some aspects of the communication revolution', in RANDELL, S.

(Ed.), *The Human Face of Technological Change*, Melbourne, The Australian College of Education.

Ministerial Review of Post Compulsory Schooling (1985) (The Blackburn Report), Vol. 1, Melbourne.

MORGALL, J. (1983) 'Typing our way to freedom: Is it true that new office technology can liberate women?', *Behaviour and Information Technology*, 2, 3, pp. 215–26.

MORRISON, D.E. (1983) 'Soft tech/hard tech, high tech/low tech: A social movement analysis of appropriate technology', *Sociological Inquiry*, 53, 2/3, pp. 220–51.

MYERS REPORT, *see* Committee of Inquiry into Technological Change in Australia (1980).

NOBLE, D. (1979) *America by Design: Science, Technology and the Rise of Corporate Capitalism*, New York, Alfred Knopf.

NOBLE, D. (1984) 'Computer literacy and ideology', *Teachers College Record*, 85, 4, pp. 602–14.

O'CONNOR, D. (1984) 'Technological change and the restructing of the global economy in the postwar period', paper presented at the US-Australia Joint Seminar on the Future Impact of Technology on Work and Education, Monash University, Melbourne, September.

O'DONNELL, C. (1984) 'Major theories of the labour market and women's place within it', *Journal of Industrial Relations*, 26, 2, pp. 147–65.

PERROW, C. (1983) 'The organizational content of human factors engineering', *Administrative Science Quarterly*, 28, 4, pp. 521–41.

POGROW, S. (1983) *Education in the Computer Age: Issues of Policy, Practice and Reform*, Beverley Hills, Calif., Sage.

REID, R. (1986) *Land of Lost Content: The Luddite Revolt 1812*, London, Heinemann.

REINECKE, I. (1983) *Microcomputers*, Melbourne, Penguin.

REINECKE, I. (1989) 'The high-tech decade', *Australian Society*, May, pp. 34–48.

RICHE, R., HECKER, D. and BURGAN, J. (1983) 'High technology today and tomorrow: A small slice of the employment pie', *Monthly Labour Review*, 106, pp. 50–8.

ROBINS, K. and WEBSTER, F. (1983) 'Information technology, Luddism and the working class', in MOSCO, V. and WASCO, J. (Eds). *The Critical Communications Review. Vol. 1: Labor, the Working Class and the Media*, Norwood, N.J., Ablex.

ROSENBERG, N. (1983) *Inside the Black Box: Technology and Economics*, Cambridge, Cambridge University Press.

RUMBERGER, R.W. (1984a) 'The growing imbalance between education and work', *Phi Delta Kappan*, 65, 5, pp. 342–6.

RUMBERGER, R.W. (1984b) *High Technology and Job Loss*, Project Report No. 84–?12, Institute for Research on Educational Finance and Governance, School of Education, Stanford University, California.

RUMBERGER, R.W. (1987) 'The potential impact of technology on the skill requirements of future jobs', in BURKE, G. and RUMBERGER, R. (Eds), *The Future Impact of Technology on Work and Education*, Lewes, Falmer Press.

RUMBERGER, R.W. and LEVIN, H.M. (1985) 'Forecasting the impact of new technologies on the future job market', *Technological Forecasting and Social Change*, 27, 4, pp. 399–417.

SAXENIAN, A. (1985) 'Silicon Valley and Route 128: Regional prototypes or historic exceptions?' in CASTELLS, M. (Ed.), *High Technology, Space and Society*, Beverley Hills, Calif., Sage.

SAXENIAN, A. (1989) 'In search of power: The organization of business interests in Silicon Valley and Route 128', *Economy and Society*, 18, 1, pp. 25–70.

SCOTT, A.J. and ANGEL, D.P. (1988) 'The global assembly-operations of U.S. semiconductor firms: A geographical analysis', *Environmental and Planning*, 20, pp. 1047–67.

STRANKS, D.R. (1983) 'Education and technological change in the eighties', *Unicorn*, 9, 2, pp. 140–8.

SWEET, R. (1987) 'Australian trends in job skill requirement. A critique of current orthodoxy', in BURKE, G. and RUMBERGER, R. (Eds), *The Future Impact of Technology on Work and Education*, Lewes, Falmer Press.

THOMPSON, E.P. (1968) *The Making of the English Working Class*, Melbourne, Penguin.

THOMPSON, E.P. (1976) 'Romanticism, moralism and utopianism: The case of William Morris', *New Left Review*, 99, pp. 88–111.

WATKINS, P.E. (1984) *Youth, Schooling and Work: Policy and Transition*, Geelong, Deakin University Press.

WATKINS, P.E. (1985) *Technology, the Economy and Education*, Geelong, Deakin University Press.

WATKINS, P.E. (1986a) *Time, Organization and the Administration of Education*, Geelong, Deakin University Press.

WATKINS, P.E. (1986b) *A Critical Review of Leadership Concepts and Research: The Implications for Educational Administration*, Geelong, Deakin University Press.

WEBER, M. (1984; original 1909) 'Energetic theories of culture', *Mid-American Review of Sociology*, 9, 2, pp. 33–58.

WEBER, M. (1961; original 1923) *General Economic History*, Trans. F. Knight, London, George Allen and Unwin.

WEBSTER, F. and ROBINS, K. (1986) *Information Technology: A Luddite Analysis*, Norwood, N.J., Ablex.

WINDSCHUTTLE, K. (1979) *Unemployment: A Social and Political Analysis of the Economic Crisis in Australia*, Melbourne, Penguin.

WINDSCHUTTLE, K. (1983) 'Technology and unemployment', in HILL, S. and JOHNSTON, R. (Eds), *Future Tense: Technology in Australia*, St Lucia, University of Queensland Press.

WINNER, L. (1977) *Autonomous Technology: Technics Out-of-Control as a Theme in Political Thought*, Cambridge, Mass., Massachusetts Institute of Technology Press.

WOOD, G.H. (1985) 'Education for democratic participation: Democratic values and the nuclear freeze campaign', *Theory and Research in Social Education*, 12, 4, pp. 39–56.

Chapter 7

Equality, Democracy and Educational Reform

Lawrence Angus

In a number of countries conservative educational reform has become a significant political issue. Margaret Thatcher, for instance, personally set the tone and pace of the education debate in Britain leading up to the 1987 general election. In the United States George Bush has declared himself the nation's 'first education president'. In Australia the results of the shift to the Right are most starkly apparent in New South Wales where Minister for Education, Metherall, in a Liberal Party government, is implementing 'reforms' that are specifically directed to the production of enhanced educational 'quality' and 'excellence'. Of even greater significance in the broad Australian context has been the establishment of a virtual national agenda for education by the Commonwealth Minister for Employment, Education and Training. Through documents like *Strengthening Australia's Schools* (Minister for Employment, Education and Training, 1989), Minister Dawkins, in adverting to themes such as national testing and centralized curriculum which are dear to the hearts of the educational Right, has largely paved the way for proponents of versions of 'quality schooling' that are destructive of public education. For, as Kenway (1986) has illustrated, quality and excellence have been attached unproblematically to private school education in contradistinction to the education provided in state schools, which is characterized as being in crisis. Public schooling, it is alleged, has failed to deliver the sort of graduates who can compete for jobs and help to shift the Australian economy towards a more secure industrial base that is oriented towards high technology, high value-added exports.

This chapter examines fundamental themes of equality and democracy that, until the 1980s, had been prominent in educational discourse and educational reform in Australia for over a century, particularly since World War II. It is argued in following sections that these ideas, while they represented positive and progressive intentions, have not necessarily contributed to greater social justice but instead have led to educational outcomes that are in important ways inconsistent with underlying principles of democracy and equality. Subsequent sections attempt to explain the persistence and general acceptance by the Australian public of continuing social and economic inequalities despite liberal educational reforms which have been intended to ameliorate such inequality. In the more recent educational climate, the educational debate, it is argued, has shifted so that liberal reform attempts have been largely discredited, both because of their actual failure and because of their alleged woolly-headed and naively optimistic intentions. Rather than themes of equality and democracy, the current climate emphasizes the logic of the marketplace with education seen as a consumer commodity. The theoretical concepts of ideology, meritocracy, reproduction and hegemony are discussed in relation to established school practices and the implications of an emerging conservative educational consensus. The chapter concludes with a tentative discussion of ways in which democracy and equality might be made more central in school practices and curriculum.

Themes in Early Australian Education

The essential argument in this chapter is that while there have been positive elements in educational changes since the establishment of mass schooling, education in Australia has generally served purposes of social control. Such purposes are especially apparent in current educational debates. This is not to deny, however, that many education reformers have advocated policies which they hoped would liberate and enlighten citizens. For the reformers in particular, a number of important ideas have been prominent in the rhetoric which has justified the development of mass education in Australia. The purpose of this section is to explore both the positive and negative aspects of several of these central themes: democracy, social harmony, equality and social mobility.

Democracy

The involvement of Australian colonial governments in education became increasingly evident in the second half of the nineteenth century and was justified on the grounds that the common good of citizens would be advanced by the spread of a common system of elementary education in each of the states. Such a claim brought the state into conflict with the churches, especially the Roman Catholic Church, which maintained a limited number of elementary schools and several exclusive secondary schools in order to instruct children in morals and religious practice. In the liberal democratic vision of late-Victorian Australia, however, only a 'free, compulsory and secular' system of education, it was argued, could mould appropriate future citizens who would maintain democratic ideals (Grundy, 1972). Such an education would take into account fundamental liberal concepts of individual rights, social justice and equality of opportunity (Bates, 1985). Under such a uniform public system, according to the rhetoric of the time, schools could erode the divisive barriers of class and religious differences by promoting a common code of citizenship and public standards.

The notion of education as a 'public good' was strongly established and not seriously challenged until the successful promotion by conservatives in the 1980s of the notion that education should properly be regarded as, in fact, a private good (Grace, 1989). The extension of popular, universal education was advocated in each of the colonies in the late 1800s as an essential prerequisite to the formation of a democratic society with an informed and dutiful citizenry (Grundy, 1972; Butts, 1955; Gregory, 1973). For if a liberal, unified and progressive society were to be built in Australia, according to a Victorian reformer of the 1860s:

> . . . the State has a duty beyond the mere duty of educating the people so as to escape the dock. It is bound to educate them so as to make them fit for the ballot box, and the political duties which in later life they may be called upon to perform. (Henry Wrixon, quoted in Gregory, 1973, p. 128)

In this statement, typical of many that were made in public debates about education in the second half of the nineteenth century and since then, several assumptions about the beneficiaries of schooling are contained. Although education was to be extended to all, the essential targets of free, compulsory and secular education were clearly the 'meaner' classes who lacked both gentility and, it was felt by the paternal reformers, a sense of civic concern. It was assumed that the children, at least the males, of the uneducated masses, although 'rough', could be picked up and dusted off sufficiently to play a part in a democratic society. However, they were to be educated to accept an extremely narrow conception of democracy and the part they would play in it. The logic behind education for a democratic society was, quite simply, 'If you gave every man the vote then you had to educate every man to understand it . . .' (Gregory, 1973, p. 132). There was an assumption that raw, uneducated working-class youths were likely to drift into a life of idleness and crime without the intervention of a benevolent state which would create worthy citizens. Again, according to Wrixon:

> ... with our rising generation reared under political institutions such as we enjoy we must not be told that we are to educate them merely for the purpose of keeping them from crime, when we know that when they grow up they may have to determine the vital questions that can affect the welfare of their country. (in Gregory, 1973, p. 128)

Citizens who were expected to play their part, however prescribed and minimal, in the political process, must, it was argued, first be educated in industrious habits and a shared view of public order. The common man was to be educated into a social order in which enlightened, responsible citizens would partake in the process of democratic elections. The notion of democratic participation here, however, was limited to that of involvement in the electoral system itself. The populace was viewed, then as now, as relatively passive bystanders in the political process.

Social Harmony

Schooling, offered to all children on an equal basis, was thought by turn of the century reformers to be the most appropriate means by which a moral consensus, a shared commitment to the social order, would be established. By means of education, the criminal and anti-social proclivities of the children of the 'lower' classes would be curbed. Schools would induct such children into the value system of the prevailing social order and so turn out 'intelligent and prosperous citizens rather than beggarly and riotous rogues' (quoted in Bessant, 1975, p. 84). The various Education Acts and regulations of the late nineteenth and early twentieth centuries were aimed at producing state education systems which would be models of efficiency in creating a literate and domesticated public.

The institutionalization of children in schools in which there was rigid control of pupils, teachers and curriculum, as well as administration, ensured that rising generations would be socialized into acceptance of the prevailing order. Through increasing regulation and supervision during the early twentieth century, the transition from youth to adulthood was to be managed to produce worthy contributors to a social and economic order which was not itself to be questioned. As a South Australian school inspector put it in 1928:

> The fact that children of today will be the citizens of tomorrow should be kept in mind by the teacher. For surely, it is not too much to expect that the habits of willing obedience to constituted authority, and of regard for the rights of others, now being formed in our schools, may promote communal peace in the future and become, in some measure, the solvent of much of the social unrest existing today. (in Bessant, 1975, p. 88)

Educators were given a mission of civilizing the wayward children from the unruly elements of society so that they would not threaten the social fabric. Social mores were not seen as being connected with politics or ideology but merely self-evident characteristics of a responsible, decent citizenry. In fact, strenuous efforts were made to ensure that politics was kept out of education. Teachers, in particular, were forbidden to express any political views in the classroom, or indeed to discuss in schools any matters of controversy. In short, during the first half of the twentieth century and beyond, as Bessant explains: 'It was taken for granted by administrators, teachers and all but the most radical politicans that the school was a bastion of the status quo. The call for political neutrality in the school was in fact an insurance against any questioning of the social order in the classrooms' (1975, p. 89).

Teachers were expected to be obedient, unquestioning, morally impeccable, utterly 'neutral' public servants who conformed to prevailing social values. They were to remain aloof from the issues of the day, maintain good discipline, keep exactly to the prescribed syllabus and employ the 'appropriate' methods of teaching to gain 'good' examination results. Initiative was not required by the teacher and could even be a handicap in the efficient provision of education in a hierarchical system. Children, for their part, were to learn basic literacy and numeracy, loyalty to country and empire, obedience to authority and acceptance of the status quo. The last of these was to be all the more effectively taught to children and their parents if they could believe that the prevailing social order offered them some possibility of advancement in terms of their relative economic position.

Equality and Social Mobility

A tradition in Australian educational reform has been one of attempting to extend the advantages of education to the more disadvantaged members of society. Although the notion of equity has now been displaced on the education agenda, an (admittedly limited) egalitarian ideal persisted in education debates for much of the past century. It held that universal education, the same for all, would provide *all* children with an opportunity of advancing their station in life. The provision of educational opportunities for the children of the poor was also seen as something of a safety valve which would relieve the social pressures built up by class conflict. If it were generally accepted that the ambitious and the industrious among the lower classes could, because of the upward mobility afforded by educational success, grasp a share of the good life, then the likelihood of class conflict would be greatly reduced. As Ely argues:

> The turbulance of the 'have-nots' was weakened by limited but real opportunities offered to their natural leaders — the more ambitious and able. The price of such opportunity has been their willing acceptance of respectable, consensus, conditional 'middle-class' society. (Ely, 1978, p. 2)

In this way, 'the educational facilities offered to the upwardly mobile have generally guaranteed their cooperation rather than confrontation with their betters' (Ely, 1978, p. 2).

The themes of social control and social mobility, then, are inextricably interrelated in the history of mass education in Australia. Social mobility was offered *within* an existing social order which was not itself to be examined as part of the educational enterprise. Contradictory intentions, which have characterized educational reforms up to the present day, are apparent in this limited view of social advancement. On the one hand, the early reformers held deeply to the aim of assisting above all the lowliest children. On the other hand, the education system was to entrench a social hierarchy which preserved disadvantage and legitimated inequality, and which could be climbed by children of the lower classes only if they became like their 'betters'. However, there were still many who saw little point in children being educated above their station. Such education was thought by some to be generally futile, and even harmful, particularly for girls of common stock. As one Member of Parliament, Mr P. Madden, put it:

> . . . I think it is a mistake to teach people more than is required for their station. Indeed it is a cruelty. Take, for instance, the girl whose place is that of a dairymaid. Is it not cruel to teach her accomplishments which make her above her station?
>
> *Dr Maloney* — Why?

Mr P. Madden — Because she will leave her dairy, come to town, fail to get employment, and perhaps go on to the streets. (in Bessant, 1975, p. 99)

Such attitudes impeded the growth of public secondary education until after World War II. The notion of education for social advancement, while it had been prominent in the thinking and rhetoric of the reformers, was not widely accepted by the general public until then. Before the war the division between education and work was rather blurred for most children, as few saw any direct connection between their school performance and their chances of getting a good job. Jobs were gained through family and social contacts, or by being in the right place at the right time, rather than by the recommendation of a school report. Moreover, many working-class children moved freely between school and work, either paid or as part of a family unit, during their school careers. A child's examination results were then often as much influenced by the number of days she or he attended school as by her or his ability. Social and economic opportunities, despite the rhetoric of reformers, had more to do with family status and connections than academic ability. In any case, as I shall argue in the following sections, the notion of 'academic' ability was also skewed to favour the already socially and economically advantaged.

It was not until the post-war years, when some secondary education increasingly became the norm for most children, that the notion of social advancement through education became widely accepted at all social levels. Hence more and more children stayed longer and longer at school. This has meant that the concept of equality of opportunity was always flawed, because many families who needed to supplement family income were hard pressed to allow children who could get any jobs at all to stay on at school after the minimum leaving age in order to accumulate the qualifications that might enable them to gain better jobs. Nevertheless, it was during this era that the idea of education as a social leveller became widespread as many parents wished their children to take advantage of educational opportunities that had not been available to themselves. Through education, it was thought, children of all ranks could compete for economic success.

Schools and Ideology

These themes in the history of education in Australia — democracy, social control, social mobility and equality — are connected to the prevailing notion that education and schools are themselves politically neutral. Public education was regarded as a public service which was offered for the benefit of all citizens and for the good of society as a whole. Education was valued as a public good, for which all could equally avail themselves. The aims of mass schooling, to fit children for citizenship and economic production, and to maintain the moral order, were not to be questioned. Educational improvement, therefore, referred to ways of doing this more effectively.

The very notion of 'education' that is used here, however, is itself both a historical and a political construct. Despite the recurring theme in liberal rhetoric that politics should be kept out of education (and vice versa), education is inherently political because, as Hall explains, 'education exists in the most complex and intimate relationship to other processes in society, and . . . it can never be isolated from those forces' (1977, p. 5). As I have argued, mass schooling in Australia has traditionally been regarded as a means to fit people for their various functions in the stable economic and social order. Such 'education', as Lundgren points out, does over time 'establish a certain pattern of thought about what education *should* be — which later assumes a more significant role as it becomes a tradition and as the state comes to play an increasingly active part in the provision of schooling' (1983, p. 144). This means that in a society that is socially and economically differentiated like Australia's:

> The content of education involved a choice of values, knowledge and skills. There was no given body of knowledge and values to be transmitted: a choice had to be made and was made, and it was one which reflected the positions of power held by various groups in the society. Compulsory education meant not only subordinaton as regards the common values and knowledge of society, but also subordination to the values and knowledge of the dominating social strata. (Lundgren, 1983, p. 145)

Once this fact that education involves choices between competing values, competing interests and, indeed, competing cultures is recognized, we are in a position to appreciate Lundgren's essential point that

> the content, and the prerequisites, which come to direct the actual processes of education and socialization are determined by the power held by various social strata and social classes vis-a-vis education. The choice of an equal education for all also means a choice of a given interpretation of society and culture. (Lundgren, 1983, p. 149)

This means that, despite the intentions of early reformers to deal with education as a neutral, public good equally available to all, education is inescapably ideological. That is, education as a part of life in a society contributes to our beliefs and dreams of what is 'true, desirable and possible' (Berlak and Berlak, 1983, p. 271) both for ourselves and for society. Ideology in this sense refers to 'the relatively formal and articulate system of meanings, values and beliefs that legitimate and justify culture as it is' (Berlak and Berlak, 1983, p. 271). Within this view education is seen essentially as a mechanical accumulation of marks and certificates that may lead to positions in the hierarchy. In individual competition with their peers, children pursue academic achievement and personal gain.

Post-War Education: Equality of Opportunity and Meritocracy

By the 1950s the major themes outlined in the previous sections had become entrenched in the educational discourse which legitimated public education. Education was generally regarded as a means to promote democracy, social harmony, social mobility and equality. These themes are part of a traditional liberal democratic view of education and society in which equal chances for all means a system that is, supposedly, both fair, at least in terms of access if not outcomes, and efficient. Social and economic inequalities can in this view be ameliorated, or partially redressed, through the all-important notion of equality of opportunity. The social structure itself was not to be altered but opportunities for advancement within that structure were to be made fairer through equal access to education. Once the notion that educational success directly contributes to economic and social 'life chances' was widely accepted, along with the view that all children did have equal chances to do well at school, it was but a small step to conceive of the ideal society as one in which those with the greatest intelligence and who make the greatest effort (and who are therefore the most deserving) are promoted to positions of power and status.

Bennett explains the legacy of this notion:

> This doctrine of equality of opportunity had enormous implications for education itself. First, it assumed that the purpose of the education system was simply personal advancement in material terms. Above all, it endorsed the principle that education, like society itself, is a competition, a process which produces winners

> and losers. The purpose of the policy is to ensure that the rules of the competition are fair — that is, that everyone has an equal chance. (Bennett, 1982, p. 165)

Bennett points out that it was in the mid-1960s that the liberal faith in the socially and economically beneficial effects of education, at the level of both the individual and society, reached its peak. Public confidence in, and support for, education grew to the point that, according to Bennett:

> The mid-1960s represented the high point of faith in education and the expectations of that period now seem hopelessly unreal, even ludicrous. Education was expected to establish an equal society, maintain economic growth and promote national prosperity, while at the same time providing everyone with higher incomes, interesting jobs and a pleasant middle-class life. (1982, p. 165)

Such faith was not confined to Australia, for during the 1960s and early 1970s, as Kogan (1979) points out, the educational policies of most Western countries were:

> based on a belief in the ability of national authorities to prescribe purposes for education on the assumption that the investment of finance, of buildings and manpower and carefully thought out systems would enable countries to reach goals of a productive economy, stronger individual freedom and choice, and a more equal society. (Kogan, 1979, p. 19)

The educational resources that were to be managed in this enterprise were, essentially, the pupils themselves. They were the human capital to be developed by national investment in schools.

One version of the 'human capital' approach to educational reform was the belief that the educational performance of disadvantaged children could be improved if schools, in their allocation of resources, were to discriminate positively in their favour. In the 1960s and 1970s such a policy of 'compensatory education' was adopted in Britain following the Plowden Report (Central Advisory Council for Education, 1967) and was the basis of the 'Head Start' program in the United States. In Australia the notion that schools should be resourced according to relative 'needs' was a major recommendation of the extremely influential Karmel Report (Interim Committee for the Australian Schools Commission, 1973). Under the Disadvantaged Schools Program particular schools still receive direct federal grants to help reduce the special disadvantages of their pupils. Such faith in public education was based on the belief that schools could deliver opportunities for social and economic success to pupils of talent from all backgrounds. The accumulation of evidence, however, even during the 1960s and early 1970s when public faith in education was at its highest, indicated that education reforms had failed to alter significantly the relative educational outcomes and life chances of children from dominant and non-dominant social groups (e.g. Coleman *et al.*, 1966; Jencks, 1972).

In the days of the post-war, long economic boom, and the accompanying growth of population and confidence, which lasted into the early 1970s, there were at least jobs for those who experienced a lack of success at school. This fact to some extent disguised the lack of substantial social movement. It was not until the recession of the mid-1970s and since then that the contraction of the youth labour market highlighted the inability of schools alone to guarantee an economically secure future for their charges. In the optimism that was at its peak from the mid-1960s to the early 1970s, however, education reflected the prevalence in other spheres of liberal progressive ideas and a faith in Keynesian economics. These justified a reasonable degree of state intervention and provision in areas of social policy such as education (Freeland, forthcoming).

There was growing confidence after the war in the ability of education to contribute to general economic advancement for the nation and also to greater social equity. Individual achievement, within the prevailing educational and social order, however, was regarded as a measure of individual worth. This view was the cornerstone of the doctrine of equality of opportunity upon which the entire edifice of meritocracy rested. It is important to recognize that behind the principle of meritocracy there *was* a positive and humane hope that education may serve as an equalizing force in society. Although education in this perspective is a competitive, individualistic process, children of talent from all social backgrounds, no matter how deprived, are given the *same* opportunity to succeed. Thus, it is claimed, education may play a part in breaking down inherited privilege and entrenched patterns in the distribution of power and wealth in society.

The point is that, despite the positive intentions of supporters of equality of opportunity, the overwhelming evidence is that at the societal level, at the level of general tendencies in overall outcomes, educational success is closely associated with family wealth and advantage (Coleman *et al.*, 1966; Jencks, 1972). This is not to deny that many individuals, children of poor families, migrants, girls, have managed against the odds to achieve both successful school careers and then commercial or professional careers. Such individual exceptions to the general tendency are important in at least two ways. First, they illustrate that there is a complex relationship between negative and positive outcomes of traditional, liberal schooling. Some children may, for one reason or another, benefit from an overall system which is generally inadequate. But even such individual 'successes' do nothing to ameliorate the inequalities that are sustained within the social hierarchy which is not challenged by minor alterations of individual places within it. Second, and related to the first point, examples of individual mobility *legitimate* both traditional school practices and the social order. That is, under the guise of equality of opportunity, education contributes to a form of social control which preserves social and economic inequality.

There is yet another level at which the policy of equality of opportunity is functional in maintaining the social order. Economic efficiency can be best served by a meritocracy in which children of ability from all social classes can compete on their merits so that the very ablest from society as a whole can reach the 'top'. The essence of meritocracy was that:

> Schools were to be reformed in such a way that they could serve as instruments for evening up 'educational opportunities', redistributing them more effectively and fairly. Both words are important. 'Fairly' meant that schools should provide the means whereby a measure of redistribution of educational chances among social classes could be affected. 'Effectively' meant that this redistribution would enable the recruitment of able students from the existing 'pool of talent'. (Hall, 1977, p. 32)

Meritocratic ideology has been increasingly attacked by a number of critics (e.g. Apple, 1982; Bourdieu, 1977; Spring, 1980), who argue that, contrary to the prevailing liberal view, life chances are not so much promoted by schools as restricted by them. Such critics do not regard schools as neutral arenas in which all children start out with equal chances in the competition for the technical knowledge and credentials that may lead to social advancement and future income. Instead, rather than holding out equal opportunities for individual mobility as promised by liberal theorists, schools are said to maintain and reproduce both a system of structured inequality over time and a dominant ideology which offers those dispossessed of political and economic power nothing more than an assurance that the competition was fair.

The above assertions should not be accepted uncritically. We must be prepared to examine critically the intentions of traditional liberal schooling against educational outcomes. Under such critical scrutiny both negative and positive elements of formerly taken-for-granted features of education may become apparent. As Hall perceptively points out:

> ... the relationship between the negative and the positive — the latent and manifest — results of schooling may not be random; there may be connections between them. Some groups may be contained, constrained, forced, won, or 'socialized' into a 'subordinate' position in society *because* some others are pushed, won or 'socialized' into 'dominant' positions. (1977, p. 10)

Moreover, any attempt to understand, much less reform, the education system in a complex industrial society must search for the connections between schooling and other aspects of society such as the economic system, the job market, the organization of work, the distribution of power, the distribution of high status knowledge (Apple, 1982). By understanding the essential unity of educational processes and social processes, we can begin to appreciate the powerful part played by schools in the maintenance and transmission of educational and social inequalities.

From the 1960s to the 1990s

Education has consistently sorted and allocated children to a hierarchy of status and opportunity while seeming to offer equal chances for all. Such allocation, because of the cultural discrimination that occurs in schools, may well have as much to do with the attitudes and attributes that people bring to schools as with their actual talent or intelligence. Such characteristics of traditional education are reinforced by the conservative elements of the current educational reform movement (Angus, 1986; Freeland, forthcoming; Seddon *et al.*, 1990) which is permeated by the values of hard-headed politicians and the 'needs' of business and industry. These translate into hopes of achieving 'the best posible educational value ... for each educational dollar spent' (Management Review, 1989, p. 31) through effective management, tight accountability, clear performance indicators, cost-benefit accounting and increased productivity.

The current educational debate in Australia and throughout much of the Western world seems to be largely characterized by notions of 'quality' and associated concepts of excellence, efficiency and standards. But these terms are usually employed without any clear referents. They are used glibly by different people to mean different things, and in the current context they have become part of a slogan system which denotes a focus on narrow curriculum, more rigid testing of pupils and teachers, and a view of education as a commodity in which consumers, parents, and their children will invest wisely in the expectation of maximal return. These predominant meanings associated with the term 'quality' perhaps best illustrate the significant shift to the Right in education discourse during the 1980s. The language of quality and excellence in education has been appropriated by the New Right into a lexicon of social Darwinism which enthuses and inspires some while signifying the exclusion of others. It is accompanied by what Kenway (1986) calls a 'language of derision' of Leftist interpretations of quality, and indeed blames Left-liberal educationalists for past experiments in state schools which, despite evidence to the contrary (including the results of recent state-wide testing of aspects of literacy and numeracy at Year 6 level in New South Wales (*Sydney Morning Herald*, 17 November 1989)), are perceived to have resulted in declining 'standards'. A particular target of attack is the notion of equity. Any suggestion that schools should contribute to 'equality of outcomes' is wilfully misrepresented by the Right as an advocacy of 'social engineering' that is designed to drag everyone, including the most talented, down to the level of 'the lowest common denominator'. As in the United States, Britain and elsewhere, the forces of technology and the marketplace are employed in the quest to lift educational standards, and to provide graduates who can compete in the 'real world' of industry and contribute to the nation's industrial competitiveness. Education, it is claimed, must be relevant to these needs.

Such views have become so pervasive that they have achieved a level of orthodoxy such that to question them, or more particularly to question the assumptions on which they are based or the implications that are drawn from them, is tantamount to questioning common sense. Even the Commonwealth Schools Commission, usually lumped by critics from the Right with the Left-liberal 'educational establishment' which caused the alleged educational mess in the first place (e.g. Partington, 1990), seems to have accepted the prevailing orthodoxy. As Smith (1987, pp. 131–2) points out about the Commission's report, *In the National Interest* (Commonwealth Schools Commission, 1986), 'In considering the demands made upon education, the Commission accepts an immutable economic imperative which shapes its view about the link between secondary education and youth policy, and the need to increase secondary education rates. . . . Other demands, including those of young people themselves and those of society at large, are considered *after* the economic ones.' This last point should perhaps not be a surprise when, in the current orthodoxy, the demands of society, too, are reduced to those of the economy.

There was a stage during the 1960s and 1970s, however, before the long economic boom of the post-war period came to an end and the links between education and the economic order were tightened, when there was in Australia and elsewhere a very limited reform movement that was very different from that which we are currently witnessing. That movement, too, was organized around attempts to make education 'relevant'. But the intention then was that the experience of schooling would be related, not so much to the demands of the 'real world' of the workplace, the labour market and national economic priorities, but to the life experience of students. Legitimacy was given to this earlier push for relevance, and companion themes of equality, diversity and participation, by the influential Karmel Report of 1973:

> The Committee's identification of educational deficiencies [i.e. lack of resources, gross inequalities, and limited quality of schooling] itself reflects the values held by the Committee, as do the remedies proposed. There is a number of values that have informed the Committee's deliberations. They are: the pursuit of quality in the sense of making, through schooling, the overall circumstances of children's education as nearly equal as possible; the attainment of minimum standards of competence for life in the modern, democratic industrial society; the concept of schooling as part of life as well as a preparation for life; the notion of education as a life-long experience, of which attendance at primary and secondary schools is one phase; diversity among schools in their structures, curricula and teaching methods; the devolution, as far as is practicable, of the making of decisions on those working in or with the schools — teachers, pupils, parents and the local community; the involvement of the community in school affairs. (Interim Committee for the Australian Schools Commission, 1973)

The school level reforms that preceded, accompanied and were influenced by the Karmel Report values were associated with innovative courses in schools, many of which incorporated 'individual progression', and which included studies in current events, political and social issues, mass media, the environment and local history. In some schools there was an emphasis on study of, and in, the community. Experiments in non-competitive and non-graded assessments were tried, and teachers attempted to make schools relevant, humane and less authoritarian.

Hostility towards broadening education in these ways became particularly strong as schools were able to be blamed for the failure of youth to get jobs. Schools can too easily be blamed for contributing to the social and economic uncertainty that is a product of the failure of capital, social and cultural change, and shifting economic relativities. Educators and the community can too easily fall back upon a general faith in managerialism that has been socially constructed in industrial societies through the institutionalization of practices of scientific management in workplaces. These practices, now represented in the discourse of public educational administration in terms of corporate management, need to be recognized as more than neutral managerial devices but as significant contributors to patterns of social relationships in which efficiency and stability are associated with hierarchical authority. The acceptance of these as standard and proper ways of managing has led to the taken-for-granted acceptance of the necessity of efficiency and effectiveness, conceived in a particular managerial fashion, for business success. In the current period of economic uncertainty, and some confusion over what is expected of education, the seemingly unproblematic notion of basic, straightforward and no-nonsense management appeals to our common sense as the right way of running schools. This is particularly the case if we accept the assumption that teachers are largely to blame for the alleged mess that schools are in. Policies to counter this perceived state of affairs are likely to be based on appeals to accountability and efficient administration. The attraction of such policies may well be as much in their symbolic value, as indicators of activity and certainty in an uncertain state, as in their substance (Popkewitz, 1988). For they reflect common sense and an aura of neutrality in that education is seen as the performance of teaching tasks as efficiently as possible. The new emphasis on basic skills and prescribed curricula in recent years, therefore, amounts to a call for:

> a return to a clearly stated, well-ordered hierarchy of school knowledge, and for an elaboration of an explicitly laid out, standardized mode of evaluation. Only this, it appears to its protagonists, guarantees the continuation of the traditional role of schooling in the reproduction of the social division of labour, and the fulfilment of expectations regarding social and occupational mobility. (Shapiro, 1983, p. 21)

The status of terms like 'effectiveness', 'standards' and 'basics' in the current education debates reflect the extensiveness of the return to such traditional schooling.

Some important qualifications need to be made here, however, lest the impression is given that the move to the Right in education is so complete that progressive educational movements have been totally obliterated. It needs to be stated, for instance, that the issues out of which curricular and organizational reforms grew and were asserted in the 1960s and 1970s — the study and understanding of contemporary life, and the attempt to understand the social and cultural context of the school — are still powerful in the minds of many educators despite recent changes. Some of these concerns may be found within recent reports, notably the Victorian Blackburn Report (Ministerial Review of Post-Compulsory Schooling, 1985), and ongoing attempts to reform the curriculum and assessment at the senior secondary years (Seddon and Deer, 1990).

Moreover, lest we become too romantic about the past, it must also be recognized that the 1960s and 1970s reforms were limited in at least two important ways. First, as the research of Rice (1983) demonstrates, despite much rhetoric, media hype and the official control of the curriculum being passed largely from administrators to teachers, there was remarkably little change in the classroom practices of most teachers:

> teachers continue[d] to produce socially and politically conservative curricula independently of formal administrative intervention or parental direction . . . [because] . . . the ideological conservatism of teachers, their limited resources, the social resolution of tensions between the pursuit of academic success and student failure, and a pattern of interlocking but exclusive social networks continue[d] to set limits to curriculum decision-making. (Rice, 1983, p. 40)

Only in a minority of schools, often dubbed 'alternative', 'open' or even 'freedom' schools, was there extensive change, and even then in many cases reform was limited in a second way — by its overriding concern for individual relativism. That is, although making substantial gains that should be protected, the reforms were flawed by an emphasis upon the individual interests and individual progress of pupils (thus preserving one of the tenets of liberalism), which arguably trivialized the notion of relevance. The individual was likely to be severed from an understanding of shared social concerns and social action. Individual interest was not harnassed towards a critical appraisal of social alternatives and possibilities. It merely celebrated individual differences. Although values were central in more open and relevant curricula, values clarification too often amounted to individual value preferences rather than a critical scrutiny of existing mores against standards of freedom, justice and democracy.

Education in Australia, therefore, has consistently offered a liberatory and egalitarian promise which has not been realized. The version of democracy that is encouraged in schools, both in school practices and in curriculum, has traditionally allowed little scope for the participation of pupils and citizens (Angus, 1986; Wood, 1984, 1985). The part played by schools in the preservation of social harmony has resulted not in any greater spirit of communitarianism but, by and large, in more subtle social control and social exclusion. This has been facilitated, especially, by the common understanding of equality as 'equality of opportunity' which offers social mobility only within the established hierarchy to those few who prove their 'worth' in meritocratic competition. It is this individual competitiveness and the assumption that the grounds of the competition are 'fair', more than anything else, that have traditionally legitimated public education as an impartial contributor to the public good.

The Shift to the Right

Current debate about so-called declining efficiency of schools and the plethora of politically conservative educational reports both in Australia and elsewhere (Angus, 1986) can be seen as symptoms of a more recent legitimation crisis in education. This crisis is manifest most clearly in attempts to restore linkages between schooling and work. The renewed emphasis on human capital and the preparation of a skilled workforce that will enhance national competitiveness is most crassly illustrated in the notorious United States report, *A Nation at Risk* (National Commission on Excellence in Education, 1983), and slightly less so in the Dawkins Green and White Papers on the restructuring of tertiary education (Dawkins, 1987, 1988). The philosophy behind this version of educational quality is blatantly utilitarian, despite a rhetoric of 'excellence'. Of particular importance is the way in which this instrumental view of education has emphasized the rhetoric of the market and has contributed to the breakdown of the former 'educational consensus' around a general liberal-democratic perspective on schooling (Freeland, 1990; Apple, 1989; Seddon *et al.*, 1990).

The attack on liberal-democratic values is accompanied by a denigration of teachers (see, for example, the series of articles in *The Australian* by Sheridan, beginning with 'The lies they tell our children', February 1985). The vitriol of these attacks has contributed to a decline in teacher morale. A lack of esteem for teachers *in general* seems to exist even in school communities where there is apparent satisfaction with the *particular* school and its teachers. Teacher deficiencies, it is argued, are largely to blame for the problem of education, which has failed to deliver adequate products for the labour market. Not only is there a problem of teacher competency, according to this logic, but also the content of the curriculum is inadequate. As Martin (1989, p. 5) points out, however, while it is only too 'convenient for critics of the education system to view teachers as unprofessional artisans who should be "made" to do their best, anyone with a smattering of knowledge in the field of organizational effectiveness knows that morale and motivation are important.'

The 'solution' from the Right is not so much to attend to teacher morale as to manage schools more tightly, test teacher competency, impose centrally determined curriculum and regularly test children to ensure that the curriculum is learned. Little thought seems to have been given, however, to the nature of the teacher-student relationship, or to the issue of student (and teacher) motivation, or to what methods teachers might employ to achieve the sorts of outcomes that various forms of testing are likely to measure. The current themes of the education debate, therefore, seem extraordinarily remote from the real world of schools, in which teachers and students are struggling to deal with each other and do their jobs well, to engage each other in various ways, and to grapple with the complex nature of teaching and learning. In the prevailing debate there is a curiously unproblematic conception of schooling in which the complex nature of education is reduced to particular problems that are represented as being amenable to direct solutions *within* the school. The narrow focus on schools as neutral institutions that are to deliver quality outputs, which is characteristic of conservative educational debate, diverts attention from the problematic nature of education in its social context. When this is coupled with the market rhetoric in which education takes the form of individual economic investment, there is also a press for 'constant measurement to determine its cost to the investor' (Preston, 1989, p. 22).

All of this reinforces a present oriented and technical orientation to curriculum which 'leads to conservative positions in educational debate because moral and political issues, such as educational standards, national core curriculum and changing forms of assessment, are defused as technical problems amenable to expert solution' (Seddon, 1989, p. 2). Knowledge is more likely to be treated as given rather than as contested and socially constructed. Teachers are more likely to teach to the syllabus and to emphasize regular testing of its mastery so that the cultural background of pupils is less likely to be regarded as a legitimate curriculum resource. In relation to equity, this type of approach is consistent with the view of equity as fair competition rather than equal participation. With students expected to compete for common credentials according to common standards, as Strike (1985, p. 412) puts it, 'perhaps the real equity issue is the extent to which all children will be expected to play the game of life on middle-class turf.'

The focus on measurement and testing, on the individual merit and qualities of individual students, teachers and principals, personalizes educational problems rather than treating them in context in relation to, among other things, the situation in which teachers work, their relationships with other members of the school community, and the nature of the school as an organization. It is features such as these that the literature indicates are significant for school improvement (Martin, 1989). Moreover, the emphasis on evaluation and pupil testing is likely to lead teachers to a concern for that which is amenable to quantified measurement, at the expense of encouraging a spirit of enquiry and a richness of the mind. At a quite fundamental level the attempt to translate complex educational objectives into measurable performance indicators either misses or trivializes much of what education is rightly about.

Even in the relatively progressive era of the 1960s and 1970s, however, the ideology that guided school practices and educational thinking was essentially conservative. The concerns of teachers and administrators have largely been about practical issues of implementation of generally agreed principles and not about the connections between education and power, culture, politics and life chances. In the remainder of this chapter it is argued that genuine educational reform can only grow out of these considerations. This means that we must think critically about education and subject to scrutiny the educational practices and concepts that we have generally taken for granted. The concepts of democracy and equality in education, in particular, must be thoroughly re-examined and related to the social and political context in which education takes place. We must also attempt to explain the failure of schools to contribute to substantial social change, and teachers' apparent compliance with education's contribution to the maintenance of an unequal social hierarchy.

Stability and Change in Schooling

Reproduction theorists, from various starting points and perspectives, argue that the ideology that is legitimated in schools supports the status quo, meritocracy and capitalist rationality. However, this does not fully explain why it is that non-dominant groups willingly lend their support to an educational and economic system which leaves them in disadvantaged positions. For if a dominant ideology were simply imposed upon an unwilling populace by coercion, manipulation, indoctrination, or even by the subtle means of economic and cultural reproduction, society would, Williams argues, 'be very much easier to move and change than in practice it has ever been or is' (Williams, 1976, p. 205). To explain such limited social and political change, and the acceptance of education which actually reinforces the status quo, the notion of 'hegemony' (Gramsci, 1971) is helpful. This difficult concept is summarized by Williams:

> [Hegemony] is a whole body of practices and expectations; our assignments of energy, our ordinary understandings of the nature of man and of his world. It is a set of meanings and values which, as they are experienced as practices, appear reciprocally confirming. It thus constitutes a sense of reality for most people in the society, a sense of absolute because [it is] experienced reality, beyond which it is very difficult for most members of the society to move, in most areas of their lives. (Williams, 1976, p. 205)

Cultural hegemony, or ideological dominance, then, implies more than simply the imposition on subordinate classes or groups of a ruling class ideology, one that simply asserts the values and beliefs of the ruling class. To maintain its dominance, the hegemony must incorporate, at least to some extent, alternative values, interests and perceptions of the world. In this way:

> By insuring that the dominant culture reflects not only the meanings and practices of the dominant class but also of other groups or classes, hegemony ensures the effective legitimation of the class structure and the consequent relations of domination and subordination. (Shapiro, 1984a, p. 28)

In relation to education, the belief that their children may climb the social and economic ladder if they 'do well' at school, or that they will at least be employable if they follow the curriculum and become competent in particular skills, reinforces in parents, teachers and the community an uncritical view of schooling as a neutral activity. Thus the public accepts, by and large, both the particular forms and structures of 'what counts' as schooling and the 'educational' mechanisms by which pupils are stratified according to a hierarchy of status and knowledge. Teachers and administrators are, of course, 'deeply implicated in the processes of identifying and using technocractic procedures for processing students' (Smith, 1985, p. 22). But even within the technocratic, meritocratic view of education the criteria by which educational success or failure are measured are unfair to many, indeed most pupils. As Smith explains:

> Individuals clearly differ and no one suggests that every student is the 'same'. The acceptance of differences however does not imply

> inequalities. The latter arise when differences are ranked as 'better', 'higher' or 'superior'. The educational criterion for identifying differences and rectifying them is testing, which itself is a competition for grades. 'Talent' or 'merit' taken as a whole range of human potentialities, has been reduced to a specific set of skills centred on classroom models of learning and a narrow conception of classroom skills.... Performance is set against quality and competence in a hierarchical scale and becomes a criterion for all manner of entry points into facilities, courses, schools and jobs. (1985, pp. 19–20)

This reduction of 'a whole range of human potentialities' to 'a specific set of skills' illustrates the hegemonic nature of curriculum. It represents the dual processes of 'selection' and 'incorporation' on which hegemony rests. What is chosen for emphasis in schools is but a narrow selection 'from the whole possible area of past and present meanings and practices' (Shapiro, 1984b, p. 369) — all else is neglected or excluded. This narrow range of special meanings and practices is incorporated into the dominant culture by being 'reinterpreted, diluted, or put into focus which supports, or at least does not contradict, other elements of the dominant culture' (Shapiro, 1984b, p. 369). This means, however, that when it comes to schooling, 'individuals are measured by attributes that are beyond personal and group control' (Smith, 1985, p. 22). More importantly, the meritocratic influence encourages and reproduces a competitive, individualistic society and does violence to alternative cultures and cultural groups. Such cultural violence is subtle, not aggressive and blatant; it operates through taken-for-granted assumptions about education, culture, and background differences. It does not forcibly or coercively reproduce inequalities but does its work in such a way as to impede the creation of conditions that might lead to social change.

That is, by mediating linkages betwen the individual and society, schools, as significant social institutions, teach pupils the 'rules' of the social order and to accept the system of status and hierarchy which largely determines their own level of participation in social affairs. Pupils generally learn to accept their lot, to accept the unequal distribution of power and wealth. In this process what Hall (1977) calls 'cultural preferencing', the complement of what I have called 'cultural discrimination', constantly occurs. Through such preferencing/discriminating, schools prepare pupils for the material world. They teach them to be more 'realistic' in their economic expectations, and introduce them to the 'realities' of a world in which power is unequally distributed:

> There is a process of cultural preferencing constantly at work. Cultures are organized in a relationship of *dominance and subordination*. The fact that schools 'prefer' and work best against the background of middle-class cultures has something to do with the fact that, outside the school, these are the dominant cultures — the ones in which the knowledge and know-how (the 'cultural capital' in Bourdieu's phrase) of society is transmitted, the values which are rewarded, which hold society together. The processes by which schools, and other institutions, prescribe the powerfulness of the preferred culture, are the same processes which tend to *reproduce* the subordinate cultures in their subordinate positions. (Hall, 1977, p. 45)

Yet this is not because schools or teachers deliberately set out to disadvantage certain pupils. Indeed, the very opposite has been the case. A principal theme in the history of educational reforms in Australia and elsewhere has been the attempt to ameliorate social disadvantage. The legitimation in schools of culturally specific forms of knowledge and social practices, however, illustrates the point that, as Giroux states: 'Schools are not merely instructional sites but also sites where the culture of the dominant society is learned and where students experience the difference between those status and class distinctions that exist in the larger society' (1984, p. 36). The suggestion is that schools help to create educational success or failure in ways other than objective teaching and testing. Because of cultural discrimination and alienation, 'working-class people are often injured, insulted and disempowered by their experiences with schools' (Connell *et al.*, 1982, p. 172). The traditional and widely accepted explanations of differences in educational outcomes, however, focus not on social and cultural forces that are played out in schools, but on the particular characteristics of individual pupils: 'They refer to attributes of individuals as the source of performance, and in the main they divert attention from school practices, so maintaining those practices and whatever social forms they reflect' (Carrier, 1984, p. 41). That is, teachers, through both the institutionalized expectations of teacher role and their training, are expected to regard educational problems as being manifestations of individual problems. The task of the teacher, therefore, is seen as being to remedy such individual problems by means of individual treatment. Within this logic both teachers and pupils are seen in isolation from each other and from their social contexts. But this view of education as the cultivation of individual students, or individual disembodied talents, denies that the education system has social functions and social consequences that are historically constituted. Individual explanations of educational outcomes are both a result of, and also encourage and sustain, the view that all children have an equal opportunity to succeed and that the key to success or failure is individual ability and individual effort which will earn rewards in the marketplace.

A set of understandings and expectations about teachers has become largely institutionalized, then, and somewhat 'taken-for-granted' since the emergence of mass education in the last decades of the nineteenth century. The notion of 'teacher role' relies heavily on the false view that education is politically neutral and that teachers are first and foremost public servants who, in doing their jobs efficiently and effectively, contribute to the 'common good'. Within this conception individual teachers play their part in the education system — each playing the teacher role for a group of students until they hand them on to the next teacher at the end of the lesson or the year.

Teacher Ideology and Educational Practice

Teachers typically enter classrooms with fairly clear ideas of what education is about and how the wider society, pupils, other teachers, principals and training institutions expect them to teach. What is generally regarded as teaching and learning in schools often boils down to a narrow range of activities which merely pass on to students 'agreed truths' and 'bodies of knowledge' which authorities and experts over the years have deemed to be that which pupils should 'know'. Knowledge in this context is regarded as unproblematic; it 'is reified, and human agency is removed from considerations of how one "knows"' (Wood, 1984, p. 225). Administrators, teachers and pupils are all expected to conform to certain established traditions and rituals in schools which, even in the pretend-school games of very young children, contain models of teacher and pupil roles, authority relations and teaching practice. In their concern to be 'good' teachers and administrators, and in the face of a range of problems in day-to-day schooling (including problems of discipline and control, marking, the allocation of time and space, diverse abilities and attitudes of class members, pressure from administrators and parents), teachers and administrators are pushed to 'do their jobs' in ways which may largely ignore the social and cultural aspects of education in favour of 'practical' concerns. Through an accumulation of craft knowledge, stories and on-the-job socialization, teachers and administrators add to the rituals and expectations of what they should do in schools and develop 'ready-made technical solutions for school problems that are part of the repertoire of being a teacher, or a principal' (Smith, 1985, p. 33). The historical and cultural notion of role, therefore, constrains teachers and administrators in their conceptions of what is possible in schools and in society. It also constrains parents and students because it operates unconsciously, as socially accepted presuppositions and taken-for-granted assumptions about what is natural and appropriate in schooling.

This relates to the pervasiveness of bureaucratic and technical rationality in schools. As Rizvi (1986) explains, such 'rationality' holds that organization members should be led and guided by experts whose task it is to apply technical or instrumental solutions to practical problems. Individual responsibility is often minimal at lower levels of the bureaucracy, as teachers are expected to adopt the established logic of the broader education system without unduly questioning it. Rather than subjecting to scrutiny much of what is taken-for-granted in education, then, teachers, like their nineteenth century predecessors, are not expected to take the initiative in critically appraising their teaching practice and the experience of schooling. Even reformist teachers are often diverted into considerations of merely efficient operation of schools rather than genuine educational concerns. This shows up in schools, as Bullough, Gitlin and Goldstein (1984) point out, 'as a pre-eminence of time concerns in curriculum matters and in the widely held belief that all learning is a simple, mechanically additive process having little to do with intuition or insight' (1984, p. 343). Such narrowness is nowhere more clearly illustrated than in the current proliferation of 'teacher proof' curriculum packages which, especially in the United States (Apple, 1986), erode the already limited autonomy of classroom teachers by removing their need to make professional judgments. Deskilling turns teachers into technicians who are even more remote from the particular concerns and interests of their pupils. The concern for the welfare and humanity of children and society that prompts many young people to become teachers in the first place can too easily become lost among concerns for effective teaching, subject specialization, administrative efficiency and the like. The 'naive idealist' may too readily be transformed into the 'pragmatic classroom manager' or 'obedient technician'. Such teachers may become blind to the social and cultural functions of education, to the stratification and legitimation of social groups, as they strive to 'do their jobs'.

It is not suggested, however, that teachers, administrators, parents and students always and everywhere accept without question the education traditions and expectations that have been largely institutionalized over time. Indeed, to some extent alternative interpretations of such concepts as 'teacher role' have been asserted from within the teaching profession. As indicated above, some limited gains that are worth preserving and extending through further critical appraisal were made within segments of the teaching profession in the late 1960s and the 1970s. The part played by teacher unionists at that time was particularly significant. Such alternatives have not yet been strongly enough asserted to overwhelm traditional conceptions of the role of teachers and schools in society.

In more recent years the role of the teacher which is implied by the corporate management approach has been challenged to some extent by Hoyle's (1980) notion of the teacher as an 'extended professional'. This concept, along with that of 'reflective practitioner' (Schön, 1983), has been widely accepted in teacher education and professional development (Ingvarson, 1990). The research of Broadfoot and her colleagues (Broadfoot *et al.*, 1988) confirms that primary teachers in England (unlike their French colleagues) value extended professionality. They regard teaching as being a problematic activity that is fraught with dilemmas; they emphasize the process of schooling rather than the product; and they develop a universalistic emphasis on the broad needs and abilities of each child rather than a particularistic approach to teaching mandated knowledge and skills (Broadfoot *et al.*, 1988).

While there are no comparable data on Australian teachers and their fundamental beliefs, the educational themes that have characterized teacher union activity in Australia (especially in regard to the curriculum debate — including support for school-based curriculum development, attempts to revise the senior secondary curriculum and attempts to engage students from disadvantaged groups) indicate that a similar teacher ideology may be present here. If this is so, then it seems clear that the current managerialist trend poses a distinct threat to such extended professionalism. Broadfoot and her colleagues (1988, p. 286) are also concerned about the effects of imposed educational change on teacher professionalism in England. They found that:

> It is the ideology or, to put it another way, the conception of their professional role, which plays the most fundamental role in determining what teachers do. If policy changes ride roughshod over such ideologies, and fail to take them into account, the result is likely to be widespread resentment, a lowering of morale, and, with it, a reduced effectiveness.

This is not to say, however, that teachers are passively subject to authority structures. The pressures on teachers' work have been variable over time and have included shifts in power relationships between teachers, administrators and the state. Within the limits of authority structures of control and supervision, administrator and teacher practice is actively negotiated. Many teachers, usually through their union, will contest and reshape the conditions of their work in an attempt to protect a degree of autonomy that is associated with their professional role.

Such considerations highlight the problematic nature of theories of reproduction, early versions of which often lacked recognition of the fact that we are social beings and, as such, are active participants in the day-to-day processes of constructing, as well as reconstructing, the practices which comprise cultural patterns, expectations and traditions. Educational practices in schools and classrooms can often be located in the context of those traditions. In keeping with prevailing ideology, they display the mixture of progressive and regressive moments outlined above. Thus, although our current forms of schooling can only be understood in relation to the history and evolution of particular traditions and conflicts in education and society, it is also true that history is characterized by a complex interrelationship between continuity and change (Popkewitz, 1983; Angus, 1988). Because education has been shaped by 'past and continuing struggles', 'the form of schooling that we actually find in a nation, a state, a school or a classroom represents the "resolution", at that moment in time, of such struggles' (Kemmis and DiCharo, 1987, p. 118).

It must also be emphasized that education has historically been related to the economy and society. This is true of the current period, in which tighter linkages have been forged between education and the economy, and there is pressure on teachers and schools to comply with narrowed curriculum, narrow testing and a managerial approach to schooling. The pressure on schools at this time is enormous, but teachers must not feel that they are powerless in the face of such pressures. It is feasible that teachers, administrators, students and school communities can alter educational practices because, as Kemmis and DiCharo (1987, p. 122) point out:

> Though schools may appear stable, we also know that their very stability is not final, fixed in space and time. Schools must be remade daily by the actions of those whose work constitutes them. When we participate in the daily reconstruction of schools in new or different ways — they become different. But even the apparent stability of schools is daily reconstituted as much through contestation as through consensus — through agreements to disagree, through the living out of oppositions, through

> the daily reconstruction of the differentiation of roles which structure the social relationships of schooling. Contestation and institutionalization go hand in hand.

Schools should be places of ongoing critical educational debate. There is no denying, however, that it may be difficult to generate such critical scrutiny in teachers. After all, many teachers are preoccupied with the incessant minutiae of day-to-day teaching requirements. Moreover, many have become socialized through their own schooling, teacher training and teaching experience to regard accepted practices as appropriate. It is, nonetheless, feasible for us to alter such practices through critically re-appraising them and working together with our colleagues and communities to achieve educational reform.

The Restoration of Democracy and Equality in Schools

Although, historically, equality has been taken extremely seriously in public education, the record of schools in contributing to a more equal society has been poor. This is largely because, although schools themselves may have been committed to the principle of equality, they have hardly practised it. They have usually been characterized by hierarchical learning styles, individualism and competition. It is true that real, but limited, progress has been made in challenging these features of traditional schooling, especially during the 1960s and 1970s. The influence of such reforms is apparent in progressive notions of teacher professionalism and in current attempts to reform the senior secondary curriculum to make it more inclusive for the broad spectrum of senior students. The recent conservative renovation in education, however, has again emphasized concerns of hierarchical management, individualism and competition. Moreover, schools exist in a society that is increasingly characterized by competition and commitment to the market. Again, the relationship between schooling and the economy has been tightened in recent educational reforms — notably in reforms in higher education — which emphasize education as a private investment.

The somewhat contradictory relationship between equality and competition partly explains the emphasis in schools on the limited conception of individual equality of opportunity — a conception which, in line with the predominant market orientation of society, fosters competition for educational commodities and credentials which may help to secure or improve individual social and economic position. If the notions of re-industrialization, competitive skills accumulation and the acquisition of marketable credentials are to reflect the types of values that a school projects, then one might anticipate that the attitude of the citizen to the school is likely to be that of an individualistic consumer, rather than a participant with a commitment to the joint creation of an institution to be organized around a notion of the common good. The interest of the consumer parent or the consumer community will be specifically in the maximization of immediate satisfaction from what the school is able to offer students in terms of their own economic advancement in a competitive marketplace. The pressure is strong for education systems to be integrated into the mechanisms of the commercial market (Apple, 1989). Yet schools are significant social institutions. By treating education as a commercial product and schools as competitors in a marketplace, we are radically altering the nature of participation in what, for many people, is the most significant social institution after the family.

Given the shift to the Right in education, and the reduction of education to the service of the economy and national interests in a competitive market, the priority given to schooling as a public good in the past will need to be reasserted. Yet the evidence of, for instance, the recent Burdekin Report (Human Rights and Equal Opportunity Commission, 1989), and lack of substantial response to it, indicates that there may already be reduced community support for our youth, particularly disadvantaged and disaffected youth. Certainly, while a greater proportion of children are staying on at school beyond the compulsory years, there is a substantial minority who do not stay, and they need to be taken account of in policy-making in relation to schooling. Such young people often will have struggled with the cultural as well as the academic content of the curriculum, and may well have been alienated by the institutional form of schooling itself. They are likely to have been powerless, confused recipients of, instead of active participants in, the schooling experience. In exposing the limited opportunities for genuine equality in education, educators, pupils and parents may have a powerful theme through which they might begin to consider curricular and organizational reforms in schools, which might lead to greater equality within them. Such a focus would raise the concepts of equality and social justice as important educational and social issues.

The issue of democracy in education is also only partially developed in current approaches to education. Wood (1984, p. 219) explains the contradiction between promise and practice:

> The promise is that of educating the children of our society in ways that will aid in their development as literate, thoughtful, and perhaps even compassionate democratic citizens. The reality

> is schooling which emphasizes the routine, rewards rule-governed behaviour, and values conformity over independence in reflecting our limited conception of democracy.

This contradiction is itself rooted in a contradictory notion of democracy. On the one hand, democracy is associated with equality before the law, equal freedoms, equal rights and responsibilities and equal franchise. On the other hand, democracy also ensures the unfettered pursuit of individual, personal gain, competitive economic advancement, and the preservation and extension of self-interest over public interest. Thus, while schools undoubtedly contribute to the production of a differentially socialized and stratified workforce for a hierarchical occupational structure, they must at the same time provide experiences that ensure the continuation of perceptions of an egalitarian democratic society. They have managed to do this by offering the illusion of equality of opportunity for all children (Shapiro, 1983; 1984c).

But the perception of democracy that historically has been associated with schools is an extremely limited one of citizen participation through the ballot-box but otherwise, in general, one of disinterest. Moreover, schools, in their organization and practices, usually have offered few opportunities for democratic participation in a full sense. In the current rhetoric of the Right, notions of democracy and schooling are reduced to calls for greater consumer 'choice' of schools in a bid to increase competition between schools and, so the logic goes, raise standards. Choice and equity are associated with the dezoning of schools so that parents can choose from the full market range which, in New South Wales for instance, includes schools with 'centres of excellence' and selective high schools.

In defending an alternative educational agenda to that of the Right, it is important for educators to point to the loose coalition of neo-conservative and neo-liberal aspirations, associated particularly with notions of the market and standards, that makes up the somewhat confusing and contradictory agenda of the New Right (Whitty, 1989). Internal contradictions make the Right's position somewhat vulnerable. The confused nature of the New Right program can be illustrated by the situation in Britain, where the 1988 Education Reform Act purports to be an example of the government 'taking action to increase the autonomy of schools and their responsiveness to parental wishes' (Department of Education and Science, 1987, in Whitty, 1989, p. 329). On the one hand, this thrust has resulted in the establishment of a dezoned market of schools, to be regulated by market choices, from which parents are to exercise consumer choice. On the other hand, the simultaneous introduction of a prescribed national curriculum and procedures for extensive national testing suggest greater centralized state control. The apparent contradiction here is of interest to Australian educationists, as a similar tension between centralization and decentralization has been noted (Angus and Rizvi, 1989; Rizvi and Angus, 1990).

Contradictions within the Right's position are apparent in Australia in the utterances of various figures of the New Right. For instance, the neo-conservative emphasis on standards, authority, tradition and national identity is espoused by such diverse figures as Dame Leonie Kramer, Michael Barnard and Bruce Ruxton, while neo-liberal free market economics are espoused by the likes of Andrew Hay and the Australian Institute for Public Affairs. This mixed agenda is met half-way by Labor governments fostering nationalism, deregulation and corporate management of the public sector. Under this rationale, equity and provision for the disadvantaged, in education as well as welfare, largely are incorporated into an idealized, efficient managerial structure which will deliver specific welfare provisions to carefully targeted groups in the name of social justice. That is, education and welfare, like good business, can and should be efficiently managed. This approach does not cut across the loose collection of conservative themes which, despite 'its internal inconsistencies and its eclectic philosophical roots' (Whitty, 1989, p. 331), appeals directly to the popular concerns and prejudices of the public.

Certainly, the view that authorities need to cut through the obfuscation and ideology of the out-of-touch and self-interested 'educational establishment' is a feature of the conservative attack on public education (Partington, 1990). The argument is put neatly by Chester Finn Jr (1989, p. 8), who says of the possibility of gaining consensus in the United States on national educational standards, 'I do not think it is going to be all that hard.... I am confident that such an agreement can be hammered out and I suggest to you that it is only educators who do not think it can be done. Ordinary citizens and voters and elected officials all know it can be done and want it to be done.'

Genuine democratic participation in decision-making about education would necessitate a far deeper sense of partnership in an educational community than is suggested by Finn. It would require, according to Wood (1984, p. 232), three conditions:

> first, the participants must be in the position of decision maker rather than decision influencer; second, all participants must be in possession of, or have access to, the requisite information on

> which decisions can be reached; and third, full participation requires equal power on the part of participants to determine the outcomes of decisions.

Such participation could be encouraged among school staffs, school communities and, importantly, among students as much as possible. This ideal is recognized in the Victorian *Ministerial Papers* which state: 'Unless the school is a place where significant decisions are made, it cannot provide a model which will assist in preparing young people for a life in a democratic community' (Education Department of Victoria, 1984, p. 9). While such a democratic ideal is far from the reality in Victorian education (Angus and Rizvi, 1989; Rizvi and Angus, 1990), it is through such a process of participation and communication that the social responsibility of teachers, parents and pupils might be developed and strengthened.

What is most important about such democratic participation is not merely that it may result in better decisions and commitment to those decisions, nor even that it stimulates greater democratic awareness and commitment to participation in a broader sense. It is most important because such genuine participation can raise for scrutiny a host of issues that are left dormant under the formerly accepted bureaucratic rationality. These include issues of relevance, justice, cultural discrimination in schools and the connections between education and society, economics and politics. Moreover, in collectively challenging the 'taken-for-granted' in education, important questions can be raised in relation to these issues, such as: What counts as education? What counts as knowledge? Whose interests are served or restricted by the selection, production and distribution of that knowledge? What aspects of society and economy are legitimated by forms of schooling? What kind of society do we want? How might schools contribute to the formation of such a society? By seriously engaging in such questions, we confront the apparent neutrality and stability of schools and begin to see institutionalized educational practices as essentially temporary and changeable. We open up these complex and tradition-bound issues for critical scrutiny and reform. As Kemmis and DiCharo explain (1987, p. 117), such a reform effort means

> to question what is in the light of what could be. It is to recognise that the classrooms, schools and society of today are the result of a process of social formation, and that to achieve a different sort of classroom, school or society, people whose work is education must embark on a process of social and historical reformation or transformation — a struggle of *reform*.

None of this is to deny that there are massive external constraints upon what even the most democratic of schools — ones which in their organization and curriculum embody principles of democracy, equality and emancipation — can do in reforming a society in which hierarchy and inequality appear to be institutionalized. Nevertheless, schools as an integral part of society have a dialectical influence upon social structures which is captured in the question: Do schools change (or at least, shape) pupils to fit the existing society; or do schools educate pupils to change (or at least, shape) society to fit them? The answer is that schools do both. Teachers have generally seen their role as contributing to the improvement of society. That is why, despite a practical classroom orientation, many are likely to resist conservative directions that would make schools less democratic and egalitarian. We must recognize that, as well as contributing in complex and subtle ways to the reproduction of culture and society, schools also have transformative capabilities. However, the overall tendency, despite continuous resistance and contestation (Giroux, 1983), has been the preservation of current arrangements because of restraints that are largely social and cultural.

Conclusion

The argument is that teachers and others (parents, pupils, education officials, citizens) may be able to work within the education system to expose the constraints on schooling and ultimately to remove them. Therefore, while schools alone cannot bring about fundamental social change, they can contribute to, and facilitate, social change by developing a critical orientation towards society and social institutions among pupils and other school participants and in school practices.

The critical movement from critique to change may come when it becomes clear to participants that current social arrangements, and the relationships between school and society, are neither neutral nor natural. At that point, as Gordon (1985, p. 2) explains:

> The question is whether we, as educators, intend education for citizenship simply to function as a mode of ideological domination, conforming students to the demands of the dominant society; or whether citizenship education should be designed to foster social reconstruction, by helping students (and others) to become creative, critical thinkers and active social participants, and to become capable of redefining the nature of their own lives in the society in which they live.

This would involve analysis not only of schooling in its social and political context, but also of the message systems of curriculum, pedagogy and evaluation, through which the dominant social order may be served (Bernstein, 1977). In the classroom such socially critical and responsible education could involve helping students to develop 'the intellectual wherewithal to criticize, reconstruct, or reform the society they will enter as adults' (Finkelstein, 1984, p. 277). In teaching literacy, therefore, teachers might consider an approach, already adopted by many, which connects the skills of literacy with cultural and political emancipation, so that students are taught not merely the techniques of, for example, reading, but to 'read' the world critically. As Tickell (1981, p. 6) explains:

> if we are teaching *literacy*, and not [merely] ciphering and deciphering, we must be teaching politics. We must be concerned with the *content* of our teaching.... If language does not address all of those dimensions of the personality, and does not help the learner to deal with those aspects of experience, then it is not developing the person as an autonomous individual, it is developing the person selectively according to someone's priorities. Secondly, it gives us a direction, a purpose, for whatever techniques are required for the learner. If we don't consider the purpose, the use to which those techniques are to be put, then we are not developing a process for liberation, we are developing a process for domestication.

Students could be educated to be alert to, and mindful of, social conditions, 'to look at things as if they could be otherwise, to envisage alternative realities' (Greene, 1984, p. 294) and to strive to achieve them. Such constructive critique of existing educational and social practice is of crucial importance in education for social and civic responsibility. It does not, as Simon (1983, p. 244) warns us, however, remove

> the old dilemma of what to do on Monday morning... Individual students face an uncertain job market and quite often are ill-prepared to cope with its 'realities'. We have responsibilities to these students. If we do not give youth a sense of how to 'make it' within the system, all too often we doom them to social marginality. We fall into yet another high-minded way of perpetuating the structural inequalities in society.

Teachers need to help students to understand about society and employment, and about getting jobs and operating within society as responsible citizens. At the same time students should be encouraged and assisted to become conscious of ways in which society might be reformed and how responsible citizens would participate in such reforms. In short, as Simon (1983, p. 246) summarized this conception of responsible education:

> I want to be straight-forward; what I have in mind is a version of education that includes real social and technological competence, but as well a critical social intelligence that refuses to let questions of compassion and justice be suppressed by the concerns of technique and efficiency.

In such an education the basics would not be simply technical competencies of literacy and numeracy, but standards of respect for fellow human beings, of justice, democracy and equality. If teachers, administrators and school communities are to be socially responsible, they must be concerned with such issues, and with the self-awareness that leads to social questioning, rather than with the regulation and control that traditional, predominantly hierarchical schooling currently entrenches.

This approach would imply that the values and knowledge of pupils and teachers become a legitimate curriculum resource. Although it is problematic in a number of ways (Ellsworth, 1989), such an approach aims to open up possibilities of sharing ourselves and our cultures through education. The aim of encouraging active rather than passive citizenship is to motivate school participants to be concerned with democracy, and with the self and social awareness that is a prerequisite for liberation, rather than with the regulation, control and mystification that the predominantly hierarchical organization of schools has long entrenched. Through a critical perspective, educators might begin to agree with the oft-quoted conclusion of Connell *et al.* that:

> Education has fundamental connections with the idea of human emancipation though it is constantly in danger of being captured for other interests. In a society disfigured by class exploitation, sexual and racial oppression, and in chronic danger of war and environmental destruction, the only education worth the name is one that forms people capable of taking part in their own liberation. The business of the school is not propaganda; it is equipping people with the knowledge and skills and concepts relevant to remaking a dangerous and disordered world. In the most basic sense, the process of education and the process of liberation are

> the same. They are aspects of the painful growth of the human species' collective wisdom and self-contol. At the beginning of the 1980s it is plain that the forces opposed to that growth, here and on the world scale, are not only powerful but have become increasingly militant. In such circumstances education becomes a risky enterprise. Teachers too have to decide whose side they are on. (Connell *et al.*, 1982, p. 208)

At the beginning of the 1990s, as this chapter is being concluded, the above exhortation seems even more urgent. The argument is that teachers, pupils, administrators and school communities should be on the side of democracy and critical scrutiny rather than that of hierarchy and institutionalized practice; participation and negotiation rather than social control and manipulation; social learning and critical cultural awareness rather than mystification and the authoritarian and dogmatic presentation and assessment of 'knowledge' that is predetermined (and often prepackaged). That is, decisions about education involve cultural and political choices and questions of value, but because of the pervasive acceptance of the ideology of meritocracy in schools, such choices are generally not regarded as problematic. They are regarded, in a sense, as not properly significant choices at all, but merely as options for effective administration from within a fairly uniform and taken-for-granted social and cultural perspective. Entrenched in the fetish of educational managers for concerns simply of effectiveness and efficiency, the management not only of educational resources but also of education itself and of educational outcomes is seen in restricted managerial terms.

The concern for community and the welfare of the disadvantaged has suffered in a climate of managerialism and economic insecurity, in which majority opinion can be tapped to oppose, rather than support, benefits that go to minorities. In the run up to the 1990 federal election in Australia the selling of Liberal Party economic policy, for instance, had Shadow Treasurer Hewson arguing that the welfare state must be 'rolled back', and Federal President Elliot justifying taxation changes, which would massively benefit the wealthy, as doing nothing more than taking from the 'bludgers' to give to the deserving 'workers', presumably like himself. The educational equivalent is the view that disproportionate resources have gone to the disadvantaged at the expense of support for the talented or 'gifted' who, in the eyes of some, are therefore discriminated against.

There are powerful reasons for teachers and educational workers to build strong linkages with their school communities, and to foster the critical scrutiny of entrenched educational practices. Not the least is the opportunity that such scrutiny provides for the exposure of internal inconsistencies in the Right's position. Another is that, in considering such issues and working towards sound and responsible education for all students, linkages between education, critical enquiry and social justice may be fostered. Moreover, in working to develop an alternative educational project to that of the Right, it may well be possible 'to construct a generalised educational program, a common learnings program, whose claim to preference over the existing academic curriculum is twofold: both that it follows the principle of social justice in education in embodying the interests of the least advantaged, and that it is intellectually better than other ways of organising knowledge' (Connell, 1989, p. 69).

Such general educational provision must be provided by, and supported by, the state, for, as Lynch correctly points out, 'While the state is by no means a perfect guarantor of democratic rights for oppressed groups, without state intervention, minority/oppressed groups have no legitimate arena within which to fight for and/or secure educational (civil) rights' (Lynch, 1988, p. 152; see also Angus and Rizvi, 1989). Therefore, the public must be encouraged to ensure that the state accepts its responsibility for the fair provision of education to all students in partnership with schools and communities. The notions of partnership and community here would exclude the kind of Thatcherite marketization of education that is currently favoured in New South Wales, elements of which have crept into the other states through an emphasis on educational managerialism.

Education, it could now argued, should explicitly assist in the necessarily ongoing process of social reconstruction 'by helping students (and others) to become creative, critical thinkers and active social participants, and to become capable of redefining the nature of their own lives in the society in which they live' (Gordon, 1985, p. 2). Such social reconstruction would necessarily be gradual, for it would build upon the positive elements in existing practice, flawed though they might be, so that all citizens may eventually be better served by schools.

A further reason for the engagement of teachers and the community in critical reflection on education is that such a project, developed collectively with the partnership of teachers and parents, can question whether the best education for children is to be provided in the individualist and competitive approach favoured by the Right. An alternative educational project that emphasizes access and justice for all pupils may be able to achieve informed popular assent rather than be dismissed as the work of self-serving educationalists. Collaboration with educational communities also would help to counter the low esteem in which teachers are held in the community. In this project it would be important to emphasize the problematic nature of the notion of quality schooling. The lack of precision in use of the term, and companion terms such as efficiency, effectiveness and standards, is itself significant, as it enables such terms to be employed as part of a slogan system which powerfully symbolizes a conservative educational ideology that has been broad enough to accommodate, for the present at least, the values of somewhat disparate groups on the Right. Such rhetorical terms are also powerful in that they have engaged the generalized fears of parents and community about the education of their children (see Kenway, 1986). This point is important because education as a major social institution is, as has been emphasized here, an arena of ideological contest. It is, therefore, important that, at a time when the educational debate has shifted to accommodate conservative New Right themes, the contest is not allowed to be one-sided.

References

ANGUS, L. (1986) *Schooling, the School Effectiveness Movement and Educational Reform*, Geelong, Deakin University Press.

ANGUS, L. (1988) *Continuity and Change in Catholic Schooling: An Ethnography of a Christian Brothers School in Australian Society*, Lewes, Falmer Press.

ANGUS, L. and RIZVI, F. (1989) 'Power and the politics of participation,' *Journal of Educational Administration and Foundations*, 4, 1, pp. 6–23.

APPLE, M. (1982) *Education and Power*, London, Routledge and Kegan Paul.

APPLE, M. (1986) *Teachers and Texts: A Political Economy of Class and Gender Relations in Education*, New York, Routledge and Kegan Paul.

APPLE, M. (1989) 'How equality has been redefined in the conservative restoration', in SECADA, W. (Ed.), *Equity in Education*, Lewes, Falmer Press.

BATES, R. (1985) *Liberalism, Marxism and the Struggle for the State: Prolegomena to the Study of Public Administration*, Geelong, Deakin University Press.

BENNETT, D. (1982) 'Education: back to the drawing-board', in EVANS, G. and REEVES, J. (Eds), *Labor Essays 1982*, Melbourne, Drummond.

BERLAK, A. and BERLAK, H. (1983) 'Towards a non-hierarchical approach to school inquiry and leadership', *Curriculum Inquiry*, 13, pp. 267–94.

BERNSTEIN, B. (1977) *Class, Codes and Control, Vol. 3, Towards a Theory of Educational Transmissions*, 2nd Ed., London, Routledge and Kegan Paul.

BESSANT, R. (1975) 'Education', in GIBB, G. and HANNAN, A. (Eds), *Debate and Decision: Political Issues in 20th Century Australia*, Melbourne, Heinemann.

BOURDIEU, P. (1977) *Outline of a Theory of Practice*, Cambridge, Cambridge University Press.

BROADFOOT, P., *et al.* (1988) 'What professional responsibility means to teachers: National contexts and classroom constants', *British Journal of Sociology of Education*, 9, 3, pp. 265–87.

BULLOUGH, R., GITLIN, A. and GOLDSTEIN, S. (1984) 'Ideology, teacher role, and resistance', *Teachers College Record*, 86, 2, pp. 339–58.

BUTTS, R. (1955) *Assumptions Underlying Australian Education*, Melbourne, Australian Council for Educational Research.

CARRIER, J. (1984) 'Cultural themes in educational debates: The nature-culture opposition in accounts of unequal educational performance', *British Journal of Sociology of Education*, 5, 1, pp. 33–47.

CENTRAL ADVISORY COUNCIL FOR EDUCATION (England) (1967) *Children and Their Primary Schools* (B. Plowden, Chairperson), London, Her Majesty's Stationery Office.

COLEMAN, J., CAMPBELL, E., HOBSON, C., MCPARTLAND, J., MOOD, A., WEINFIELD, F. and YORK, R. (1966) *Equality of Educational Opportunity*, Washington, D.C., United States Government Printing Office.

COMMONWEALTH SCHOOLS COMMISSION (1986) *In the National Interest: Secondary Education and Youth Policy in Australia*, Canberra, Australian Government Publishing Service.

CONNELL, R. (1989) 'Curriculum politics, hegemony and strategies of social change, *New Education*, 11, 2, pp. 63–71.

CONNELL, R., ASHENDEN, D., KESSLER, S. and DOWSETT, G. (1982) *Making the Difference*, London, George Allen and Unwin.

DAWKINS, J. (1987) *Higher Education: A Policy Discussion Paper* (Green Paper), Canberra, Australian Government Publishing Service.

DAWKINS, J. (1988) *Higher Education: A Policy Statement* (White Paper), Canberra, Australian Government Publishing Service.

DEPARTMENT OF EDUCATION AND SCIENCE (1987) *Grant Maintained Schools: A Consultation Paper*, London, Department of Education and Science.

EDUCATION DEPARTMENT OF VICTORIA (1984) *Ministerial Papers 1–6*, Melbourne, Government Printer.

ELLSWORTH, E. (1989) 'Why doesn't this feel empowering? Working through the repressive myths of critical padagogy', *Harvard Educational Review*, 59, 3, pp. 297–324.

ELY, J. (1978) *Reality and Rhetoric: An Alternative History of Australian Education*, Sydney, Alternative Publishing Coop.

FINN, C. (1989) 'National standards for American education: A symposium', *Teachers College Record*, 91, 1, pp. 4–30.

FINKELSTEIN, B. (1984) 'Education and the retreat from democracy in the United States, 1979–198?', *Teachers College Record*, 86, 2, pp. 275–82.

FREELAND, J. (forthcoming) 'Quality of what and quality for whom?', in J. CHAPMAN, L. ANGUS and G. BURKE (Eds), *Improving the Quality of Australia's Schools*, Melbourne, Australian Council for Educational Research.

GIROUX, H. (1983) 'Theories of reproduction and resistance in the new sociology of education: A critical analysis', *Harvard Educational Review*, 53, 3, pp. 257–93.

GIROUX, H. (1984) 'Rethinking the language of schooling', *Language Arts*, 61, 1, pp. 33–40.

GORDON, B. (1985) 'Towards emancipation in citizenship education: The case of African-American cultural knowledge', *Theory and Research in Social Education*, 12, 4, pp. 1–23.

Grace, G. (1989) 'Education: Commodity or public good?' *British Journal of Educational Studies*, 37, 3, pp. 207–21.

Gramsci, A. (1971) *Selections from the Prison Notebooks of Antonio Gramsci*, Ed. by Q. Hoare and G. Nowell-Smith, New York, Lawrence and Wishart.

Greene, M. (1984) '"Excellence", meanings, and multiplicity', *Teachers College Record*, 86, 2, pp. 283–97.

Gregory, J. (1973) *Church and State*, Melbourne, Cassell.

Grundy, D. (1972) *Compulsory, Free and Secular: The Education Act of 1872*, Melbourne, Melbourne University Press.

Hall, S. (1977) *Review of the Course*, Unit 32, E202 Schooling and Society, Milton Keynes, Open University Press.

Hoyle, E. (1980) 'Professionalization and deprofessionalization in education', in Hoyle, E. and Megarry, J. (Eds), *World Yearbook of Education 1980: Professional Development of Teachers*, London, Kogan Page, pp. 42–54.

Human Rights and Equal Opportunity Commission (1989) *Our Homeless Children: Report of the National Inquiry into Homeless Children*, Canberra: Australian Government Publishing Service.

Ingvarson, L. (1990) 'Places where teachers learn', in J. Chapman, (Ed.), *School-based Decision-making and Management*, Lewes, Falmer Press.

Interim Committee for the Australian Schools Commission (1973) *Schools in Australia* (Karmel Report) Canberra, Australian Government Publishing Service.

Jencks, C. (1972) *Inequality: A Reassessment of the Effects of Family and Schooling in America*, New York, Basic Books.

Kemmis, S. and DiCharo, G. (1987) 'Emerging and evolving issues of action research praxis: An Australian perspective', *Peabody Journal of Education*, 64, 4, pp. 101–30.

Kenway, J. (1986) 'Left right out: Australian education and the politics of signification', Mimeo, Deakin University, School of Education.

Kogan, M. (1979) *Educational Policies in Perspective: An Appraisal*, Paris, Organization for Economic Cooperation and Development.

Lundgren, U. (1983) 'Social production and reproduction as a context for curriculum theorizing', *Journal of Curriculum Studies*, 15, 2, pp. 143–54.

Lynch, K. (1988) 'Reproduction in education: An elaboration of current neo-Marxist models of education', *British Journal of Sociology of Education*, 9, 2, pp. 151–68.

Management Review (1989) *Schools Renewal: A Strategy to Revitalize Schools within the New South Wales State Education System*, Sydney: Management Review: New South Wales Education Portfolio.

Martin, R. (1989) 'Improving the quality of education', Mimeo, Adelaide, South Australian Institute of Teachers.

Minister for Employment, Education and Training (1989) *Strengthening Australia's Schools*, Canberra, Department of Employment, Education and Training.

Ministerial Review of Post-Compulsory Schooling (1985) (Blackburn Report) 2 vols, Melbourne, The Ministerial Review of Post-Compulsory Schooling.

National Commission on Excellence in Education (1983) *A Nation at Risk*, Washington, D.C., US Government Printing Office.

Partington, G. (forthcoming) 'Conceptions of quality in education', in Chapman, J., Angus, L. and Burke, G. (Eds), *Improving the Quality of Australia's Schools*, Melbourne, Australian Council for Educational Research.

POPKEWITZ, T. (1983) *Change and Stability in Schooling: The Dual Quality of Educational Reform*, Geelong, Deakin University Press.

POPKEWITZ, T. (1988) 'Educational reform: Rhetoric, ritual and social interest', *Educational Theory*, 38, 1, pp. 77–93.

PRESTON, N. (1989) 'The Dawkins *et al.*, managerial assessment push', *Education Links*, 35, pp. 21–3.

RICE, A. (1983) 'After bureaucracy, what?', *Urban Education*, 18, 1, pp. 40–58.

RIZVI, F. (1986) *Administrative Leadership and the Democratic Community as a Social Ideal*, Geelong, Deakin University Press.

RIZVI, F. and ANGUS, L. (1990) 'Reforming bureaucracy: An attempt to develop responsive educational governance', in CHAPMAN, J. and DUNSTAN, J. (Eds), *Bureaucracy and Democracy*, Lewes, Falmer Press.

SCHÖN, D. (1983) *The Reflective Practitioner*, San Francisco, Calif., Jossey Bass.

SEDDON, T. (1989) 'Curriculum history: A map of key issues', *Curriculum Perspectives*, 9, 4, pp. 1–15.

SEDDON, T. and DEER, C. (Eds) (1990) *A Curriculum for the Senior Secondary Years*, Melbourne, Australian Council for Educational Research.

SEDDON, T., ANGUS, L. and POOLE, M. (1990) 'Pressures on the move to school-based decision-making and management', in CHAPMAN, J. (Ed.), *School-based Decision-making and Management*, Lewes, Falmer Press.

SHAPIRO, H. (1983) 'Class, ideology, and the basic skills movement: A study in the sociology of educational reform', *Interchange*, 14, 2, pp. 14–24.

SHAPIRO, H. (1984a) 'Crisis of legitimation: Schools, society, and a declining faith in education', *Interchange*, 15, 4, pp. 26–39.

SHAPIRO, H. (1984b) 'Ideology, hegemony and the individualising of instruction: The incorporation of progressive education', *Journal of Curriculum Studies*, 16, 4, pp. 367–78.

SHAPIRO, H. (1984c) 'Choosing our educational legacy: Disempowerment or emancipation', *Issues in Education*, 2, 1, pp. 11–22.

SIMON, R. (1983) 'But who will let you do it? Counter hegemonic possibilities for work education', *Journal of Education*, 165, 3, pp. 235–56.

SMITH, B. (1987) Review of *In the National Interest, Discourse*, 8, 1, pp. 131–6.

SMITH, R. (1985) *The Inequalities Debate: An Interpretive Essay*, Geelong, Deakin University Press.

SPRING, J. (1980) *Educating the Worker-Citizen*, New York, Longman.

STRIKE, K. (1985) 'Is there a conflict between equity and excellence', *Educational Evaluation and Policy Analysis*, 7, 4, pp. 405–16.

TICKELL, G. (1981) 'Literacy and transition', *English in Australia*, 56, pp. 3–8.

WHITTY, G. (1989) 'The new right and the national curriculum: State control or market forces?', *Journal of Educational Policy*, 4, 4, pp. 329–41.

WILLIAMS, R. (1976) 'Base and superstructure in Marxist cultural theory', in DALE, R. (Ed.), *Schooling and Capitalism*, London, Routledge and Kegan Paul.

WOOD, G. (1984) 'Schooling in a democracy: Transformation or reproduction?', *Educational Theory*, 34, 3, pp. 219–34.

WOOD, G. (1985) 'Education for democratic participation: Democratic values and the nuclear freeze campaign', *Theory and Research in Social Education*, 12, 4, pp. 39–56.

Notes on Contributors

Lawrence Angus has taught in both state and private schools in Australia and England. He is currently a senior lecturer at Monash University where he teaches educational policy and administration, and social foundations of schooling. He is the author of *Continuity and Change in Catholic Schooling: An Ethnography of a Christian Brothers College in Australian Society* (published in the Falmer Press 'Explorations in Ethnography' series) and of a number of monographs and articles on educational administration, educational reform, power and ideology in education, and pupils' perceptions of schooling. His principal academic interest is in critical approaches to educational administration and educational reform.

Jill Blackmore is a lecturer in social and administrative studies in education at Deakin University. She has had fourteen years' experience teaching mathematics, history and general studies in state schools in Victoria, and came to Deakin after two years teaching educational administration at Monash University. Her research interests include gender relations, teacher unionism, school-based decision-making, the school-work relationship, evaluation and educational history. Current projects include a feminist critique of managerialist reforms in education, case studies of representative committees in schools and the reception of gender policy in schools.

David Dawkins spent ten years in a variety of occupations before entering university as a special entry student. He has been a secondary school teacher in Papua New Guinea, a lecturer in sociology at the State College, Geelong, and is now a senior lecturer in social and administrative studies in education at Deakin University. His work focuses on culture, the culture of schools, and the connections between education and employment.

Jane Kenway is a senior lecturer in social and administrative studies in education at Deakin University. Her research and publications concentrate on the connections between education and social inequality. One focus of her work is on the macro and micro class and gender politics of private schooling and on the private school-state school interface. A second focus is on gender and education, with a particular concern to appraise critically gender reform programs for schools. She is an active participant in education debates in academic and professional journals and in a number of public forums organized by teachers and parents.

Paige Porter works in the sociology and politics of education, and has been Head of the Department of Education and Dean of the Faculty of Education at the University of Queensland since July 1988. Previously she has worked at Murdoch University and the University of Western Australia. She has been a member of the National Innovations Committee of the Commonwealth Schools Commission, a member of the WA Education Department's Research Advisory Committee on Equal Opportunity, and Chairperson of the Council of the WA College of Advanced Education. She is currently a member of the Queensland Board of Teacher Registration. Her research and publications focus on innovation in education, federal-state relations in education, gender and education, and education policy.

Fazal Rizvi is a senior lecturer in social and administrative studies in education at Deakin University. He has published papers on multiculturalism as an educational policy, the politics of democratic reforms in education and ethical issues in educational administration. He is currently conducting a study of 'new' expressions of racism in Australian schools.

Peter Watkins is a senior lecturer is social and administrative studies in education at Deakin University. He was a secondary teacher in Victoria before joining the tertiary education sector. He has published numerous monographs dealing with work, technology and education, and papers in such journals as the *British Journal of Sociology of Education, Australian Journal of Education, Journal of Education Policy* and *Discourse.* His current work is on notions of flexibility in the workplace and education.

Index